STUDY SKILLS FOR
SPORTS STUDIES

Starting university can be a daunting prospect, as students come to grips with new ways of working, learning and thinking. Studying sport at university poses particular challenges, with students often engaged in playing or coaching sport alongside their studies and having unconventional working patterns.

Study Skills for Sports Studies is the only complete guide to degree-level study to be written specifically for students on sports-related courses, outlining the core academic competencies needed to succeed at university. The textbook offers tips and techniques for all aspects of higher education, including time management, critical thinking, academic research and writing, e-learning, presentations, group work and exams. The practical processes are supported by sports-related examples, and each chapter ends with useful exercises to test your skills as well as reflect on your prior learning experiences. Designed as either a self-paced text or a companion to an introductory class, *Study Skills for Sports Studies* demystifies the academic skills needed to succeed and helps you make the most of your time at university.

Tara Magdalinski lectures in the UCD Centre for Sports Studies, University College Dublin, Ireland. As an inaugural recipient of a UCD College Teaching Award (2008), she is committed to ensuring undergraduate students are equipped with the necessary skills to succeed in tertiary education. Her most recent monograph, *Sport, Technology and the Body: The Nature of Perform-ance*, was published by Routledge in 2008.

STUDY SKILLS FOR SPORTS STUDIES

Tara Magdalinski

Routledge
Taylor & Francis Group

LONDON AND NEW YORK

First published 2013
by Routledge
2 Park Square, Milton Park, Abingdon, Oxon OX14 4RN

Simultaneously published in the USA and Canada
by Routledge
711 Third Avenue, New York, NY 10017

Routledge is an imprint of the Taylor & Francis Group, an informa business

British Library Cataloguing in Publication Data
A catalogue record for this book is available from the British Library

Library of Congress Cataloging in Publication Data
Study skills for sport studies/Tara Magdalinski. – First edition.
    pages cm
    Includes bibliographical references.
    1. Sports – Study and teaching (Higher) 2. Study skills. I. Magdalinski,
    Tara.
    GV361.S83 2013
    796.07'7 – dc23   2012051296

ISBN: 978-0-415-53381-2 (hbk)
ISBN: 978-0-415-53382-9 (pbk)
ISBN: 978-0-203-11397-4 (ebk)

Typeset in Aldus and Scala Sans
by Florence Production Ltd, Stoodleigh, Devon, UK

Printed and bound in Great Britain by
TJ International Ltd, Padstow, Cornwall

TO THE TWO TEDDIES:
MARCUS AND ARES

CONTENTS

ILLUSTRATIONS

FIGURES

TABLES

PREFACE

The study skills market is extensive with texts on every conceivable part of the academic process. From those dealing with note taking to critical thinking and research methods, there is a publication to suit every need. Increasingly, study skills texts are targeted at particular disciplines, where relevant examples are used to situate generic skills within a subject specific context. *Study Skills for Sports Studies* is similarly designed with the sports studies student in mind. 'Sports studies' is used here as a collective term to refer to the broad range of disciplines that have the study of sport, exercise, leisure and recreation at their core, including biophysical and socio-cultural approaches. Furthermore, it may appeal to student athletes who, while studying other fields, appreciate the familiar examples. Although it is aimed primarily at students in tertiary education, the book is accessible enough to suit students in further education, community colleges and the final years of secondary school.

Overall, the book aims to:

- introduce students to the challenges of higher and further education as they start to study sport;
- familiarize students with their roles and responsibilities as a sports studies student;
- highlight the role and responsibilities of the lecturing staff/faculty;
- outline the expectations that lecturers/faculty have of students;
- provide useful techniques and tips to help students succeed in their studies;
- guide students through the process of producing high-quality academic work in a variety of forms;
- help students prepare for exams;
- encourage students to be critical thinkers and independent learners.

Students are often expected to arrive on campus primed for study, already competent in academic conventions and aware of the expectations of the academy. Yet in the absence of specific guidance, critical skills are either learned through trial and error or missed entirely, as students struggle to find their bearings during the first weeks and months. Few sports programmes have the luxury of a dedicated study skills module, such as the one delivered though the UCD Centre for Sports Studies that inspired this book, and yet the competencies outlined within are identified across courses, institutions and national borders. For this reason, *Study Skills for Sports Studies* was conceived as both an introduction for students embarking on a new course as well as a reference guide that can accompany them throughout their time in higher education. It can be used either as a companion to an introductory or skills-based course or as a self-paced guide. The terminology and examples within the book are written with a global and cross-disciplinary market in mind. As an introduction to tertiary education, it functions as a precursor or complement to more advanced skills texts, such as Gratton and Jones (2010) *Research Methods for Sports Studies*, which guides students through the process of designing and executing their own research projects.

Like any guide, the techniques and strategies can be used as much or as little as the user needs. Some students will be well organized and already learning independently with great confidence in their abilities; others, however, will be more anxious about the transition to higher and further education and will appreciate the advice that *Study Skills for Sports Studies* offers. The techniques presented herein demystify many academic conventions, while the exercises at the end of each chapter reinforce skills by urging students to 'have a go' at practical examples. There are case studies in each chapter for students to think about, as well as advice from students who have experienced similar challenges. In addition, there is a glossary of common terms, and the appendices include some checklists and other useful materials to assist their studies. Finally, students are encouraged to reflect upon their current abilities, their learning processes as well as the challenges they may face as they embark upon higher education, so that they are more aware of how various skills may apply to their studies as well as the steps they need to take to implement and practise them.

The following icons are used to guide students through the chapter and to identify tasks, case studies and advice:

Case study: Students are encouraged to utilize the skills outlined in the text by applying them to a case study in each chapter.

Student viewpoint: Throughout the text, real students provide feedback and suggestions based on their experience.

Tip: Shortcuts, suggestions or important points to keep in mind are provided in each chapter.

Checklist: These provide a list of key points that students should keep in mind.

Of course, no textbook can purport to cover the full range of skills needed within and across a wide variety of sub-disciplines, but *Study Skills for Sports Studies* does alert students to the different types of activities they might be expected to engage in at college as well as the key competencies that they should be able to demonstrate by the time they graduate. For further information on each of the various skills discussed in this book, specialist, albeit mostly not sports-related options for further reading are listed at the end of each chapter.

The book begins by welcoming students to university and providing an initial overview of the higher education sector, identifying the differences between secondary and tertiary education, and outlining the roles and responsibilities of students and faculty. It then moves to the first days, where students are learning to work independently by managing their time, organizing their study schedules, attending classes, taking notes and thinking critically. Chapters 4 to 8 focus on preparing good-quality academic assignments, concentrating on research essays and laboratory/business/field reports as well as online formats such as blogs and wikis. The processes of breaking down assignment topics, searching the library for relevant resources, 'reading' academic sources and extracting meaningful notes, planning and writing assignments with appropriate citations to avoid plagiarism are explained in detail. The final part of the book examines other popular forms of assessment, such as group work and oral presentations, before discussing the process of aligning theory and practice through labs, pracs and internships/work placements. The final chapter prepares students to take a range of examination formats.

I am fortunate to have a study skills module that outlines to students in their first semester how to learn, research, write, collaborate, present and prepare for exams, and I was reminded of the value of this module in a recent student submission. In a weekly reflective piece, a student explained that he was not aware of how much he had learned in the Core Academic Skills module until he asked a peer from another course whether he had 'found all his references' for a particular coaching assignment they were both completing. 'It was only when my friend said "What's a reference?" that I truly understood how far I had come.' It is my hope that in the absence of a dedicated course, students of sport in its many disciplinary guises can use *Study Skills for Sports Studies* to learn the basic skills needed to succeed at university.

Tara Magdalinski
April 2013

ACKNOWLEDGEMENTS

As always, there are more people who have contributed to or made an impact on this book than actual names on the front cover, so I would like to take this opportunity to thank all those who have assisted in large or small measure with this project. Even the briefest of conversations or suggestions in passing have been appreciated more than I can express here.

First and foremost, I want to thank Simon Whitmore for first encouraging me to write this book. Although initially thinking the market was already saturated, we eventually realized that there is something to be said for study skills texts that target particular disciplines with relevant, accessible examples. It is a rare joy to work so closely with such a skilled editor, and his ideas and suggestions have made for a much stronger book. The anonymous reviewers also provided insightful additions and clarified areas of common concern, for which I am thankful.

A number of generous colleagues took the time to offer national and institutionally specific information to provide the book with a global relevance, so I would like to thank them for their thoughts: Daryl Adair, Susan Birrell, Patrick Delaney, Sarah Fields, Rob Hardin, Keith Harrison, David Hassan, Rob Hess, Barrie Houlihan, Shelley Lucas, Dan Nathan, Vicki Paraschak, Dil Porter, Jaime Schulz, Amanda Schweinbenz, Maureen Smith, Alvy Styles, Jan Todd, Patricia Vertinsky, Kevin Walmsley and Alison Wrynn. I am very grateful for your input.

I think I must have had a worthy past life in order to deserve so many colleagues – friends – who are supportive of my endeavours and are willing to provide advice and encouragement, or just lend an ear, where and when desperately needed. With much love, thank you in particular to Jane Prince, Malcolm MacLean, Murray Phillips, Doug Booth, Doug Brown, Gary Osmond, Mike Cronin and Moynagh Sullivan.

My ever suffering colleagues in the UCD Centre for Sports Studies, who have been hearing about 'the book' for quite some time, allowed me the latitude to develop a specific study skills class and to test out many of my 'formulae' on our unsuspecting students. I owe an enormous amount to the past and present students of SMGT 10260 Core Academic Skills for Sports Studies; your feedback has been invaluable, and while you probably did not realize you were guinea pigs at the time, your engagement with the weekly exercises and reflections helped me to refine many of the techniques and clarify relevant examples outlined in this book. I am also grateful to Maeve Caraher, my co-conspirator in the development of Core Skills, for her support and encouragement.

Grateful thanks go to Ruth Whelan for her invaluable service as my research assistant on this project, and particularly for being at my beck and call during the final few days. I am notoriously hopeless at examples, and I was fortunate to be able to rely on her to make excellent suggestions and additions to the book, particularly from a student perspective. I am so fortunate that the talented Caragh Brooks added her inimitable style through her artwork.

On a personal note, there are a number of friends and family who have helped in their own way to give me the space and time to bring this book to completion. The Aveta witches, who avidly (or not!) followed the progress, receiving regular Facebook updates, whinges and late-night questions that demanded immediate responses, kindly offered their insight into their college and workplace experiences.

With much love, I'd like to thank Natalie and Helmut Wehr for letting me clutter up their kitchen bench and dining-room table – any surface, really – with my laptop, notes and drafts. I'm sure you wonder why I'm always working when I'm supposed to be on holidays!

As ever, I am so grateful to my sister, Anna . . . Anna Magdalinski, who listened to weekly updates in between discussions of THE MOST EXPLOSIVE ROSE CEREMONY EVER, as well as my father, Lloyd, who I can never thank enough for setting me on the path to a career in sports studies.

And finally, as every academic knows, a book can never be written without a significant amount of time and space on weekends and in the evening to just 'get on with it', and so to my husband, Marcus, I am incredibly grateful that you shouldered the bulk of the homefront duties and squirrelled the little one out of the house while I stared at a computer screen for what seemed like months. The ducks, I'm sure, have been more than well fed, the play equipment at the local parks is well worn, and every coffee shop for miles around knows to expect you and Ares on the weekend as you seek refuge from the maniac occupying the dining-room table. Your support, love and patience sustained me through this process and beyond.

WELCOME TO UNIVERSITY

Settling in and getting started

OVERVIEW

This chapter outlines:
- what it means to study sport at university;
- the difference between secondary and tertiary education;
- the importance of time management and organizing college, sporting, social and family commitments;
- the most efficient way to incorporate study sessions into a weekly schedule.

INTRODUCTION

Welcome to the exciting field of sports studies, and congratulations for embarking on an educational path that leads to so many interesting careers. Whether you want to manage sports events, improve athletic performance, work in sports federations or coach athletes, there are many ways that people study sport, and each incorporates a variety of intellectual approaches, academic disciplines and fields of knowledge. 'Sports studies' is used in this book as an overarching or 'umbrella' term that includes both biophysical and socio-cultural perspectives of sport. Your course might have a general name, such as sport and exercise science, human kinetics, kinesiology or human movement studies, or the name may be more specific, such as sports management or recreation studies. If you are interested in the biophysical study of sport, then you might be taking classes in exercise physiology, biomechanics or motor learning. If, however, you are more business or industry oriented, then you might have enrolled in a sports management major that includes areas such as sports marketing, sponsorship, operational management and event management.

The socio-cultural approaches examine sport from a philosophical, historical, psychological or sociological perspective, whereas those with a practical or applied outlook might be studying coaching or athletic training. Finally, some will be considering sport as part of broader studies in leisure, recreation or tourism. Regardless of the specific sub-discipline or the kind of programme you are enrolled in, this book guides you through the academic conventions and processes, the skills and the techniques that will help you study sport successfully.

Do you remember what it is like to try a new sport for the first time? You might be excited, though nervous – perhaps even a little unsure of what will be expected of you. Yet after learning a few basic skills, your nerves dissipate and you find yourself more at ease and confident in your abilities. Entering any new learning environment can be daunting. Whether you are a school leaver or a mature-age student returning after time away from formal education, you will face challenges as you navigate your way through college. For many students, it takes no time to settle in, whereas for others, it takes longer, particularly when faced with larger classes, few contact hours and uncertainty about what you are supposed to be doing. Understanding what is expected of you and knowing where to turn for assistance will ensure you make the best possible start to your studies, and this book outlines the basic skills you will need to ease your transition into higher education.

TERMINOLOGY

Before getting started, it is important to clarify the terminology used through-out the text. Some general terms are used to describe the study of sport, and as these may not be familiar to you, it is important to define them so that you can establish the equivalent at your institution (see Table 1.1 for a summary).

Table 1.1 Summary of common terminology across different national contexts*

	Overall programme of study	Teaching staff	Subject	Class	Practical
USA	Major	Professor	Course	Class	Lab
UK/Ireland	Programme	Lecturer	Module	Lecture	Prac/Lab
Canada	Degree	Professor	Course	Class	Lab
Australia	Degree/Course	Lecturer	Subject/Unit	Lecture	Prac
New Zealand	Degree	Lecturer	Paper	Lecture	Practical
Other terms		Faculty/Tutor		Tutorial/Seminar	

* These are not exclusive terms and there can be a wide range of variation among institutions within a country.

This book is intended for students in 'higher education', which encompasses all forms of education after high school, such as university, college, institutes of further or higher education, technical colleges and other educational organizations that teach students who have left secondary education. To simplify the text, 'university' or 'college' will generally be referred to throughout, though the skills and tips will be applicable to anyone studying sport in any kind of higher educational setting and may, in fact, also be useful for those in the upper levels of high school/secondary education.

Higher education providers offer different programmes of study. These might be known as a 'course', 'programme', 'degree', 'diploma' or 'certificate', though yours might have another name. You might be doing a general degree and be taking a 'major', 'specialization', 'concentration' or 'focus' in sports studies, which means most of your studies will centre on this field. If you are taking a 'minor', then only some of your studies – and not the bulk of them – will focus on sport.

The academic year is typically divided into two semesters, though some institutions have trimesters (or three teaching periods per year). The length of the semester will vary by institution. In some colleges, you might have as few as twelve weeks of teaching, whereas in others there might be fifteen. Some institutions will give you a revision week between the end of classes and the beginning of exams, whereas others might not have a break – or might even schedule exams within the teaching period. You might be entitled to a mid-semester break from classes, such as 'Spring Break' in the USA or a 'reading week' in the UK. It is important that you familiarize yourself with the way your institution schedules classes so that you can create a complete semester timetable and study plan, which will be discussed later in this chapter.

Once you have started your degree or major, your studies will often be broken into individual units of learning, which may be referred to as 'modules', 'units', 'subjects', 'papers', 'courses' or 'classes'. These are essentially self-contained units focused on specific topics, where a lecturer or professor (or a team) takes you through content in a 'lecture', 'class' or 'seminar'. If you are attending lectures with a large number of students (maybe several hundred), you might later have the opportunity to attend smaller 'tutorials' with perhaps fifteen or twenty students, where you discuss the lecture content with the same lecturer or a different 'tutor', often a graduate student. In the biophysical sciences, you might be required to take 'labs' or 'pracs', where you will conduct experiments or learn how to apply the theory outlined in the lecture to practical situations. Some institutions will offer fieldwork, service learning, internships/work placements, activity courses or other experiential learning opportunities. Depending on the programme or module, you might have one lecture or class per subject per week whereas others will have two or three weekly contact hours. Regardless of how the subjects are delivered, a basic expectation across all institutions is that you attend all contact hours. Some institutions or individual lecturers may make this mandatory and will take a physical or electronic attendance list; others will simply assume you are in class.

WHAT DOES IT MEAN TO STUDY SPORT AT UNIVERSITY?

For many people, the idea of studying 'sport' sounds fantastic – almost like playing fantasy football all day long. Yet, studying sport is more than simply chatting about your favourite team, analysing match reports or discussing the merits of individual players. It is even more than training to be a great coach or exercise physiologist. Studying sport is a chance to think creatively and critically about a phenomenon that touches almost every person on the planet. This means taking a step back from what you think you already know about sport, opening yourself up to new perspectives and sometimes challenging your preconceptions about the sport industry and the people in it. Studying sport requires more than blindly accepting ideas at face value: it requires delving below the surface to gain a deeper understanding of sport's role in society, its impact internationally or locally and its significance and meaning to different groups of people. You will engage with theoretical perspectives that take you outside your comfort zone and question common myths and assumptions about the value of sport. In the biophysical sciences, you will learn about the intricacies of the human body so that you can make scientifically justified adjustments to improve athletic performance, enhance health outcomes or generate superior rehabilitative techniques, rather than relying on 'the way it has always been done'. In short, you will be expected to think beyond the sports pages and engage critically with the field and your sub-discipline.

Regardless of your particular focus, one basic tenet applies to every student in higher education: this is *your* learning opportunity. It is up to you, and you alone, to make the most of it. You really do get out of college what you put in, and as you prepare for your future career, keep an open mind about what you are learning and look at how each class contributes to your overall understanding of the field. In other words, always keep one eye on the big picture. It is a privilege to be able to spend time learning, discussing and critiquing an area as popular as sport, so enjoy exploring ideas and challenging yourself and your ways of thinking, and make a valuable contribution to this important field of study both as a student and as a professional.

TRANSITIONING FROM SCHOOL TO UNIVERSITY

Being a university or college student differs significantly from being at school, and knowing what to expect from the outset will make the transition a lot less stressful. Probably the most important difference is the expectation that you will be an independent learner, which means you will need to take primary responsibility for your learning. The pace of learning also increases considerably, and although there is a brief introductory period, learning begins straight away. In order to keep up with classes, additional study and assessments, you will need to apply yourself from day one; otherwise you may quickly fall behind.

Some of the main differences between school and college include:

- *Larger classes*: In some modules, you may be seated with several hundred students in a lecture theatre, which can be overwhelming if you come from smaller high school classes. You may not get to know the lecturer on an individual basis, and there might be few opportunities to ask questions. Being little more than an anonymous number on a class register can be quite confronting to those who are used to their teachers knowing them personally.
- *Fewer contact hours/more 'free' time*: Unlike school, studying at college may not require you to be in class all day, every day with only a few short breaks. In some institutions, you may have as few as twelve face-to-face, or 'contact', hours per week. It might seem as if there is quite a lot of 'free time' for you to meet friends, have coffee, join a few casual sports clubs and – best of all – sleep in. But do not be fooled.
- *More independence*: What looks like 'free' time in your weekly schedule is actually time when you should be studying. University requires a lot more autonomous study, and students are expected to become independent learners. You will be responsible for organizing your schedule, finding supplementary study materials, remembering to prepare assignments and studying for exams; at the same time you will be keeping up with extra-curricular activities such as training or part-time work, as well as balancing your social and family lives.
- *Less 'spoon-feeding'*: The corollary of more independence is less 'spoon-feeding'. In high school, you are typically provided with much, if not all, of the information you will need to know for tests, and there is less of a requirement for you to source important materials to prepare you for assignments and exams. At university, you will not be given everything you need to know, and a lecture or class is generally just the starting point, or an introduction, to an area. You will need to use your initiative to supplement what you learn in class with additional independent study.
- *Less direct supervision/monitoring by teaching staff*: Part of the process of being an independent learner is keeping up with required readings, study, assessments and preparation for exams without your lecturer, tutor or professor monitoring your progress. Some may give you reminders, whereas others will just assume you are working steadily, so it is up to you to manage your college commitments. It is not unusual for you to be given an assignment to do with no further mention of it in class; you are simply expected to submit it on time.
- *Less feedback*: There is less individual feedback and guidance when it comes to assessments. You might be used to a teacher looking over drafts of your work and giving you suggestions before submitting your final paper. At college, while professors are usually happy to help, they normally do not have the time to read drafts, though they may be willing to discuss your general ideas. Assignments or exam papers may be returned to you

with only a grade and no specific feedback on how to improve. It will be up to you to solicit more detail if you need it.

- *New faces*: You may begin college not knowing anyone in your course, and in large classes, you may not even see the same people from week to week. It can take time to find peers who share common interests. Forming a study group will prompt you to meet weekly to discuss classes and assignments, and having some friends will come in handy if you need to work on projects in groups.

STUDENT VIEWPOINT

I went from a small high school in a very small town to a very large university, where I didn't know a single person. I felt pretty lost to start with, but realized quick smart that the only one who could make a difference was me. I joined some clubs and a basketball team and developed some really strong friendships. I also learned to be confident enough to ask for help if I needed it, because trying to figure it all out on my own just wasn't working.—Lucy.

ROLES AND RESPONSIBILITIES

The teaching staff at your institution will have a number of different responsibilities. At large universities, most professors will be engaged in research and publishing as well as administration, so teaching might be only a reasonably small part of their overall position. Teaching-focused faculty will have fewer, if any, research commitments, and so may be more available to students. Regardless of the type of university, all faculty will have administrative responsibilities and committee work, and many will supervise graduate students and engage in other professional activities that mean they are not at your beck and call. Utilize published 'office hours' when professors make themselves available for students, or make an appointment to meet at another time, but unless you are explicitly told it is acceptable, do not assume you can just drop in to their office whenever it suits.

When it comes to teaching, lecturers are responsible for designing and delivering module content, setting assessments and exams, and grading students' work. In higher education, lecturers are not teachers as such but guides who lead you through the subject matter. In essence, they introduce you to topics and create frameworks to help you learn. It will be up to you, however, to find additional resources to develop a comprehensive understanding of the material. This means you will need to ask questions, interpret and analyse material, find extra readings and/or visit relevant, specialist websites. In short, it is vital to recognize your role and to accept that you are at the centre of your learning experience. How much or how little you choose to put into your studies is entirely a personal decision, but bear in mind it is not the lecturing staff's responsibility for you to learn.

In terms of students, it is expected that you adopt a professional attitude towards your studies. If not mandatory, full attendance is certainly expected, and there is a strong correlation between attendance at classes and successful completion of a subject, just as there is a strong correlation between attending training sessions and improving at your chosen sport. It should come as no surprise that being aware of the class content results in better grades, but this seems to escape students when first starting out, particularly when there are many other pursuits to tempt them away from lectures.

RESPECT

It is important that both faculty and students show respect for one another. Both should arrive on time and prepared for the class. Both should not talk when others are talking. Before class starts, switch off all electronic communication and music devices. If you need to keep your phone on vibrate for an emergency, then mention this to your lecturer and quietly absent yourself from class to take the call. As students, you should submit all assessments on time and in the required format. Finally, both staff and students should behave and communicate in a professional manner at all times. When sending emails, begin with a salutation and the recipient's name, use formal language as opposed to 'text-speak' to state the issue and what you need, and sign off with your full name and student number. Respond promptly to requests from professors.

TIME MANAGEMENT

One of the most important skills to learn at university is time management, and getting this right from the start will establish valuable habits for the rest of your degree and beyond. Time management is more than ensuring you attend class on time, but in reality is little more than *self*-management. We cannot create more time; we can only control what we do with it. In order to best organize yourself, make a frank assessment of your life – including your studies and your extra-curricular commitments such as sport and social life – to design the best strategy to manage each one. Although you may need to prioritize certain activities at certain times, the overall key to time management is to be honest about what you can realistically manage.

The first step to good time management is to create an overall schedule of your week and fill in all fixed or 'non-negotiable' commitments. These will include your lectures, seminars and labs, other on- or off-campus activities and personal or family responsibilities. If you have fixed sporting obligations, make sure you have copies of training schedules. Mark all of these 'non-negotiables' on your calendar in red so that you know they cannot be changed. Next, fill

CASE STUDY

Although for many students, waking up in time for a 9am lecture is a struggle, consider the rigours of elite athletes who are trying to combine achievement in sport with success at university. Here is a typical day in the life of a modern pentathlete who had to disrupt his second year at college to compete at the Olympics.

6:45am	Wake up
7:00am	Carb shake (pre-run)
7:30am	Run; 15 minutes cool down
8:50am	Arrive home (put breakfast on stove)
8:55am	Shower
9:05am	Breakfast (porridge, raisins, flaxseed, banana), coffee
9:30am	Travel to college
10:00am	Lecture (2 hours)
12:10pm	Eat (carbs)
12:30pm	Study (2.5 hours)
3:00pm	Eat
3:30pm	Foam roll/stretch
4:00pm	Swimming training (2 hours)
6:00pm	High-calorie shake (900 kcals)
6:15pm	Shooting practice (40 minutes)
7:00pm	Fencing training (2 hours)
9:15pm	Dinner/relax
10:00pm	Emails, stretch, prepare food for tomorrow
10:30pm	Bed

→ What strategies can you learn from his schedule to help you better organize your time?

→ If you could give him one suggestion about finding balance between sport, study and relaxation, what would it be?

→ What advice do you think he would give to other students struggling to combine outside activities with college?

in your flexible activities: 'date night', going out with friends, workouts and other activities that can be rescheduled if needed. Add these in a contrasting colour, such as green, to indicate they are movable. Once you have gone through this process, you will see how much 'free time' you have left each week. It is easy to fritter away an hour here and there by having a coffee with friends after class, a lunch break that extends into the late afternoon or regular sleep-ins. While the occasional sleep-in or long lunch is no big deal, indulging on a regular basis wastes precious time that will just add to your stress levels when assessment deadlines and exam dates loom.

The final step is to identify periods of time that can be set aside for study and assessment preparation. Most subjects will expect a larger time commitment from you each week than just the class contact hours, so allocate additional study time to each class. Start with two hours per subject on the understanding that as the semester progresses, you will probably have to increase it. The two hours do not need to be one continuous block. If you find thirty minutes is all you can manage before your mind starts to wander, simply find four thirty-minute sessions across the week for each class. Before scheduling study periods, be realistic about your personal characteristics and study habits. Do you like to wake up early? If not, there is no point scheduling study sessions early in the morning. If you work best in the quiet, do not schedule study sessions at dinner time in the family home. If you have to share resources, such as a computer, schedule sessions when you know you will have access. If you are normally wiped out after training, do not plan to sit up for a few more hours to study. You are in control of your timetable, so make it work for you and do not set yourself up to fail by being unrealistic or overly ambitious.

TIP

Remember that study periods are not 'maybes' or only 'if I have time' sessions. Once they are on your calendar, they are fixed, non-negotiable appointments that you need to commit to keep. They are as important as attending class or going to practice and need to be treated as such.

HOW DO I 'STUDY'?

For many people, studying equates to long days and nights furiously memorizing and cramming before an exam. Yet this is not the most efficient way of learning, nor the most sensible use of your time. Studying means to examine and review ideas, work through concepts presented in class, discuss them with others and gradually come to a point where you know and can apply the subject matter. While it sounds like a lot of work, it is actually a reasonably small weekly investment for a large return at the end of the semester.

In terms of the practicalities of studying, the most successful sessions are those that are planned. Each week, spend half an hour or so identifying your study priorities to utilize your time as efficiently and as effectively as possible. Study blocks are part preparation, part revision and part assessment oriented, so there are a number of tasks that can be completed during this time:

• Review, edit and annotate your lecture notes.
• Revise key points raised in class and identify any that are unclear.
• Meet with your study group to discuss lectures.
• Find additional materials to help you broaden and deepen your knowledge.

- Complete any required readings for the next class.
- Examine any notes that might be provided ahead of the next lecture.
- Research and complete assessments. You may need to allocate more time to assignments as due dates approach.
- Prepare for quizzes, tests and exams.

Once you have worked out your weekly schedule, the next step is to design an overall semester schedule. You can list all important class times, assessment *start* and *due* dates, exam dates, any tournaments or training camps you will need to attend and other extra-curricular activities that could impact on your studies. Keep this schedule pinned in a prominent place in your study space so you have a visual reminder of what is coming up and set yourself alerts through your smartphone or electronic calendar to remind you to begin assignments.

ASSESSMENT MANAGEMENT

Part of the process of time management is managing the assessments for each subject. These may vary from written papers to multiple-choice quizzes to short exercises and essay exams, as well as online interaction and collaboration. Each one will need a different type and level of preparation, depending on the relative weighting and due date. No matter what the assessment, it is important that you do not leave everything to the last minute, as the quality of your work will suffer, and professors are more than familiar with rush jobs. To schedule in your assessment preparation, you need to work backwards from the due date to establish the start date. The only value in a due date is to let you know when you need to submit the finished piece of work. It is more important to know when to start. Your start date for a written assignment will depend on several factors, including the time it takes you to locate, read and summarize relevant research as well as write your paper, whereas the start date for a quiz or exam will depend on how long you think it will take you to revise each week's lecture material as well as supplementary readings. Some students like to schedule in each component of their assessments to ensure they remain on track through the semester.

REVISING YOUR TIME MANAGEMENT PLAN

After the first few weeks, review your study habits. Look at your diary and note the number of times you successfully completed your study sessions. If you have missed some, can you see any patterns? If there are no acceptable reasons for missed study sessions, identify the steps you need to take to get your time management plan back on track. If there is a regular conflict, simply revise your plan and reschedule. Be honest when reviewing your plan. Excuses do not matter, only the actions you take, so if something is not working, make the changes to fix it. Of course, you do need to have some flexibility, but too much just means you are not following any plan at all.

A QUICK NOTE ON PREPARING FOR EXAMS

While Chapter 13 is dedicated entirely to the exam process, it is important to think early in the semester about how you prepare for exams. There is no point leaving everything to the last minute and trying to cram in four or six courses' worth of lectures. Your weekly study sessions are a time to revise and learn the material that you will need for exams at the end of the semester. Learning slowly and steadily as you go through the content each week means that by the time you begin revising for exams, you will already *know* and understand the content, so that revision will simply be revision, not learning the entire course from scratch. Small investments each week mean that you will have a large return by the time the exam begins. You will then be rewarded with less stress and more confidence as you enter the examination period.

SUMMARY

1   Sports studies is a multifaceted and exciting field that provides a broad range of career opportunities. It embodies a number of sub-disciplines and scientific approaches.
2   There are significant differences between secondary and tertiary education, and it is important that students understand from the outset their role within their learning experience.
3   Time management and self-management are among the most important skills to learn as students transition to become independent and autonomous learners.
4   A commitment to review and study course content each week is a small investment in learning that will yield strong gains as the revision and examination periods begin.

EXERCISES

1   Familiarize yourself with your institution's semester structure. When do classes start? How many weeks is the teaching semester? When are exams scheduled? Is there a mid-term break and a revision week?
2   Establish your own semester schedule, including breaks, revision time, assessment due dates, training sessions, match schedule, travel home and any other activities in which you are involved.
3   Create your weekly schedule including your class timetable and other 'non-negotiables', and find at least two hours of study time (either as a block, or divided as you like) for each of the classes you are taking.
4   Design an assessment management plan by working out how much time you will need for each assessment item.
5   Find out about the various support services in your institution that will help you with everything from writing assignments, handling exam anxiety and dealing with personal issues.

REFLECTION

Think about what it will be like to start university. What might be the main challenges you will face? How will you overcome these? Are there any obstacles that might prevent you from maintaining your study schedule? How will you deal with them? How do you best study? Can you think of some techniques to assist your learning?

FURTHER READING

Ferrett, S. (2012) *Peak performance: success in college and beyond,* 8th edn. New York: McGraw-Hill.

Light, R.J. (2001) *Making the most of college: students speak their minds.* Cambridge MA: Harvard University Press.

2

LEARNING AND THINKING

What and how to know

OVERVIEW

This chapter outlines:
- what it means to be an independent learner;
- how to use different learning styles to suit individual needs;
- the process of critical thinking and how to apply reason to readings, lectures and other information sources.

INTRODUCTION

One of the most important skills you will learn at university is the ability to 'know how to know', which is developed by 'learning how to learn'. In many cases, 'knowing how to know' is considered more important than the substantive content of your course and sets you apart from those without higher education. It is more than just having the ability to look up appropriate sources of information; it allows you to think about those sources, to delve beyond the surface to understand a text, issue or situation more deeply, to identify connections and relationships between ideas and to offer informed decisions about the content you are reviewing.

To understand the process of 'knowing how to know', imagine you have been asked to write a feasibility report on the inclusion of pesäpallo at a local sports facility. You probably do not know this sport, so you would begin by finding out what pesäpallo actually is. Like most people, you would turn to the internet to discover that pesäpallo is a popular Finnish activity that resembles baseball. As it is a fast-paced sport, you feel it is exciting enough to propose to the club, but unfortunately your personal opinion is not enough for a report, and you will need to know more about the sport and the feasibility of including it before making a confident recommendation. At this point, you will have to decide what type of information you require, the most appropriate sources of that information and how the information will be accessed before you will be able to filter the relevant details from the unhelpful. Finding, selecting, discarding, interpreting and analysing the right information are critical components of knowing how to identify the right knowledge base to suit each situation.

Knowing how to know begins with an awareness of what knowledge is, how it is produced and the agendas it might serve, and requires you to be cognisant of the way that you learn. This chapter outlines the processes by which we learn and what it means to be an independent learner, briefly examines different learning styles and introduces the concept of research from an academic perspective. Finally, it covers the most crucial aspect of knowing how to know: the ability to be a critical thinker and to employ critical thinking skills in any educational, professional or personal context.

HOW DO WE KNOW?

Most people would think they have a good understanding of what 'knowledge' is – namely, the outcome of learning. This might be understood as a series of facts and figures that can be recalled at will, so a game show contestant, for example, might demonstrate a 'good level of knowledge' as they answer questions. To gain a 'good level of knowledge', we may sit in a classroom where a teacher imparts information or we might read some books or website pages, so that at the end of the process we know more than when we started. We have, therefore, entered some data into our brain or 'gained knowledge'. Nevertheless, while the brain can certainly store significant amounts of data, knowledge is more than a collection of individual 'facts'. It is the process by which we gather, form and assimilate ideas, information and experiences, identify patterns or differences, evaluate and critique, draw conclusions and determine or predict outcomes or consequences.

While knowing how to know sounds time consuming or even quite difficult, it is worth considering that we engage daily in this process from birth. Babies and toddlers are among the greatest scientists in the world and spend their days conducting increasingly sophisticated experiments. Under the guise of 'play' they are establishing patterns of behaviour, cause-and-effect relationships, their influence on others and the limits of their existence:

> If I throw the ball at the wall, what happens? OK, if I throw it harder, will it go further or bounce harder? What if I roll it? And if I throw it to Mummy, will she throw it back or take it away? Oh, she threw it back! If I stand here, I wonder if I can hit the cat with the ball? Hmm, the cat. If I pull the cat's tail, what happens? If I pull it again, I predict the cat will hiss at me. Am I right? Let me try that again, just to be certain. Oh no, it scratched! I guess the cat doesn't like it . . . will she like it if I try now?

We engage in these tests every day as we navigate through life, though the subject matter might be a little more involved than balls and cats. For the most part, however, we are unaware of *how* we are learning or even *that* we are learning. It is so ingrained as part of our everyday life that it does not seem particularly noteworthy. For this reason, understanding how we learn may help us learn more efficiently.

Psychologists regard learning to be a relatively permanent change in behaviour potential that results from experience (cf. Klein 2012). It is a fundamental change in who we are and how we might choose to behave in the future. The toddler in the passage above will have learned that pulling the cat's tail results in discomfort and so, over time, will modify their behaviour. We could look at a similar example of learning in sport. Most combatants in mixed martial arts come to the sport from martial arts that are performed in an upright position. Encountering specialists in groundwork without knowing how to defend oneself on the ground or how to avoid being pulled down would place most of these combatants at a disadvantage. Learning how to avoid being brought to ground or get out of the situation if they are means they have the potential to respond if they need to. In other words, after we learn a new skill, we have the capacity to use that skill, even if we do not need to use it all the time. This is the change in 'potential behaviour' that results from learning. So the learning you engage in at university will change your potential behaviour as you have new knowledge bases and experiences to draw upon to inform your actions. To make the most of the opportunity, it is important to identify strengths and weaknesses in your learning practices so that these skills can be more consciously applied when studying at university.

BECOMING AN INDEPENDENT LEARNER

Understanding our learning practices is an important step in becoming an independent learner. Independent learners are those who accept their central role in, and responsibility for, their own learning experience. They are motivated to learn and actively seek resources to help them study rather than relying on others to facilitate their learning. Independent learners are adept at organizing themselves and their lives to ensure they manage their various obligations and deliver assessments on time. Most importantly, being an independent learner means understanding that learning is something that *you* do, not something that is done *to you* or *for you*. It suggests you are willing to try to work out ideas for yourself rather than being given the answers or being told what to believe. An independent learner thus thinks critically and creatively, and questions information rather than accepting everything at face value.

Independent learning is enormously liberating for some students, but can be quite overwhelming for others. It can be difficult shedding years of conditioning that teaches us to expect knowledge to be handed to us rather than discovered on our own. Without the 'right answer', students can sometimes feel as if they are treading water with nothing to hold on to for support. For this reason, it is important to recognize that being an independent learner does not mean having to do everything on your own or without any help. Indeed, being an independent learner also means knowing when and how to ask for assistance. There is no expectation that you will already have all the answers, so not only should you explore ideas for yourself but you also need to be self-reflective enough to know when you have reached an impasse. In sum, being a successful independent learner means appreciating how you best learn.

CASE STUDY

Jack is a second-year exercise science student specializing in strength and conditioning. He arrives at his practical session on plyometrics without having attended the preparatory lecture. He is called upon to demonstrate a simple exercise but is not sure what he is supposed to do, so he asks his tutor to explain the basic principles to him.

→ How do you think the tutor reacted to Jack's request?

→ How would Jack's request for the tutor to recap the lecture impact the rest of the students in the class?

→ If Jack could not attend the lecture, what should he have done to prepare for the practical?

→ Jack clearly does not understand what is going on. At what point do you think it would be reasonable for him to ask for help from the tutor?

LEARNING STYLES

The most effective way to learn differs considerably from individual to individual, and to this end, a number of different 'learning styles' have been identified. It is thought that through various inventories it is possible to determine what kind of learner each person is, so that they can utilize study techniques that are best tailored to their individual needs. The main learning styles include:

- *Visual learners*: Visual learners learn best by seeing. They thrive on diagrams, images, flashcards and demonstrations, and like to see how ideas fit together rather than listening to content. They like taking notes and organizing their ideas on paper, making lists and otherwise recording ideas in black and white.
- *Aural learners*: Aural learners like to hear information. They work best by listening to others speak, having ideas explained to them or even listening to lectures or podcasts online. They follow spoken instructions well and like to engage in debates and discussions. They prefer presentations to written papers and recording lectures to taking notes.

- *Kinaesthetic learners*: These learners learn by doing. They need to feel or experience the information by using all their senses, so this might include building models, conducting experiments, or going on field trips, rather than listening or watching. It would be likely that those who enjoy sport might like elements of kinaesthetic learning, given that learning a new athletic skill requires you to perform it.

As attractive as these styles seem, the concept of learning styles is highly contested, and there is no specific evidence to suggest that conforming to a particular learning style will yield better academic results. Indeed, an individual may prefer one learning style over another in particular subject areas, but thrive with a different style when it comes to another discipline. Moreover, their preferred learning style may change as they become more confident in their overall study skills. If you decide to complete an online inventory to determine 'your' learning style, do not change all your study habits to conform to the identified structure, but do try different learning strategies, and pick and choose the techniques that best suit you. The real value in learning styles is being aware of the varied ways that people learn, so that you can add to your repertoire of study skills.

KNOWING HOW TO KNOW

'Knowing how to know' simply means having the ability to find, assess and critique relevant information in response to any knowledge gap you might have. It is a process of problem solving by actively and systematically soliciting knowledge. It differs from 'learning how to learn' in that it concentrates on developing skills of research and critical analysis rather than on our personal learning styles or strategies. Knowing how to know develops through exposure to systems of knowledge and by applying research conventions in a range of contexts.

We each have the ability to conduct basic research and to solve problems on a routine basis, but this is often conducted without the same level of awareness required of formal research. For example, imagine you are visiting your grandmother and you discover a box of old photos and sporting memorabilia in the attic. You pause to look at the photos and examine the rusty inscriptions on the trophies. You wonder who the people in the photo are. Is your late grandfather pictured? Where are they? What are they doing? Do you stop there, forever curious about what this box represents, or do you actively seek more information? You ask your grandmother, who cannot remember all the details, so she refers you to your grandfather's letters and diaries. You learn that he was competing at national level. Many people might be satisfied that the mystery is now solved. But you are still curious about the others, so you search though old newspapers at the local library and find the names of the remaining athletes. You learn that two of them went on to compete at the Olympics. Through your natural curiosity, you manage to collect relevant information through rudimentary archival research.

What distinguishes your casual searching for information inspired by a box of memorabilia and the research actions of a sports historian, for example, is the level of formality in documenting and recording archival evidence, analysing the significance of artefacts, situating the uncovered details in a broader social, historical or political context and perhaps applying a theoretical framework to make sense of the results. Simply put, the difference between everyday research and academic research is that the latter is systematic and organized, based on accepted methodologies, and is subject to higher levels of analysis to test the strength of the data. It requires more specific intent, dedication and actions and relies less on informal situations or anecdotal evidence. As you engage in these processes at college, your ability to know how to know will be greatly enhanced, so you will have a wider knowledge base and set of skills to draw upon when problem solving.

> ### TIP
>
> Conquer the feeling of being overwhelmed about academic learning by realizing it is just a systematic, organized approach to how we learn on a daily basis.

A BRIEF INTRODUCTION TO RESEARCH

For most assessment tasks at university you will be required to conduct some level of research. This might range from gathering previously published materials to develop an argument in response to a research question to collecting your own data to analyse. Many students baulk at the idea of conducting research instead of simply presenting their own opinions because research seems like hard work and they feel that everyone is entitled to their own opinion. Yet we all conduct research by collecting information and using it to inform our decisions or actions. Even just the act of reading reviews before deciding which movie to see is an example of engaging in research. As such, carrying out scientific research is simply a matter of honing and applying these skills within a scientific context.

Academic or scientific research is the systematic collection, organization and analysis of data (cf. Gratton and Jones 2010). Researchers carefully design studies to gather relevant information, record the results in a logical manner, draw conclusions about the significance of their findings, and confirm or refute previous theories about the subject matter. Each researcher makes small contributions of ideas and theories that collectively create the knowledge base in any given field of study. It is necessarily a time-consuming, meticulous and methodical process; an informal, disorganized or casual approach would not yield the consistent or trustworthy results that are needed to form a reliable basis for future research. This should suggest that your own research will need to be careful, considered and systematic, and that a haphazard or random approach to gathering materials does not lead to effective outcomes. The research process will be discussed in more detail in Chapter 4.

CRITICAL THINKING

The most important skill that you will use in all aspects of your university career and the one that will stay with you throughout the rest of your life is the ability to think critically (cf. Ryall 2010). Critical thinking does not mean 'being critical' but rather suggests that you have the capacity to think beyond your own preconceived notions, understand a multitude of perspectives and, simply put, not accept ideas and information at face value. It means that you are actively questioning concepts and propositions until you are satisfied that they are based on a logical and rigorous foundation. Rather than just sitting back and passively letting information wash over them, critical thinkers carefully evaluate information and arguments to determine their worth. The ability to think critically and ask questions means that you will be able to assess the arguments you read in books and journal articles, and will be able to appraise the quality of conclusions and recommendations of scientific reports. A critical thinker tries to examine the context of various events to find comprehensive explanations for actions or reactions, and evaluates material to establish patterns, trends or other relationships. Likewise, as you develop the skills of critical thinking, you will be more competent in the art of writing lucid arguments based on logic and evidence.

For the amount of analysis that exists in the print media, online, on television and in bars around the world, it would be fair to think that the study of sport is founded on the basic principles of critical thinking. Every pundit can look at a curve ball fifteen different ways to explain its context and significance to the pitcher, catcher, batter, team, match and competition, and outline in some detail how an alternative selection would have had notably different outcomes. Yet there are many ways in which the popular analysis of sport is devoid of critical thinking. There are many assumptions and presumptions that are simply accepted as absolutes rather than critically assessed to see if they hold true. For example, for the average person on the street, it is completely antithetical to think of sport as anything other than a positive, character-building exercise that teaches values such as hard work, discipline and respect, and that these traits translate to other aspects of a participant's life. Parents, for example, would not be inclined to sign their children up to junior sports if they thought their kids would learn how to use violence to assert their will and take advantage of the weakness of others. Yet if we think critically about competitive contact sports, these might be precisely the skills and qualities that are privileged and perhaps even translated into other aspects of participants' lives. There are some areas of sports studies where critical thinking might make us feel uncomfortable, and in other areas the alternative perspectives will be less confronting, but no matter which discipline you focus on, you will be required to become a competent critical thinker.

BECOMING A CRITICAL THINKER

Critical thinking is not something that comes naturally to everyone, and it can be challenging or even confusing when starting out. It is incredibly difficult to overcome years of socialization that tells us we are all entitled to our own opinions and instead try to set aside our perspectives in favour of having an open mind that is flexible enough to respond to evidence, reasoning and logic. Nevertheless, like any complex physical skill, critical thinking is an intellectual endeavour that can be learned and, with practice, can become second nature. In college, you will mostly be required to exercise your powers of critical thinking when you are presented with research assignments and problem-based learning activities or during lectures when the professor poses questions. In every case, knowing that you are required to think beyond just a simple or obvious response means that you will start to look for alternative explanations or ways of thinking about a topic, and will be able to assess arguments you encounter in the research literature.

Starting the process of critical thinking begins with a simple question: how do you know? By applying these four words to any idea or concept, you can start to peel back the layers of knowledge until you find a more appropriate solution or are convinced by the evidence that supports the original proposition.

Consider this example:

> The Olympic Games brings the best athletes in the world together to compete against one another.

This is a fairly standard description of the Olympics. We know that athletes come from all over the globe to excel in their given sport, and a reasonable person would trust that 'the best in the world' means those athletes who at that moment are the very best competitors in each event. The statement suggests explicitly that what we witness at the Olympics is a test of human ability on a level playing field to see which athlete is the best of the best. But is this really the case? Do we really witness a test among the world's most elite sportspeople? We will need to apply our powers of critical thinking to this statement to see if the evidence supports or refutes it.

We begin by examining the statement itself and breaking it down to the key ideas:

- the Olympics;
- best athletes in the world;
- compete against one another.

The first and third points seem reasonable. We can agree that there is an event called 'the Olympics', and to some degree we can agree that athletes compete against one another, recognizing, of course, that in some events not all athletes compete against all other athletes, because of heats, knock-out competitions or other methods of weeding out weaker competitors. The next step is to take a closer look at the second part of the statement, 'the best athletes in the world', and apply our 'how do you know?' test.

Looking more closely at the second point, we can, of course, agree that *athletes* compete at the Olympics – it is a sports event after all – but can we agree that they are the *best* athletes? And do they represent the best athletes *in the world*? In order to test this proposition, we should first decide what 'the best athletes in the world' means. Everyone will have their own criteria, but given there are around 10,000 athletes competing at the Olympics, it might be fair to suggest that the top twenty in any one event might be considered 'the best in the world'. You might think the top ten or the top fifty are better representations of 'the best in the world', and part of the process of critical thinking will be establishing your own parameters for the analysis. Determining the top twenty would also need a timeframe, as the list will change. For this exercise, we will select the time period between 1 January and 30 June 2012 – in other words, the six months leading up to the Olympics. Finally, we need to select some sports to determine whether the top twenty athletes from the first half of 2012 were indeed competing at the Olympics. Let us consider the men's marathon, the 50m men's freestyle and the 100m women's sprint.

According to the website of the International Association of Athletic Federations (IAAF), the twenty fastest male marathon runners in 2012 prior to the Olympic Games were from either Kenya or Ethiopia. The IAAF selection criteria, however, only permit up to three representatives from any nation to compete at the Games. Not taking into consideration injury or any other factors that would reduce the number available to participate, this means fourteen of the top twenty runners in the world were not allowed to compete at the Olympic Games. It is worth restating this point. Fourteen of the best marathoners in the world were not invited to compete at the Olympics, whereas other, less accomplished runners were able to compete. Similarly, of the top twenty men's 50m freestyle swimmers in the first six months of 2012, five were from the United States, four were from France and four were from Australia. National swimming federations may send only two swimmers for each event to the Olympics, so many of the world's fastest swimmers over fifty metres were precluded from competition, including the swimmer who had posted the fourth fastest time. Finally, in the women's 100m, the top twenty sprinters included seven from Jamaica and five from the USA, with only three competitors accepted from any one nation. As in the swimming example, one of the top ten sprinters was ineligible for the Olympics. Imagine being in the top ten in the world and being passed over for selection, while someone slower than you has the honour of competing.

From this analysis, it is increasingly difficult to accept the proposition that the 'best athletes in the world' compete against one another at the Olympic Games. It would be more accurate to state that 'the best two or three athletes from each country compete against each other at the Olympics', but this is not quite as catchy. It demonstrates that even a seemingly innocuous statement can be examined critically to determine its veracity, and at university you will be expected to gradually become more adept at evaluating the quality of the information you are analysing.

STUDENT VIEWPOINT

Critical thinking is a vital skill for me to develop because having the ability to filter and evaluate information is just as important as learning to identify and discard false ideas. I find my lack of experience or practice a barrier in critical thinking, and I know I need to read more texts to improve this skill. Another area of weakness for me is that I don't have the confidence yet to critique experts. I find this quite difficult as the authors are usually experts in a particular area, and I am reluctant to critically analyse their ideas, methods and argument. I know it will take practice in order to overcome these barriers and improve my confidence, but I'm willing to put the work in because becoming a good critical thinker will improve my standard of work at college.—Carly.

PRACTISING CRITICAL THINKING

There are different ways that you can hone your critical thinking skills, but for the most part it just takes a conscious decision to start asking more questions. You can practise critical thinking sitting on the bus reading the newspaper, watching the game on television, looking at analyses of current events, reading blogs or considering topical issues within your field. Start by watching some stories on the evening news and ask yourself the following questions:

- What is the story about?
- Who is speaking? In other words, who has been given the opportunity to comment on the issue?
- Why has this person been selected?
- What are the qualifications, credentials, position or experience that gives them the authority to speak on the matter?
- What questions are they being asked?
- What questions are they *not* being asked?
- What questions would you like to ask them?
- To what extent is their position being challenged or supported?
- Is their position reasonable and supported by evidence? Or are they merely expressing personal opinions with no logical rationale?
- Who else might be able to offer a perspective on this situation?
- Why have they *not* been chosen to speak?

These questions encourage you to think beyond the surface presentation and to come to a more reasoned conclusion about the story or event. It is not difficult to start practising critical thinking, and once you are more confident with asking questions, you can start to apply these skills to more complex situations.

CRITICAL THINKING IN LECTURES

Although the process of how to listen actively in lectures and take notes will be discussed in Chapter 3, it is worth discussing here how to think critically during lectures, seminars, labs or other classes. The process begins with good preparation so that you are familiar with the topic before you arrive at the lecture. Being prepared enables you to listen actively because you will recognize key ideas as they are mentioned. Thinking critically takes you one step further to evaluate ideas as they are presented. Why does the professor choose this perspective? Are there other ways to examine this topic? Does the lecturer's material contradict or affirm the reading you have done on the topic? What conclusions can be drawn from the differing ideas? Make notes of the ideas that spring to mind as you evaluate the material and follow these up later with your study group or professor.

CRITICAL THINKING WHEN READING

When you read academic works, such as journal articles, or popular sources, such as web pages, it is important to think critically about the information you are looking at. Start by thinking about the text as a whole:

- Who is the author?
- What are their credentials?
- What is the source?
- Who is the publisher?
- Has the research been funded?
- Is there a conflict of interest?
- Who owns the publication/website?

After you have considered the document as a whole, it is time to delve into the actual content and critically assess the material contained therein. Begin by trying to identify the main purpose of the piece, as this will confirm the authors' stated intention and allow you to determine whether they successfully met their objectives:

- Examine the research methods: how has the author collected data?
- Identify the main findings of the paper: translate these into your own words to ensure that you understand what these points mean.
- Are there any obvious theoretical frameworks being used? Are these appropriate in this context?
- Is the argument logical, consistent and well supported by evidence?
- Are the conclusions a logical extension of the findings? Could you think of other ways of explaining the results?

The next step is to consider this paper in the context of other related research you have read. How does this paper compare? Does it have similar or different findings? If they are different, why do you think they are different? What does the paper add to our understanding of the issue? What future research does it propose and has anyone else followed up on these suggestions? Finally, evaluate the overall value of the piece in terms of the quality of its argument and its reliability as a piece of research.

BARRIERS TO CRITICAL THINKING

Many students just starting out can be reluctant to think critically about readings, lecture content and other materials they are provided with, and they are certainly not prepared to contradict or challenge a professor in class. There are several reasons for this reticence, beginning with the fact that critical thinking is challenging, and most people are quite happy not to be confronted with alternative ways of thinking. It takes an open mind and flexibility to expose one's position to critique. This is coupled with an expectation that 'critical thinking' is just being 'negative' or 'judgemental', rather than encouraging rigorous debate. No one wants to open themselves up to being ripped to shreds. Furthermore, students often lack confidence in both their knowledge of the field and their ability to critique more accomplished experts. This is understandable; however, students are not expected to engage on the most sophisticated level right from the start. Critical thinking starts by asking a few simple questions – 'Why?' and 'How do they know?' – and gradually develops as a student's skills and confidence grow.

SUMMARY

1   One of the most important skills students learn at university is 'knowing how to know'. Understanding the mechanisms by which they learn and know helps students demystify the academic process and employ effective learning strategies in both their studies and their future careers.

2   Successful students are able to become independent learners who take responsibility for, and invest in, their own learning experience. Independent learners manage their activities, time and themselves effectively, seek out additional resources to aid their learning and understand that they are at the centre of their quest for knowledge.

3   The concept of learning styles may give students an insight into the variety of techniques that may help them learn more effectively. Though the concept is contested, the various strategies can be mixed and matched to suit an individual's study needs.

4   Critical thinking is a central part of tertiary education and requires learners to be willing to evaluate lecture content, readings and other materials. A lack of familiarity with the subject area does not preclude a student from critically thinking about the materials they are exposed to.

EXERCISES

1   Complete an online learning styles inventory to see which type of learner you might be. Examine the different techniques associated with the various learning styles and select ideas that you feel best suit your current study patterns as well as one or two others to try.
2   Select a short sports-related magazine article or blog of your choice and use the questions in the text to think critically about the content. Try to determine what the author's perspective might be, the evidence used to support the position and whether the position or conclusion is justified.
3   Write a short response to the article you chose in the previous exercise, outlining a different perspective or way of interpreting the situation. You might be able to identify more than one alternative standpoint.

REFLECTION

What changes will you need to make to your current study habits to become an independent learner? Consider your previous learning experiences. What were your most effective study strategies? Can you identify your learning style from your study preferences? Can you see techniques to enhance your learning style? Think about the difference between 'being critical' and 'thinking critically'. How might you learn to look at issues from different perspectives? Would you regard yourself as flexible and open to new ideas? What is the relationship between critical thinking and being an independent learner?

FURTHER READING

Jarvis, P., Holford, J. and Griffin, C. (eds) (2003) *The theory and practice of learning*, 2nd edn. Abingdon: Routledge.
Ryall, E. (2010) *Critical thinking for sports students*. Exeter: Learning Matters.

3

MAKING SENSE OF LECTURES

Listening in class and taking notes

OVERVIEW

This chapter outlines:
- the purpose and structure of a lecture;
- how to listen actively to get the most out of a class;
- several note-taking systems to record lectures effectively;
- how to augment lecture notes through the semester to prepare for exams.

INTRODUCTION

One of the main activities that students engage in at university is attending lectures. At its simplest, a lecture is an oral presentation that communicates information from the lecturer to students in a format that has existed for centuries. Lectures might be held in large auditoriums with hundreds of students, or they might be more intimate classes with smaller groups. Large lectures typically provide fewer opportunities to interact with the professor, while smaller classes or seminars might be more interactive, so you will be expected to contribute to the discussion. In many ways lectures are similar to training sessions where the coach outlines the tactics for the next game or season. There might be a chance to ask questions, but it is largely a situation where the coach speaks and the athletes listen. Like lectures, these sessions are only the start, not the end. The athletes still need to review, learn and practise the tactics many times before executing them on the field of play.

Whatever size or form they take, lectures, classes and seminars are used to introduce students to subject matter in a structured manner, though the way information is presented will vary dramatically between lecturers. Some might use complex multimedia presentations; others might speak to a few notes on an overhead, while others still might employ the 'chalk and talk' method of writing on a whiteboard as they speak. The lectures might be interactive and require a lot of student input, or they might be more traditional, with a professor 'professing' and students listening. As web technologies are further integrated into learning systems – or if you are a distance learner – you may be viewing online lectures or listening to podcasts, and engaging interactively via discussion boards.

To support lectures, most universities will have a virtual learning environment (VLE), such as Blackboard, WebCT or Moodle, which will be used to differing degrees by individual lecturers. Some will upload a lot of information, lecture notes, additional resources, review questions, links and other relevant materials; some will post brief lecture overviews and announcements; others will only offer the bare minimum, if any, detail. Some faculty will provide detailed notes for students to study; some will offer only a lecture summary; and others will not provide any written material, expecting you to take your own notes instead.

Each year, students end up disgruntled, even angry, when they cannot access lecture notes through the VLE, and this is usually at exam time when they realize that their lecturer expected students to take their own notes in class. To avoid this situation, familiarize yourself with how your lecturers use the VLE by browsing through each subject's portal in the first week of term. Regardless of how much information is posted, remember that the one constant in every lecture is you. It is up to you to make as much or as little of the module as you like, and this chapter outlines how to extract meaningful information from each class, tailored to your individual needs. Being able to take your own notes frees you from relying on handouts, so if class notes are not provided, you are not left floundering. Notes that you have written yourself are customized to your knowledge base and are expressed in your own words, which makes them the best materials to support your learning.

PURPOSE OF A LECTURE

The purpose of a lecture is to introduce you to new subject matter. Whether it is outlining the structure of the human skeleton, identifying key strategies for successful sports marketing or highlighting the role of sport in disadvantaged communities, lectures present themes, issues and examples to students, pitched at an appropriate level. Although a lecturer can appear to talk effortlessly about a particular topic, a lecture is not personal opinion. Each lecture takes hours of preparation as the professor reads widely on a topic, analyses the key concepts, and summarizes decades of knowledge and research into a format that is accessible to students.

The process of condensing an entire area of study into a single lecture means that professors need to make significant decisions about what to include and what to leave out, revealing that a lecture cannot possibly provide every single piece of relevant information on a topic. Think of lectures like a window that gives you a glimpse of a new field, but limits what you can see by the structure of the window frame. Nevertheless, the view is enough to make you aware of some key features. Independent learners will not be satisfied with the partial picture, and will find their own way outside to experience it for themselves. In other words, for every lecture you attend, there is a wealth of information beyond what is presented in class, and part of your responsibility as a learner is to source relevant materials to complement the lecture content so that you can develop a comprehensive understanding of the topic.

TIP

Lectures do not provide everything you need to know. It is up to you to fill in gaps by finding additional sources of information.

STRUCTURE OF A LECTURE

Like any good presentation, lectures are structured with an introduction, a middle and a conclusion. Each part of the lecture has a specific function, so being aware of these will help you to recognize relevant information. Professors often provide 'signposts' or cues during the lecture that flag the points they expect you to remember. Learning how to read these 'signposts' helps you to take useful, relevant and, above all, meaningful notes.

INTRODUCTION

At the start of a class, a professor will usually preview the lecture, indicating the main issues to be discussed. They will locate these issues within the context of the module, perhaps even providing a recap of the last class to show how they fit together. If there is a slide or overhead outlining the lecture's key points, write these down so that you can check that you understand each one when it comes to revision. Introductory statements that preview the lecture include: 'This lecture covers internal and external forces on the body', 'In last week's class we discussed the history of the Olympics, but today we're turning our attention to the commercialization of the Games' and 'There are three main ways of looking at player salary caps – we will discuss the first two today and the last one on Thursday'.

MIDDLE

Not surprisingly, the 'middle' of the lecture delivers the content you need to learn. Lecturers not only present 'facts' but also concepts, theories, ideas, transitions and trends, and then link these ideas to one another. They will break the topic down to key areas and main points, which may be written explicitly on a slide or be implicit in what they are saying. You will need to distinguish between information such as concepts, examples and case studies, and less critical information and asides that provide some additional background. This is a skill, and it may take a little while to separate the big picture ideas from the less significant examples. Statements to listen for include: 'Here are the three key ideas', 'The main point you need to remember is', 'Now that we've outlined the theory, let's look at a practical example' and 'This case study highlights the key issues we have been discussing'.

CONCLUSION

In the conclusion, lecturers will reiterate the key points, so check that you have recorded these accurately in your notes. They might summarize the main ideas, suggest additional resources for more information and outline what the next class is about. During the conclusion ensure you understand the main ideas, and if something is not clear, make a note to come back to it later. Concluding statements include: 'Let's review the main points', 'In summary . . .' and 'Looking forward to next week, we will be discussing . . .'.

TIP

Do not start packing up when the lecturer starts the conclusion, as this is the time when ideas are drawn together. If you are putting away your things, you might miss a key idea or resource.

NOTE TAKING

Note taking is a useful skill primarily because it allows you to record relevant and meaningful notes that are tailored to your individual knowledge base. By taking notes, you can document what the lecturer regards as the most important points, and skip over material that you already know. Furthermore, note taking increases your understanding of a particular topic and also flags relevant ideas and concepts for you to follow up in your supplemental readings. Finally, taking notes gives you something tangible to start with as you prepare for exams.

Note taking is a highly individual activity and no two students will have exactly the same lecture notes (see Figures 3.1 and 3.2 for examples of individual notes). Each student will have a different base knowledge, which will influence the ideas that seem important enough to write down. If you are listening to a lecturer discuss the marketing mix using Nike as a case study, and you happen

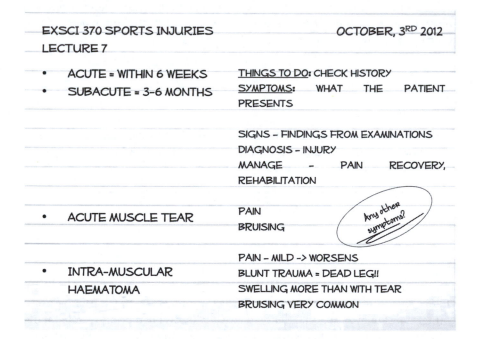

EXSCI 370 SPORTS INJURIES: LECTURE 7   3 OCTOBER 2012
                        ACUTE MUSCLE INJURY
                          - short onset or sudden
                          - identify symptoms
                          - examine signs, diagnose, manage
ACUTE MUSCLE TEAR   INTRA-MUSCULAR HAEMATOMA
   ✓   Sudden pain   ✓   Pain – initially mild, then worsens
   ✓   Bruising – due to associated bleeding   ✓   Blunt trauma
   ✓   Swelling – unusual   ✓   Bruising common
                                          ✓   Swelling common

Figure 3.1 An example of student lecture notes

EXSCI 370 SPORTS INJURIES   OCTOBER, 3RD 2012
LECTURE 7

   •   ACUTE = WITHIN 6 WEEKS   THINGS TO DO: CHECK HISTORY
   •   SUBACUTE = 3–6 MONTHS   SYMPTOMS: WHAT THE PATIENT
                                     PRESENTS

                                     SIGNS – FINDINGS FROM EXAMINATIONS
                                     DIAGNOSIS – INJURY
                                     MANAGE – PAIN RECOVERY,
                                     REHABILITATION

   •   ACUTE MUSCLE TEAR   PAIN
                                     BRUISING   Any other symptoms?

                                     PAIN – MILD -> WORSENS
   •   INTRA-MUSCULAR   BLUNT TRAUMA = DEAD LEG!!
       HAEMATOMA   SWELLING MORE THAN WITH TEAR
                                     BRUISING VERY COMMON

Figure 3.2 An example of student lecture notes

to have already taken an introductory marketing class, then you will already be familiar with the 'four Ps': product, place, price, promotion. When your lecturer introduces and explains this concept to the class, you might only need to write down 'four Ps' to remind yourself that it was raised, and then focus your attention on how the four Ps relate to Nike. Your classmate, who has never heard of the four Ps, will be furiously writing down what each one stands for and why the concept is important before they even start thinking about applying it to the case study. Note taking allows you to record what is important *for you*, which is why sharing written notes is not always helpful. Your notes will not reflect everything delivered in class, and what you write down might not be what your friend needs to understand. This is not to say you cannot assist friends, but rather than photocopying your notes, it would be better to discuss the lecture with them.

Significantly, research suggests that if you know that critical information is stored elsewhere – such as on a handout or Wikipedia – or is accessible through a search engine, you are *less* likely to remember it yourself (Sparrow *et al.* 2012). This is because our memory is finite so our brains decide between retaining information and simply remembering where that information can be found. For example, if you are grocery shopping without a written list, your brain is forced to remember all the items you need to buy. If, however, you have a written list, you are less likely to remember individual items because your brain knows where the information is stored and the only work it needs to do is remember where that written list is.

Similarly, class notes provided by your lecturer do not help you remember relevant information – they merely encourage your brain to remember where that information can be found, which is of little help in an exam. Printed notes are also problematic because these are simply words on a page without the nuanced explanation provided in class, and the content on slides may not reflect the position the lecturer is expressing. Indeed, if only the lecture notes were important, your professor would simply email these around to the class rather than wasting time explaining the concepts in person. When it comes to demonstrating your understanding of a topic, you are expected to do more than simply memorize and repeat lecture notes back to the examiner, so printing these out at the end of the semester and expecting that they will help you understand the material is a flawed approach on every level. You should be recording the lecturer's argument, examples and the subtle or explicit emphasis on some issues and not others, rather than memorizing a series of PowerPoint slides.

Effective note taking is a skill that needs to be learned and practised. It is more than simply copying down everything you see and hear in a lecture. Taking good *quality* notes is more valuable than recording a large *quantity* of notes. Note taking requires you to listen, interpret, select and write, all at the same time, so the more you practise the more proficient you will become. The construction of useful study notes does not, however, begin and end in the lecture; it requires both preparation and review to get the most out of the process.

CASE STUDY

Have a look at the two sets of lecture notes below. The first is provided by the lecturer, and the second is a record of what Rebecca, a first-year student, heard in class.

Lecturer's notes	*Rebecca's notes*
Technology in sport	Technology in sport

Technology in sport
- Focus is on public perceptions and concerns about technology in sport and discusses possible reasons why some are banned and others are permitted
- Growing concern over influence of technology in sport
  - results from popular idea that sport is natural/organic/human mastery over nature
  - BUT sport is made by humans; industrial – a technology in itself
  - athletes need technology – diet, skill, fitness, equipment
  - concerns about technology are limited to notion of 'performance enhancement'
- Performance enhancement
  - A term used to denote the 'evils' of sport
  - Suggests that an athlete is going beyond 'natural limits'
  - Constructed as an immoral act when in fact all training is designed to 'enhance performance'
- Question? Why are some technologies rejected as performance enhancing, whereas others are accepted as a fundamental part of sport?
  - General consensus that some technology is necessary for sport, e.g. equipment (EXTERNAL)
  - BUT uneasiness with technologies that enter the body (INTERNAL)
- Answer? 'Authenticity' of sport is thought to be corrupted by presence of

Technology in sport
- technology in sport should be banned
- Technology
  - o performance enhancement
- Performance enhancement
  - – evil; needs to be banned
  - o Athletes going beyond their natural bodies
  - o immoral
- Why should we ban technology?
  - o changes body
  - o community
- Authenticity of sport is corrupted
  - o Sport is no longer pure
  - o Training is not technology
- Drugs/altitude chambers should be banned
- Earning training adaptations should be respected

technology, i.e. the 'purity' of 'natural sport' is disrupted by technology

- Expectation that sport is designed to test the absolute limit of human capacity
  - Training is considered appropriate to reach these limits
- So performance enhancement per se is not the problem, but the manner in which the body is pushed to the limits IS a concern. Popular perception:
  - Training = hard work/discipline (concepts respected in sport)
  - Drugs/altitude chambers = perception that they are a short cut or 'passive' way of reaching limits; no way to know the extent to which technology is operating
- EARNING training adaptations using EXTERNAL means is more respected, but that does not mean that INTERNAL technologies are inherently immoral
  - Athletes still need to train hard
  - Athletes still need to perform

→ How accurate are Rebecca's notes?

→ What are the main ideas that she missed from the lecture?

→ What can she do now to improve the notes?

HOW MEMORY WORKS

Think about the best sporting achievement of your life, a moment where you performed at your very best. Describe what happened. What led up to that moment and what followed? Who was with you? How did you feel? Now write a list of the last fifteen people you have seen. Write down their names – or a description if you do not know their name.

Which of the two is more difficult? The second one is almost impossible, because you are relying on information captured in your short-term or working memory, whereas the first task comes more easily as it is firmly encoded in your long-term memory. Understanding the difference between short-term memory and long-term memory will help you understand how note taking is a critical step to support your ability to understand lecture content.

Short-term memory is notoriously brief. Information that passes into it is retained for only around twenty seconds (up to thirty seconds if information is repeated). Short-term memory contains only around seven slots, which means that only seven pieces of information can be held at any one time. As we are constantly bombarded with new information, these seven slots are continuously overwritten.

We simply could not cope with the information overload if every single thought, idea, encounter, image, song and so on moved into our long-term memory, and so the short-term memory is a filtering space where your brain makes rapid decisions about what information it needs to send to storage, and which details it can discard. Long-term memory, by contrast, is a long-term repository with a rapid recall system. It is so integrated into our being that our memories hardly seem like discrete bits of data; they seem more like a fundamental part of who we are. The stored information is easily and immediately retrieved, and while memories might degrade with time, it is difficult to instruct our brains to deliberately remove them.

Our short-term memory can hold only so much detail, and this short-term memory is being erased and re-recorded as new information comes in. Some have suggested that as soon as we leave class we will have already forgotten around 40 per cent of what we heard. By the next day we will have lost up to 80 per cent of the detail, and after a month we may remember only around 2 per cent. This means that if you are trying to rely on your memory for an entire semester – and for multiple subjects – you will have next to nothing to draw upon when it comes to revising for exams. The University of Waterloo's (2012) 'Curve of Forgetting' suggests that revising notes within a day of the class for only ten minutes will return the memory close to 100 per cent; after a week it will take only five minutes of revision, and after a month just a few minutes will be enough to remind yourself that you know the content. Use your brain's natural strengths to your advantage and review lecture notes at least weekly.

BEFORE THE LECTURE

Just as competing in the highest levels of sport requires preparation, so, too, note taking begins even before setting foot in the classroom. To get the most out of the lecture, it is important never to attend a class 'cold'; you need to 'warm up', or prepare, in order to recognize what is relevant and important. First of all, consider how the lecture fits into the course in terms of past and future topics, and think about what points might be raised. Skim through your notes from the last class to remind yourself of main points and try to predict how the next one will link to these ideas. If your professor has recommended some supplementary readings, read those and make note of any key terms or concepts. Look up unfamiliar terms so that you already know what they mean if they are raised in class. Having a grasp of some of the main ideas beforehand means that the lecture will not be entirely new and will reinforce concepts with which you are already familiar.

Another important part of your preparation for a lecture is to identify questions about the topic that you would like answered. You might have some preliminary understanding of the topic, or there could be some issues that confuse you, so think about the information that you need in order to improve your comprehension of the material. Write a list to remind yourself to keep these ideas in mind during class.

There are a few practical steps you can take in preparation for the lecture. Have an individual notepad for each class and start each lecture on a fresh page. Loose pages are easily lost if not filed systematically, and one book for all subjects can become confusing when revising. Write the name of the class, the title of the lecture and the date at the top. Decide on a note-taking system and ensure that your notepad is set up in advance. Arrive early and find a seat with a clear view to the lecturer and the screen so you do not miss the introduction. Watching the lecturer rather than the screen will alert you to important clues about the material that the lecturer regards as most important. Avoid distractions, such as a noisy air-conditioning unit, sitting next to the door or sitting near chatty friends, and as you wait for the class to begin, think about what you already know about the topic and the kinds of issues you expect to be presented.

DURING THE LECTURE

Once the lecture starts, there are several techniques for ensuring you get the most out of the class. The first tip is to engage in 'active listening', which means 'listening for meaning' or listening with a specific purpose. Listening is not the same as hearing; it requires engagement on your part. When listening actively, you are evaluating ideas as you hear them, linking lectures to one another, and pre-empting the next point, not simply letting sounds wash over you. Active listening also helps you to take effective notes, because not only will you write down useful and meaningful information from the lecturer but you will also be noting questions and ideas as they occur to you. Material that you have already encountered in the readings will not need to be noted, as you already know where to find those ideas and they can be added in later. Additional questions raised in the lecture can be followed up during your study session.

Here are some additional tips to help you take effective notes in class:

- As the class gets underway, anticipating what will be raised next helps you concentrate on the content.
- Remember to listen to the end of class; do not jump to conclusions and do not stop listening because you might disagree.
- Although they may not look directly at you, maintaining eye contact with lecturers keeps you focused on what they are saying.

Finally, do not worry about the 'style' of delivery, as every professor will be different. Some will be more animated and interactive; others will be more reserved and matter of fact. It really is just a matter of personal taste, so if you are prepared for the lecture and are actively listening to the content, the delivery style will matter less and less. Your main priority is to extract as much meaningful information as possible to create a comprehensive set of notes that will form the basis for your study and revision.

NOTE-TAKING SYSTEMS

The key to effective note taking is being organized and systematic, so that if you look at your notes tomorrow, next week, next year or ten years later, you will recognize key points, secondary points, examples, and so on. Note-taking systems can provide the necessary structure to ensure that your record is clear, and as there are a number of options, each with their advantages and disadvantages, the best strategy is to try some and decide on the most useful approach for you. There are no hard-and-fast rules, so you can also modify one or combine different elements to create a system that suits. The note-taking strategies that will be outlined here include:

- Cornell system
- split page systems
- PowerPoint notes
- mind mapping.

Regardless of the strategy you use, you need to develop a structured approach to taking and reviewing notes.

Cornell system

The Cornell system is a well-respected approach to note taking developed by Cornell University professor, Walter Pauk. It is based on the five 'Rs' of note taking – record, reduce, recite, reflect and review – which together present an effective, and efficient, learning strategy (Pauk and Owens 2010). The key feature of the Cornell system lies in the division of a page into three key areas, each with its own function, as seen in Figure 3.3. You will need to set the page up in advance or use a template in your word processing package.

After noting the course code, the lecture title and the date at the top of the page, notes are *recorded* in the larger right-hand column. Always leave plenty of space when taking notes so that you can fill in missing or additional information after class. Following the lecture, notes are *reduced* to key ideas, terms or subheadings that are written in the left-hand column. The section at the foot of the page is for a summary of the key lecture points. If you can write a summary of the class, then you can be confident you grasp the subject matter. When studying, cover the right-hand column and use the cues to prompt you or your study group to *recite* as many of the key points as you can. You can then either individually or collectively *reflect* upon the key ideas and link these

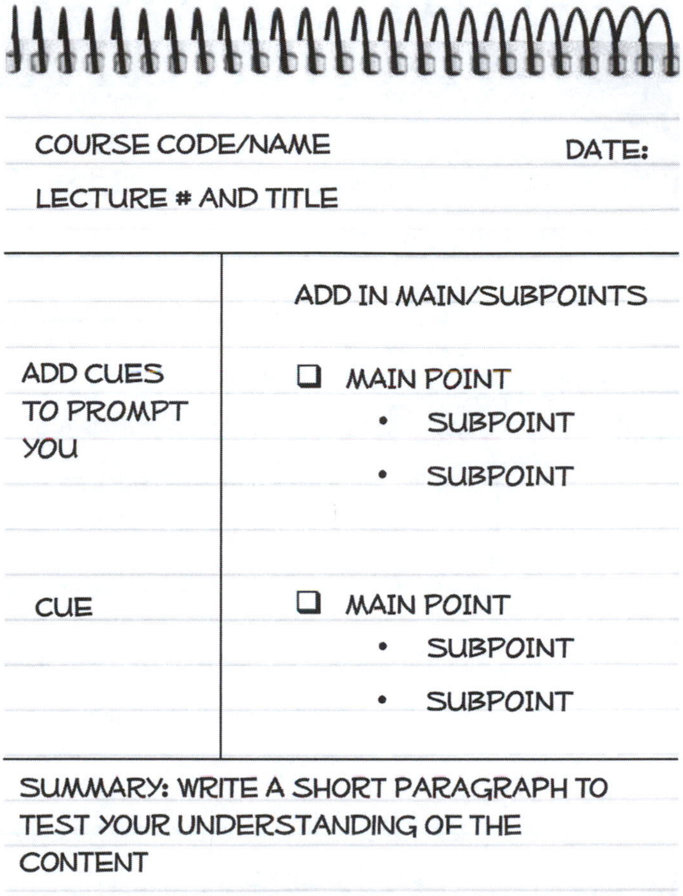

COURSE CODE/NAME	DATE:
LECTURE # AND TITLE	

	ADD IN MAIN/SUBPOINTS

ADD CUES TO PROMPT YOU	☐ MAIN POINT
	    • SUBPOINT
	    • SUBPOINT

CUE	☐ MAIN POINT
	    • SUBPOINT
	    • SUBPOINT

SUMMARY: WRITE A SHORT PARAGRAPH TO TEST YOUR UNDERSTANDING OF THE CONTENT

Figure 3.3 Page layout for the Cornell note-taking system

to other parts of the module, to other modules being studied and to relevant additional sources. Finally, these notes should be *reviewed* weekly, just prior to the next class, to ensure you remember the key points. See Figure 3.4 for an example of notes recorded in the Cornell system.

Variations to the Cornell system include preparing for your lecture by drawing up a series of relevant points derived from the readings, a list of terms or ideas that you need to know more about, and a list of points you feel are important and should be raised in the lecture. At the end of the class, compare your notes to these lists to see whether your expectations have been met. If not, there may be additional areas that you need to research in order to round out the topic. You can add a list of follow-up points or questions that the lecture raises at the end of the summary or provide room for notes from supplementary readings.

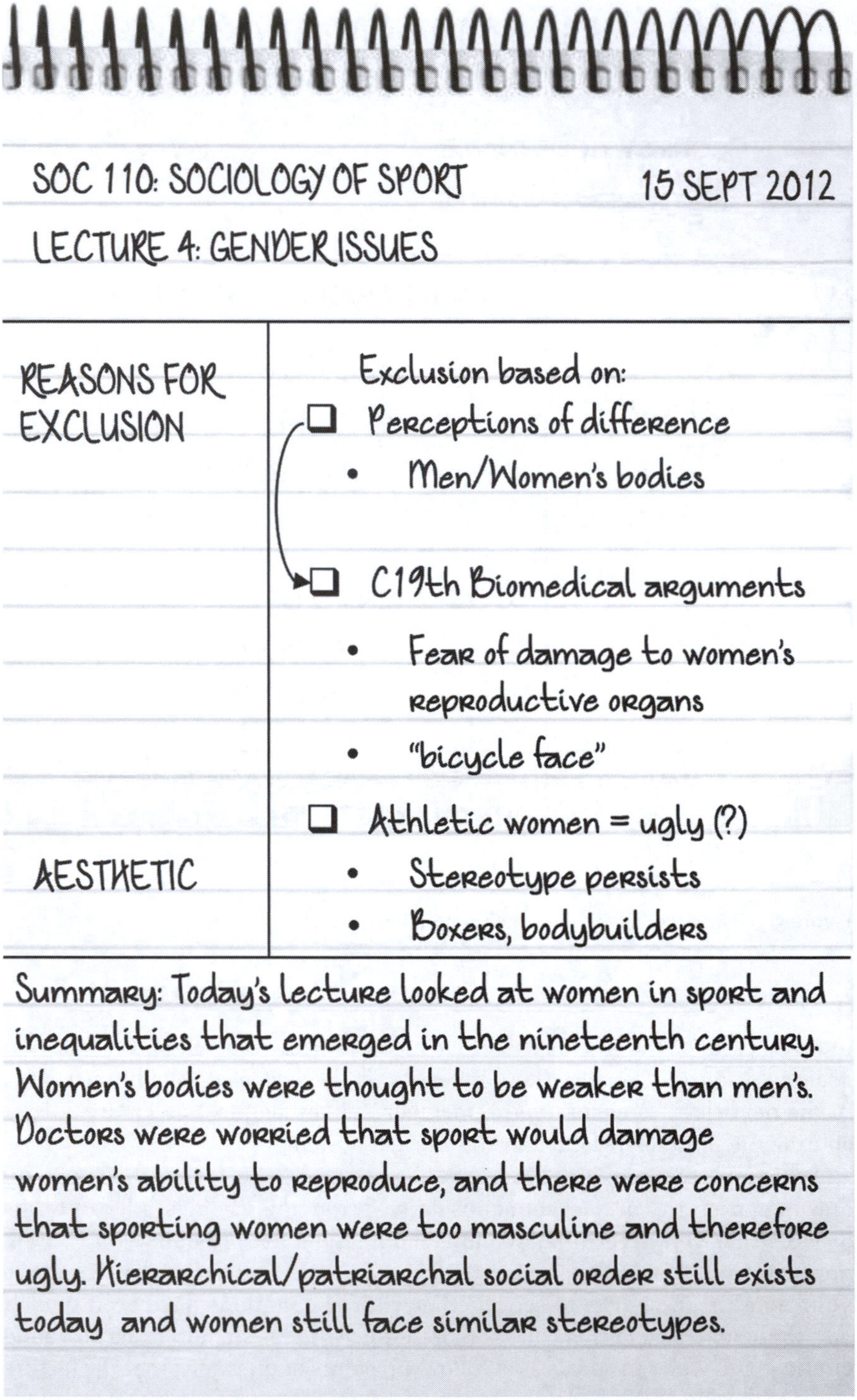

SOC 110: SOCIOLOGY OF SPORT   15 SEPT 2012

LECTURE 4: GENDER ISSUES

REASONS FOR EXCLUSION	Exclusion based on: ☐ Perceptions of difference • Men/Women's bodies ☐ C19th Biomedical arguments • Fear of damage to women's reproductive organs • "bicycle face" ☐ Athletic women = ugly (?)
AESTHETIC	• Stereotype persists • Boxers, bodybuilders

Summary: Today's lecture looked at women in sport and inequalities that emerged in the nineteenth century. Women's bodies were thought to be weaker than men's. Doctors were worried that sport would damage women's ability to reproduce, and there were concerns that sporting women were too masculine and therefore ugly. Hierarchical/patriarchal social order still exists today and women still face similar stereotypes.

Figure 3.4 Lecture notes using the Cornell system

STUDENT VIEWPOINT

Note taking is a crucial part of a lecture, and it has an enormous impact on my learning. There are many advantages to taking your own notes. I think it is a great way to evaluate information critically, as only the essential points are written down. You can always go back and add in information later. I find that taking my own notes helps me when revising as they are in my own words and I am able to think back to when I first wrote the notes in the lecture, and the cues and summary notes I wrote during my study period that week. Clear notes are also extremely valuable when revising for a test. Personally, I still have a lot to learn about note taking. For me, the biggest challenge is being able to write fast enough to keep up with the lecturer, but I now use abbreviations and this really helps. It is also difficult to maintain a clear structure. I am a perfectionist, and in the past would rewrite my notes after each lecture to maintain a neat and organized notebook. I have learned, however, that rewriting notes wastes time and prevents me from studying efficiently.—Toby.

Split page system

The split page system is similar to the Cornell approach, but it encourages greater interaction between lecture notes and additional readings and resources. A page is divided in half, either horizontally or vertically, and one half is used to take notes (the left-hand column or the top half) and the remaining half is used to record additional material from readings (see Figure 3.5). You can also add a summary to the end of the lecture notes, as per the Cornell system, and a list of questions to follow up. This system creates a comprehensive overview of the topic in a single document.

PowerPoint notes

If your professor posts PowerPoint lecture notes ahead of time, print these out as 'notes' in the 'three to a page' format. This means that you will not have to write down everything on the slide, but can focus on adding ideas and examples raised in the class next to the corresponding slide. The pages are not large enough to allow for supplementary notes, but you could affix these pages to the left-hand page of your notebook and write corresponding information from the readings on the facing page.

Mind mapping

Mind mapping can be a useful tool for visual learners or for those who like to have an overview of an entire topic on one page. Mind mapping is free-form

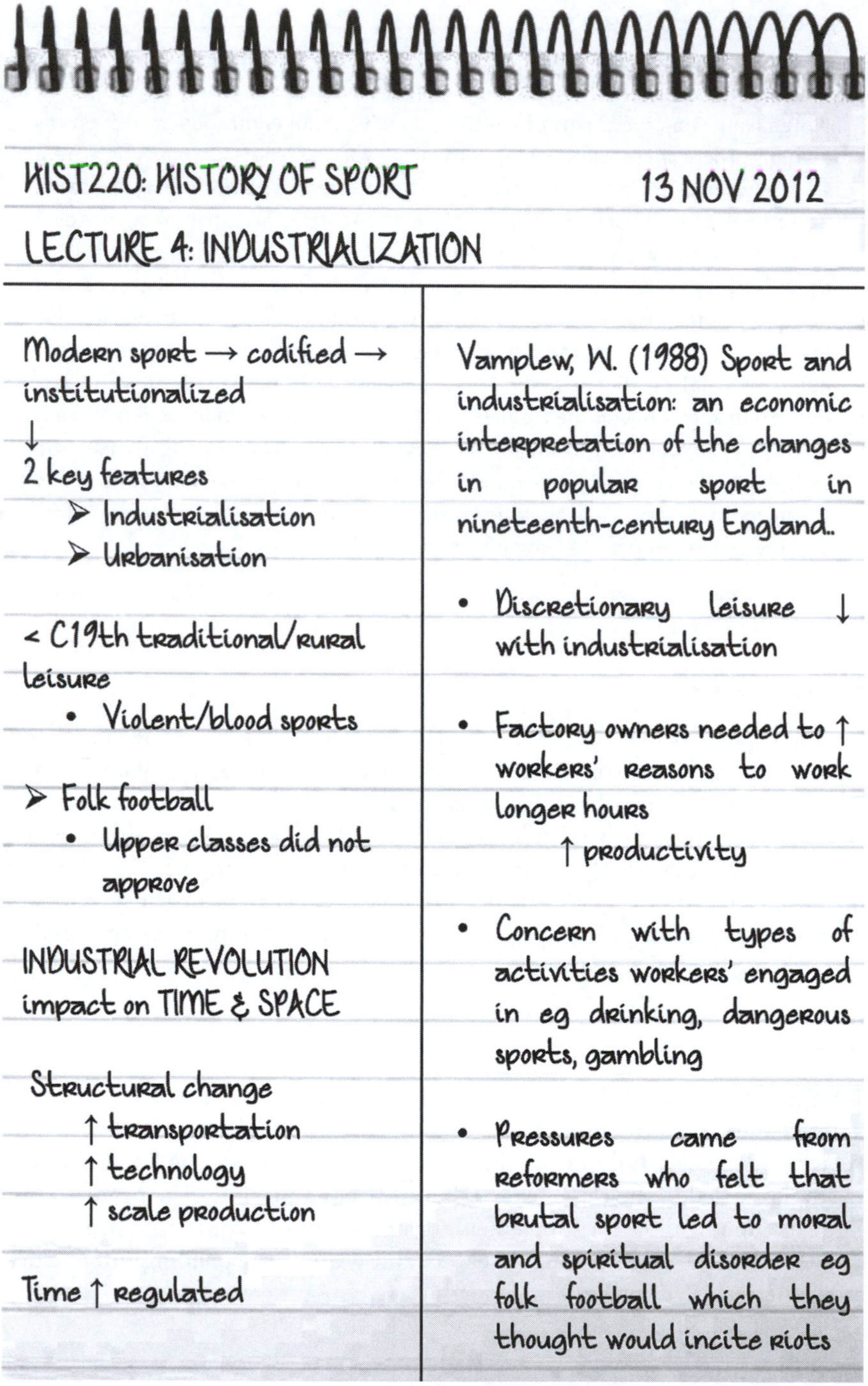

HIST220: HISTORY OF SPORT   13 NOV 2012

LECTURE 4: INDUSTRIALIZATION

Modern sport → codified → institutionalized
↓
2 key features
  ➤ Industrialisation
  ➤ Urbanisation
 	
< C19th traditional/rural leisure
  • Violent/blood sports
 	
➤ Folk football
  • Upper classes did not approve
 	
INDUSTRIAL REVOLUTION
impact on TIME & SPACE
 	
Structural change
  ↑ transportation
  ↑ technology
  ↑ scale production
 	
Time ↑ regulated
	Vamplew, W. (1988) Sport and industrialisation: an economic interpretation of the changes in popular sport in nineteenth-century England.
	
	• Discretionary leisure ↓ with industrialisation
	
	• Factory owners needed to ↑ workers' reasons to work longer hours
	   ↑ productivity
	
	• Concern with types of activities workers' engaged in eg drinking, dangerous sports, gambling
	
	• Pressures came from reformers who felt that brutal sport led to moral and spiritual disorder eg folk football which they thought would incite riots

Figure 3.5 Lecture notes using the split page system

in its approach, but it should have a logical flow. The main topic should be located in the centre of the page, with sub-topics radiating out from the central hub (see Figure 3.6). Key words and images can be used to trigger associations, and there is no end to the number of branches and ideas that can be included.

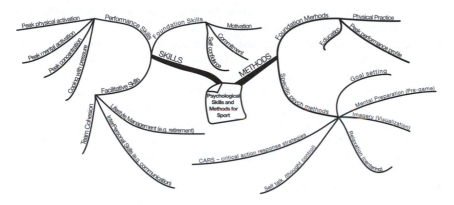

Figure 3.6 Lecture notes using a mind map

HOW DO I TAKE NOTES?

Although it is not difficult to understand the need for thorough notes, where many students come undone is in the practical steps associated with taking them. They are not sure what to write down or how to distinguish between important and interesting details, and struggle with trying to record as much as possible in a lecture. As mentioned earlier, note taking is individual, and what is meaningful for you may not be for someone else. Information, however, will be significant only if you have some context for it. If you attend the lecture unprepared, every single thing the lecturer says might seem critically important for you to record; if you have completed readings in advance, however, you will be better able to discern the points that are worthy of your attention.

Here are some practical steps for successful note taking:

- *Wean yourself off slide presentations*: Never just copy everything down without thinking about the ideas because you are not writing down what is meaningful for you or points that your professor has identified as important. Copying slides does not require understanding, interpretation or selection, though slide headings might be a useful indicator of key topics.
- *Do not write out full sentences*: You will waste a lot of time if you try to note down full sentences. Use phrases or words as prompts, and fill in the gaps with more a detailed explanation after class.
- *Select only what is relevant to you*: It may seem that everyone around you is writing furiously, but you do not have a single thing written down on your pad. This may be because you are not hearing the key points, but if you came to class prepared, it is more likely that you have yet to hear

something new or useful. Do not feel compelled to write for the sake of writing. If you find you are taking down nothing at all in most classes, then you will need to review your approach. You do need to record the key ideas because even if the material is familiar, you need to remember which points were emphasized in class. Returning to an earlier example, unless you write 'four Ps' on your notepad, you may not remember that these were raised in the class.

- *Keep notes short and to the point*: Be concise; you can elaborate later when editing and annotating your notes. Use abbreviations to speed up the process. If you are using your own, keep a list of abbreviations in the front of your notepad and be consistent. There is no point making up new abbreviations in every class, as you want note taking to become effortless.
- *Use your own words*: You are more likely to understand and remember ideas and concepts that you have 'translated' into your own words. Similarly, use your own examples where possible to confirm that you can apply the lecture content.
- *Leave space between notes*: You need to have space to edit and annotate, or simply fill in information that you missed in class. If you do not have time to write down an example, you will have the space to add it in later.
- *Do not panic if you miss something*: Leave space and discuss it with your study group, peer or even the lecturer after class. Do not disturb the person next to you (and the class and professor) by asking what you missed, as you will miss the next three points.
- *Avoid getting stuck in explanatory detail*: You need to remember the key points raised in a lecture, not the nitty-gritty detail. If you understand the point, there is no need to record every last thing the professor says. Keep a record of some key words that will remind you of the examples raised in class.
- *Look for visual/verbal cues*: A lecturer normally 'signposts' key information by using visual/verbal cues.

VISUAL/VERBAL CUES

Lecturers signal the most important points of the class using visual and verbal cues, and learning to read these will enhance your note taking. Visual cues include material that appears on the board or screen that is highlighted or emphasized in some way, but it does not include *all* material on a slide. Visual cues may also include the lecturers' body language. They might use their fingers to number key points, or emphasize an idea with their hands. The more animated your professor is about a point the more important it is likely to be.

Verbal cues include the lecturer repeating or emphasizing particular points. This might be apparent through their intonation, how much time they spend on a particular topic or how many examples are used to ensure students understand the point. Lecturers often repeat key points in different ways to ensure that everyone understands, so listen carefully and avoid the temptation of writing the same ideas down over and over. Use an asterisk to highlight that this is an important point. Lecturers might explicitly state 'This will be on the exam' or 'A critical issue is XYZ'. They might suggest that 'It is significant to note that . . . however . . .', which suggests there are several points of view to consider. They may enumerate or sequence ideas: 'There are three points of view on . . . First, . . . Second, . . . The third reason is . . .'. They may compare and contrast ideas using terms such as 'similarly', 'likewise', 'however', 'on the other hand', and they may highlight cause and effect through terms such as 'therefore', 'as a result', 'thus', 'hence', 'for this reason', 'because'. Learn to recognize these cues and use them to guide your note taking.

RECORDING LECTURES

Recording lectures on a Dictaphone or cell phone can assist those who have difficulties listening and writing at the same time or students who simply want to be able to hear the lecturer's words again. It means that you have the opportunity to revisit the lecture, pause when you want to write something down, listen to a passage again to ensure you understand it and generally take time to process the material.

There are some disadvantages to recording lectures. Listening to the lecture again is time consuming. If you have four subjects in a semester and three hours of lectures per subject per week, you not only have to sit through twelve hours of lectures but you also need to find the time to listen to *at least* twelve hours again – *at least* because stopping and starting the recording to take notes takes longer.

If you choose to record, there are some issues to note:

- *Always seek the permission of the lecturer*: A lecturer does not have to grant you permission to record their lectures, but if they do, remember that you are not entitled to circulate the recording without their permission.
- *Take notes during the lecture*: Recording the lecture does not mean you can sit back in class and do nothing. You should still take notes and use the recording only as a back-up to fill in the gaps you have missed rather than starting from scratch. If you have difficulty with a particular issue during the lecture, record the time so you can go straight to that part of the recording, rather than listening to the entire lecture again.
- *Commit to listening and processing recorded lectures each week*: If you decide to record lectures, you should commit to listening to and processing the lectures the same week they are held. If you have ten, twelve or more hours of lectures to listen to each week and do nothing with them, you are simply compounding the workload later in the semester.

TIPS FOR EASY NOTE TAKING

It is worthwhile developing a system of abbreviations and symbols so you can record ideas quickly. When using abbreviations, remember to be consistent, and if you 'invent' one during a lecture, either write down what it means straightaway, or make a note immediately after class. Here are some common abbreviations:

&	and	esp.	especially
∴	therefore	min.	minimum
~	approximately	max.	maximum
w/	with	#	number
w/o	without	↑	increases
i.e.	that is	↓	decreases
e.g.	for example	→	leads to
etc.	et cetera (and so on)	+	more/positive
NB	note well	–	less/negative
b/c	because	<	less than
b/4	before	>	more than
re:	regarding	=	equals
wrt.	with respect to	≠	does not equal

Make good use of asterisks or underlining to convey significance or importance, but avoid using different coloured pens or highlighters as it wastes time to change pens in class. Use a different coloured pen to annotate your notes when reviewing the lecture. Devise a system of hierarchy to determine main points and subsidiary ideas (see Figure 3.7 for an example). It may be that you can only identify the relationship between ideas after class, in which case, you can add in notations to record the relative importance of the various ideas.

AFTER THE LECTURE

Just as lectures do not begin when lecturers open their mouths, the work associated with lectures does not end when you walk out the door. To ensure the greatest level of recall, you should review your notes as soon as possible after class. This will reinforce what you have learned and ensure that you have understood the main ideas. Importantly, it also allows you to fill in any gaps while the information is still fresh in your mind. If you are using the Cornell system, this is the time to write the summary of the lecture, using your notes as a guide, and to condense the lecture material into single-word prompts to add to the left-hand column. Reciting the information through discussion with your study group is an excellent way to review the lecture content. Each of you can identify the key points you took from the lecture, and any differences between group members can form the basis for discussion.

The review process enables you to identify any gaps in your knowledge and to make note of areas that require further reading. You can compare what you actually learned with what you expected to learn. A good technique to test your understanding is to write a paragraph about the lecture in your own words without referring to your notes. What was it about? What were the main points? How did the lecture fit into the module overall? What points did you

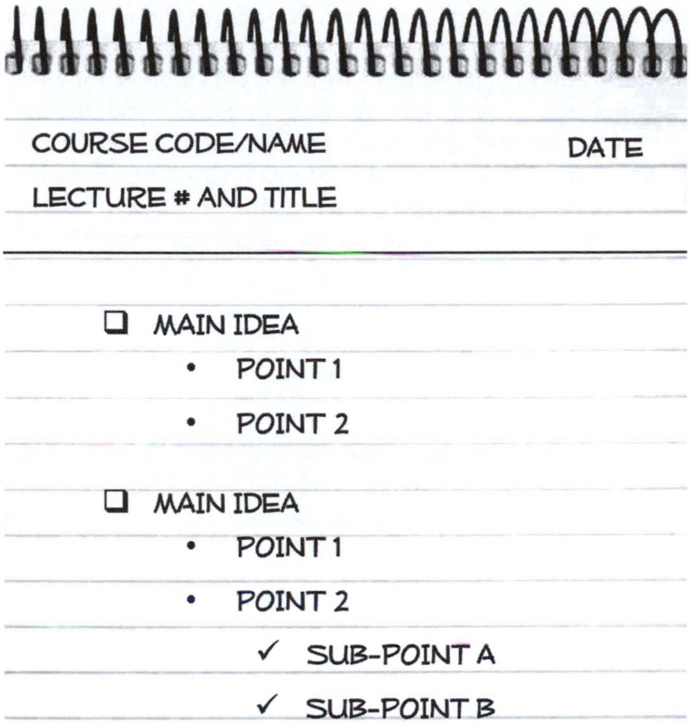

COURSE CODE/NAME   **DATE**

LECTURE # AND TITLE

❑ MAIN IDEA
  • POINT 1
  • POINT 2

❑ MAIN IDEA
  • POINT 1
  • POINT 2
      ✓ SUB-POINT A
      ✓ SUB-POINT B

Figure 3.7 Hierarchy of points in lecture notes

not understand? Successfully summarizing the lecture will indicate a good grasp of the material, and writing questions about what you need to find out will help guide your study of the topic.

ANNOTATING LECTURE NOTES

Many students like to rewrite their messy class notes; however, this is a repetitive task that does not help you learn or understand the material, and there are better ways to utilize your time. A more effective strategy is to edit and annotate your notes, which is why leaving plenty of space is important. Editing allows you to add information that you might have missed in class or to add more to a point that was raised. You might want to explain the examples in further detail or add in one of your own. Underline key points or highlight ideas to add emphasis.

Annotations are additional explanatory notes that will create a more comprehensive overview of the topic. You can add in your notes from your preparatory reading or from other relevant resources. Listen to podcasts on the topic or find books that explain the ideas from a different perspective so that you develop a strong summary of the area. Note down useful websites or videos that explain the topic area in more detail. You might also highlight links to other lectures in this subject or to lecture content in other modules, or note common themes that are emerging in the course and try to predict how the ideas might further develop during the semester. Think about how this material relates to your entire programme of study and decide whether the pieces of the puzzle are coming together for you. An annotated set of notes will make preparing for exams straightforward as all the relevant information is in one place.

TIP

When editing or annotating your notes, use a different coloured pen from the one you used to take the notes. This way, you have a visual distinction between notes taken in class and extra points and ideas that you have added in later.

A FINAL NOTE

Well-prepared, organized and comprehensive notes are your best tool for preparing for exams. The strategies in this chapter take little time to implement, but they do require planning and commitment. If you follow the review process, by the time of the final exam you will not need to 'cram' but simply review your notes as, for the most part, you will already have a clear and thorough understanding of the lecture content. You will not need to waste time trying to create effective study notes because you already have a solid basis from which to study. You might need to remind yourself of small details, but you will already know the overarching themes of the module, and this is a powerful position to be in prior to a final exam.

SUMMARY

1   Lectures should be considered a starting point for a topic rather than an end point. Students should regard lectures as a framework for under-standing key issues and then seek additional information to provide richer detail and more nuanced analysis.
2   Taking notes records concepts and examples that are relevant to the student, increases understanding and retention, and provides the basis for later revision and study.
3   Students should prepare for class in advance by completing required or recommended readings, thinking about how the material links to previous and future topics, and familiarizing themselves with key concepts and terminology.

4   There are a number of recognized note-taking system that appeal to various styles of learner, including the Cornell system and mind mapping. A combination of techniques serves most learners well.

5   Lecture notes should be revised, edited and annotated with additional material to create a comprehensive review document that will form the basis for study and revision in preparation for assessment.

EXERCISES

1   Find a podcast of a lecture online and identify the main parts of the lecture. Can you hear verbal cues? Does the presenter provide an overview at the start and a summary to finish? Decide whether the overall structure was systematic or haphazard.

2   Using the same podcast, use one or two of the note-taking systems to practise taking notes. You can replay the lecture and look at your notes to see how many of the key points you managed to note down and whether you recorded these accurately.

3   Find some readings related to the subject matter in the podcast and try annotating the notes you created in the above exercise.

4   Use different note-taking systems in your classes over a week and see which one is easier and inspires you to create the most comprehensive notes.

REFLECTION

Think about your previous note-taking experiences. What has worked for you and what has not? How might good note taking impact on your learning, and what changes do you need to make to become a more effective note taker? Can you think of additional techniques that might enhance your note taking? What challenges might you experience in trying to take meaningful notes in class? Reflect on your study habits and think about how you can incorporate weekly revision of notes into your study sessions.

FURTHER READING

Buzan, T. (2012) *The ultimate book of mind maps*. London: HarperCollins.
Kesselman-Turkel, J. and Peterson, F. (2003) *Note-taking made easy*. Madison WI: University of Wisconsin Press.

4

STARTING ASSIGNMENTS

Breaking down questions and effective research

OVERVIEW

This chapter outlines:

- different types of research, including appropriate and unconventional sources;
- the process of conducting good-quality academic research;
- three clear steps to help students begin written research assignments;
- how to navigate library holdings using electronic search engines.

INTRODUCTION

During your time at college you will be asked to write many different types of assignments. These might be research papers where you review and evaluate literature on particular topics, such as gender discrimination in sport, or reflective pieces that ask you to consider your personal responses to issues, such as the use of sporting boycotts to sanction errant nations. You might need to write applied reports that seek solutions to real world problems, such as developing a sponsorship proposal for a junior sports event, or even creative pieces where you are encouraged to use your imagination to think about, for example, how it might have been to be a professional athlete during the amateur era. In each case, you will be given a topic or parameters for your paper, and the successful completion of the assignment will depend on the extent to which you have fulfilled the criteria. This chapter outlines the basic steps to begin the process of writing an assignment. It focuses on producing a research paper, as this is one of the most common, and most challenging, pieces of work you will be asked to submit at college. Having a clear understanding of the requirements for such a piece of work is critical, and knowing the process of good research will help you write effectively across a number of formats.

PURPOSE OF ASSIGNMENTS

An assignment is essentially a piece of writing on a topic based upon relevant research literature in the field. Lecturers set assignments for many reasons, but in most cases they are a way to evaluate your progress through the unit. They demonstrate your understanding of, and engagement with, the course content and determine the degree to which you have met the stated learning outcomes. Assignments also have other, more strategic, purposes. For example, writing an assignment deepens a student's learning of the subject and develops independent research skills. A research paper asks you to *argue* an intellectual position rather than state personal opinions, which means you are demonstrating your ability to gather relevant research and make judgements on the value of the evidence you collect. Assignments also extend and refine your thinking processes, enhance your capacity to manage projects and develop your writing skills.

Writing a research paper develops a range of critical thinking skills, including selecting evidence, synthesizing an argument and formally presenting results. These are not skills that every student has going into college, and they cannot be taught in one simple lesson. Instead, the ability to research and evaluate is acquired over time and refined as you engage in research activities. As you progress through your degree, your skills will improve so dramatically that it will be almost cringeworthy to read assignments you wrote in your first semester.

Many students are unsure how to write assignments to an appropriate standard when they first start college, so this and the next few chapters prepare you for these challenges. The first key point to note is that good-quality assignments take time to produce. You will be shown how to break assignments down into smaller components that can be completed each week rather than trying to do the entire project a few days before it is due. The second key point is that the quality of your assignment is directly related to the quality of your research, so the better the research the stronger your argument will be. To identify good-quality research, you first need to understand what research is, how it is created and how it is presented.

WHAT IS RESEARCH?

In Chapter 2, research was briefly introduced as a systematic, methodical and organized process of gathering data and generating ideas in order to contribute to humankind's knowledge. It is a diligent process of inquiry that is essentially inspired by the desire to know, interpret and understand the world and ourselves. Research is predicated on natural curiosity and begins with a simple question: why? To answer that question, researchers design studies to examine observable or theoretical phenomena, test and analyse both existing knowledge and new hypotheses and draw informed conclusions about their significance and meaning. These conclusions then become the stimulus for debate and further research, which reminds us that the quest for new insights is necessarily founded on the knowledge we already have. This is a critical point. The research process slowly builds upon itself, reviewing past ideas based on new evidence, and slowly but surely driving forward our conception of the world and beyond. Figure 4.1 depicts the research process.

As students, you are being apprenticed in the techniques of finding, evaluating and creating knowledge that date back thousands of years, and not only will you learn to become effective researchers but the contributions you make will add to the way that we understand sport. Research is thus an exciting part of the college process as well as a lifelong skill that can be employed in all manner of personal and professional situations. There are a number of categories of research that you may encounter at college, and these are outlined below.

SCIENTIFIC/UNSCIENTIFIC RESEARCH

Scientific research utilizes recognized and accepted research methodologies to collect and analyse data in order to describe observed phenomena or behaviours,

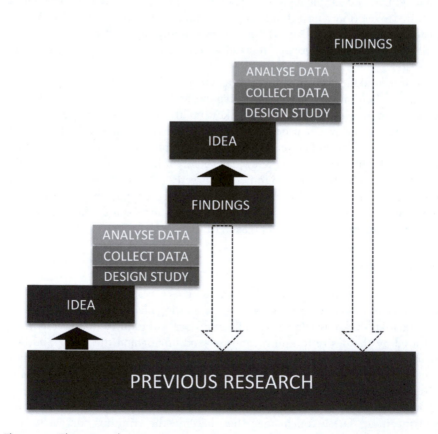

Figure 4.1 The research process

TIP

It is highly likely that you will take a specific research methods class as part of your overall degree, and this will be the time to delve more into the research process and the different methods used in various sports studies disciplines.

to predict likely outcomes to experiments or interventions, to determine the cause of a particular result and then to explain those results with reference to the existing literature. Accepted methods might include experiments, surveys, content analysis and field observations, and within these there are many research designs. Once the data are analysed, informed conclusions, based on the presented evidence, are drawn, which may then be generalized across a specific research population. Different research methods are used across sports studies. Within the biophysical sport and exercise sciences, you will most likely encounter training studies, where a group of participants are subjected to an intervention to compare their resulting performance with a control group who did not receive the intervention. There might be experiments to examine the effect of exercise on blood lipids, which will require laboratory analysis. Within the socio-cultural study of sport, you are likely to encounter field observations, where, for example, a researcher examines how women interact in a boxing club, or content analysis, which drills down into government policies on the provision of recreational facilities in specific neighbourhoods.

Unscientific research, on the other hand, relies on anecdotal evidence and personal experiences. There is no systematic collection or evaluation of data, and personal opinions directly influence conclusions. Students often try to rely on their own knowledge of an issue to write an assignment rather than drawing on scientific research, but the main point of a research paper is to conduct research on an issue to educate yourself further about the range of ideas and perspectives that may exist on any given topic.

PRIMARY/SECONDARY/TERTIARY RESEARCH

There are essentially three levels of information with which you should be familiar:

- *Primary data*: These are the raw, unprocessed facts that you gather. Primary research might include survey results, photographs, websites or tweets on Twitter, blood lactates, DEXA scan results and sales figures. If you are a historian, it might be sports memorabilia, newspaper clippings or personal letters; if you are a biomechanist, it might be the measurements you collect as your subjects perform a tennis serve. In most cases, you will not be expected to collect primary data until you are skilled in research.

- *Secondary data*: These are the sources of information that have already processed and analysed raw data and drawn conclusions about their significance. This means that rather than having to survey a large number of people or scan a group of athletes every time you want to find out about an issue, you simply refer to research that has already collated this data. Secondary research includes government or industry reports that detail participation rates in various demographics or policies for elite sport funding, and published academic research (journal articles, chapters, books, conference proceedings) on any relevant topic. In most cases, you will be expected to examine secondary sources to learn more about specific issues.
- *Tertiary data*: These are the weakest sources of information for research as they are several steps removed from the primary data. Tertiary sources gather together secondary sources, and condense the many and varied ideas down into straightforward and easily understood summaries. Textbooks are an example of a tertiary source, and although they provide an excellent introduction to, or overview of, a field of study, they are not always the best source of information when it comes to research, particularly as you move into the latter stages of your degree.

As you begin your studies, your assignments will probably focus mostly on collecting secondary data, and as you progress, you might be required to collect primary data to analyse yourself. If you complete a final year dissertation or capstone project, it is highly likely that you will need to design a study, collect data and interpret the results before writing up and formally presenting your findings. If you are not sure which sources of information you should be using in your own research, your professor will be able to give you specific direction.

PURE/APPLIED RESEARCH

Pure research is conducted simply for the sake of understanding concepts and theories, and generating knowledge. It may be motivated by curiosity or based on previous results, but a key characteristic of pure research is that there is no expectation of a direct application. In other words, it is the production of knowledge only for the sake of knowledge and may not be utilized in the 'real world' for decades or even centuries. An example of pure research would be researchers determining the chemical make-up of sweat.

Applied research, by contrast, is intended to apply scientific theories and principles to solve specific, practical problems in the 'real world'. It is inspired by actual challenges in industry, business, education or other fields and translates pure research into evidence-based solutions. An example of applied research would be identifying whether any of the electrolytes lost through sweating could be returned to the body via a sports drink and then determining whether such a solution helps the body during endurance events.

QUANTITATIVE/QUALITATIVE RESEARCH

Quantitative research generally counts something or 'measures' the relationship between variables, and may be either descriptive (observational only) or experimental (intervention with pre- and post-testing). Data are processed statistically and presented numerically, often in graphs, charts and tables, and conclusions are generalized to the broader research population. Biophysical research tends to be largely quantitative, though this form of research can also be used in the socio-cultural study of sport, particularly in sports psychology, sociology of sport and sports management. A quantitative research project might be 'A comparison of the number of women who have experienced discrimination in sport in Australia, New Zealand, the United States, Canada and the UK'. The data would consist of a lot of numbers that might be compared and contrasted with one another to determine the nations where there is a greater degree of discrimination.

Qualitative research typically 'collects' observations of what people say or do and how they respond to various events or stimuli. It records experiences, opinions, perspectives, motivations, feelings and behaviours through open surveys, interviews, focus groups or observation. Qualitative data are not easily reduced to numbers, nor are they typically generalizable. Instead, researchers try to interpret why people think or behave the way that they do in particular situations and what themes, differences or trends might be identified across a number of subjects. Qualitative research is more prevalent in the social sciences, though it can certainly be used in the biophysical sciences. A qualitative research question might be 'Understanding women's experiences of discrimination in football in Australia, New Zealand, the United States, Canada and the UK'. The results are likely to be written or verbal responses that researchers will analyse to build a picture of how the participants felt if and when they experienced discrimination in each of these nations. These experiences might then be compared to determine any cross-national similarities or differences.

A word of caution: 'numbers' do not equate to 'objective', nor does the collection of experiences or observations equate to 'subjective'. Both types of research have established methods and data collection protocols that are designed to ensure the reliability and validity of data. Both types of research are equally subject to personal bias on the part of the researcher, and neither is 'better' quality research than the other; there are just more and less appropriate methods to gather particular types of data depending on the research question and objectives. Each piece of research should be judged on its own merits by scrutinizing its design, methods and analysis. It is not uncommon for studies to contain both quantitative and qualitative research components.

DISSEMINATION OF RESEARCH

After a study has been conducted, researchers disseminate their findings as widely as possible so that they may contribute to the overall body of knowledge on that particular topic and inspire new research. Without sharing the results of academic research, our knowledge would remain fractured and incomplete. Researchers in one institution would have no idea what researchers in other universities – in their own country and elsewhere – are working on, although by the time it appears in print, research can already be a few years old. It takes time to design the project, conduct the research, analyse the findings, write the paper, submit it to a scholarly journal for review, receive feedback and corrections, re-submit and then wait for it to be published. Again, the research process is slow and methodical, relying on a number of checks and balances to ensure quality.

There are several ways that scientific research is published in the academic world and then communicated to the broader community. These publications are the secondary sources that you will use to study sport, prepare for exams, write assignments and perhaps inspire your own research. Not all of these sources are as highly regarded as others, so it is important to have an understanding of each format and the reasons why you should focus on good-quality research in your assignments. See Figure 4.2 for a general overview of the quality of various sources of information for your research papers.

JOURNAL ARTICLES

An academic journal is a small booklet published by a scholarly association or reputable publisher as little as once or twice a year or as often as weekly. Journals are normally quite specific in terms of the subject matter that they

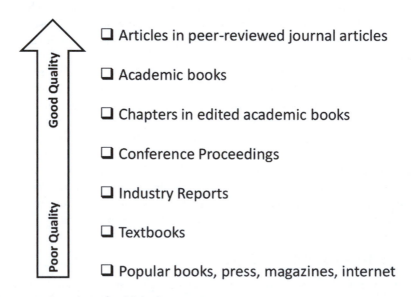

Figure 4.2 Overview of published sources

deal with, and as you become more familiar with the journals in your field, you will start to know which ones to consult for specific topics. Examples of academic sports studies journals are listed in Table 4.1. Each small booklet, or 'issue', contains a number of different sections, such as articles, book reviews and research notes. There may be only three or four articles in any one issue or there might be a larger number, depending on the size of the journal. Each article is written by a separate author or group of authors on topics that are linked to the overall subject area of the journal, although an individual issue sometimes has a specific 'theme' where most, if not all, articles will be related to the stated focus. Although journals are technically small booklets, you may never actually hold an issue of a journal in your hand because you will access most journals and articles electronically; however, it is worth going to the journals section of your library to see what they look like.

A journal has an editor (or co-editors) and a panel of experts (known as a review or editorial board) who examine each submission and decide whether

Table 4.1 Examples of academic journals in sports studies

European Journal of Sport Science	www.tandfonline.com/toc/tejs20/current
European Physical Education Review	http://epe.sagepub.com/
Exercise and Sport Sciences Reviews	http://journals.lww.com/acsm-essr/pages/default.aspx
International Journal of the History of Sport	www.tandfonline.com/toc/fhsp20/current
International Journal of Performance Analysis in Sport	www.ingentaconnect.com/content/uwic/ujpa
International Journal of Sport Policy and Politics	www.tandfonline.com/toc/risp20/4/1
International Journal of Sport Psychology	www.ijsp-online.com/
Journal of Biomechanics	www.jbiomech.com/
Journal of International Society of Sports Nutrition	www.jissn.com/
Journal of Sport and Tourism	www.tandfonline.com/toc/rjto20/current
Journal of Sports Economics	http://jse.sagepub.com/
Journal of Sport History	www.journalofsporthistory.org/
Journal of Sport Management	http://journals.humankinetics.com/jsm
Leisure Studies	www.tandfonline.com/toc/rlst20/current
Medicine and Science in Sports and Exercise	http://journals.lww.com/acsm-msse/pages/default.aspx
Sociology of Sport Journal	http://journals.humankinetics.com/ssj
Sports Coaching Review	www.tandfonline.com/toc/rspc20/current
Sport Management Review	http://journals.elsevier.com/sport-management-review/

it is worthy of being published in the journal. When an author submits an article, several experts in the field will review the paper without knowing who wrote it. This is known as 'blind peer-reviewing' and is considered the highest standard of publication because it is anonymously assessed. The reviewers recommend the paper for publication, suggest major or minor corrections or reject the paper. This process is designed to ensure that only good-quality articles are published so that the development of the field is based on rigorous inquiry.

A journal is organized numerically by volume and issue. Generally, the volume is associated with the year of publication, so all issues of *Sport Marketing Quarterly* published in 2012 are part of Volume 21. Within a volume, there will be several issues, and these are typically numbered in order – Issue 1, Issue 2, Issue 3. Here are three examples of journal articles:

> Abernethy, P.J. and Wehr, M.S (1997) Ammonia and lactate response to leg press work at 5 and 15 RM. *Journal of Strength and Conditioning Research*, 11(1): 40–44. Available at: http://journals.lww.com/nsca-jscr/Abstract/1997/02000/Ammonia_and_Lactate_Response_to_Leg_Press_Work_at.9.aspx.

> Devine, A., Bolan, P. and Devine, F. (2010) Online destination marketing: maximizing the tourism potential of a sports event. *International Journal of Sport Management and Marketing*, 7(1/2): 58–75. Available at: www.inderscience.com/info/inarticle.php?artid=29712

> Osmond, G. (2010) Photographs, materiality and sport history: Peter Norman and the 1968 Mexico City Black Power Salute. *Journal of Sport History*, 37(1): 119–37. Available at: http://muse.jhu.edu/journals/journal_of_sport_history/summary/v037/37.1.osmond.html.

ACADEMIC BOOKS

An academic book presents original research on a specific topic. It is written by a single author, two authors or a group of authors, who are normally, but not always, employed at a university. Academic books can be quite dense, even impenetrable, as they sustain a complex, specialist argument over many pages and chapters. They typically take a lot of time to conceive, develop, research and write, and are considered significant milestones in the authors' careers. Academic books are usually published by a reputable academic or university press (see Table 4.2 for examples). Here are three examples of academic books:

> Fields, S.K. (2008) *Female gladiators: gender, law, and contact sport in America.* Champaign IL: University of Illinois Press. See: www.press.uillinois.edu/books/catalog/64fks9qh9780252029585.html

> Magdalinski, T. (2008) *Sport, technology and the body: the nature of performance.* Abingdon: Routledge. See: www.routledge.com/books/details/9780415378765/

Schiller, K. and Young, C. (2010) *The 1972 Munich Olympics and the making of modern Germany.* Berkeley CA: University of California Press. See: www.ucpress.edu/book.php?isbn=9780520262157

Table 4.2 Examples of reputable academic or university presses and their location

Cambridge University Press, Cambridge	www.cambridge.org
Columbia University Press, New York	www.cup.columbia.edu
Harvard University Press, Cambridge, MA	www.hup.harvard.edu
Human Kinetics, Champaign, IL	www.humankinetics.com
Oxford University Press, Oxford	www.oup.com
Princeton University Press, Princeton, NJ	www.press.princeton.edu
Routledge, Abingdon	www.routledge.co.uk
Sage, London	www.sagepub.com
University of Queensland Press, Brisbane, QLD	www.uqp.uq.edu.au

EDITED BOOKS

An edited book is a collection of chapters, each of which is written by different people. Edited books are generally focused on a specific theme, and each contributor will write an independent chapter that relates to the overarching concept of the book and examines the issue from different perspectives or by using case studies. Each contribution is either original research or a summary of the author's previous work in the area. The chapters are edited by a single, pair or group of editors, who will write an introduction contextualizing the chapters in relation to the overall theme of the book and explaining the rationale for developing the collection. The editor(s) may also write their own chapter(s). Edited books are easily recognized as the cover will specify who the book is 'edited by', and the table of contents will acknowledge the author of each individual chapter. Here are three examples of chapters in edited books:

Brown, D. (2004) Olympic legacies: sport, space and the practices of everyday life. In: J. Bale and M.K. Christensen (eds) *Post-Olympism: questioning sport in the twenty-first century* (pp. 99–118). Oxford: Berg. See: www.bloomsbury.com/uk/post-olympism-9781859737194/

Davids, K., Bennett, S.J. and Beak, S. (2002) Sensitivity of children and adults to haptic information in wielding tennis rackets. In: K. Davids, G.J.P. Savelsbergh, S.J. Bennett and J. Van der Camp (eds) *Interceptive actions in sport: information and movement* (pp. 195–211). Abingdon: Routledge. See: www.routledge.com/books/details/9780415241533/

Holmlund, C. (1997) Visible difference and flex appeal: the body, sex, sexuality and race in the *Pumping Iron* films. In: A. Baker and T. Boyd (eds) *Out of bounds: sports, media, and the politics of identity* (pp. 145–60). Bloomington IN: Indiana University Press. See: www.iupress.indiana.edu/product_info.php?products_id=20909

TEXTBOOKS

A textbook is typically an overview of, or introduction to, a broader field of study. It differs from an academic book in that it does not present original research, but rather condenses current research into key ideas that are easily communicated to students or those starting out in the discipline. Textbooks are an excellent way to start learning about an issue and will introduce you to the main concepts that have developed over time as well as the key researchers in the field. Here are three examples of textbooks:

> Fullerton, S. (2007) *Sport marketing*. New York: McGraw Hill. See: http://highered.mcgraw-hill.com/sites/007338111x/information_center_view0/
>
> Gamble, P. (2012) *Strength and conditioning for team sports*, 2nd edn. Abingdon: Routledge. See: www.routledge.com/books/details/9780415637930/
>
> Weinberg, R.S. and Gould, D. (2011) *Foundations of sport and exercise psychology*, 5th edn. Champaign IL: Human Kinetics. See: www.humankinetics.com/products/all-products/Foundations-of-Sport-and-Exercise-Psychology-wWeb-Study-Guide-5th-Edition

OTHER SOURCES OF INFORMATION

Although they might be easier to access, newspapers, magazines, blogs, websites and other popular media are not considered good sources of information for research papers because they are not usually produced to the same high standards as academic research. In other words, the requirement for evidence may be absent, the method of collecting and analysing data may not be foregrounded and the process of rigorously checking and reviewing the material prior to publication might be neglected. Furthermore, newspaper and magazine journalists are paid for their opinions and interpretations, and the political agenda of the parent company or the influence of advertisers may not be apparent. Material on a website is contentious as it can be difficult to find out who the author or owner is and the degree to which the material represents personal opinions rather than research evidence. If you do not know the author, who is funding the site or how the material has been produced, then it is difficult to trust the veracity of the information being presented.

If there is one online source that generates a lot of debate and concern among lecturers, it is Wikipedia (www.wikipedia.com). Unlike the clunky encyclopaedia sets of old, Wikipedia is a quick, accessible online repository with pages on almost every conceivable topic. For many students, Wikipedia is their first point of call, which typically alarms their professors. While the reliability of Wikipedia entries cannot always be guaranteed, the self-regulating nature of wikis means that there are some checks and balances that correct inaccuracies when they appear. Wikipedia promotes a neutral rather than biased account, and citations are required to support assertions. Even though the 'facts' might be in order, it is important to remember that Wikipedia is still just an encyclopaedia that presents information with little analysis or interpretation.

A good rule of thumb might be to use Wikipedia as a starting point to familiarize yourself with broader ideas and concepts, much as you would use a textbook; the entry may have academic references that you can examine once you have a general overview. It is a useful source if you need a basic or straightforward introduction to a topic, but it is limited in terms of developing a sophisticated overview of that topic and is not at all designed to engage you in spirited intellectual debate. At the end of the day, like any encyclopaedia, Wikipedia is a helpful entry point, but it can never be an end point for your research assignments, because these must be based on formal, published academic research.

THE IMPORTANCE OF ACADEMIC RESEARCH

We live in an information age, and facts and figures overwhelm us at the click of a mouse. No matter what the topic, an online search yields all manner of websites, articles and blogs. In a university setting, however, there is an expectation that the information used to construct a rigorous argument will be good-quality academic research. Academic research is typically scientific, presenting informed argument that carefully builds upon the existing knowledge base. Data are collected according to specified protocols and interpreted using accepted methods and theories, and the resulting evidence is used to support the author's argument. Before it is published, an academic research paper will have been stringently reviewed by experts and specialists. In order to find and use appropriate sources, it is important to know how to distinguish between strong and weak research.

PEER-REVIEWED RESEARCH

When looking for good-quality research, the gold standard is 'peer-reviewed' journal articles. This means that the article has been rigorously examined by independent reviewers who read the submission and provide comments, revisions and suggestions to the author(s). The author(s) are then expected to make those revisions before the journal's editor will accept their submission for publication. In other words, your professors are still having their work 'graded' each time they submit a paper for publication. Reviewers will determine whether the research is valid, rigorously conducted, based on appropriate methodologies, well argued and well written with logical conclusions. Although it is an important process to ensure the quality of the journal, it is not infallible, and there have been occasions when journals have published sub-quality research. It is always important that you make your own evaluation of the research material you find.

CHECKLIST: IDENTIFYING GOOD QUALITY RESEARCH

There are a number of ways you can check your sources to determine whether or not they are of a suitable standard:

- *Consider the publication*: Is it an academic journal, book or edited collection? Is it an online journal? Is it published by a recognized academic or university press? Is it associated with a scholarly society or association? Is the journal peer-reviewed?
- *Consider the authors*: What are their institutional affiliations? Are they recognized researchers in the field? Have they published other scholarly works?
- *Consider the article*: Does it 'look' scholarly or are there large headings and lots of photos? Is the language scholarly or chatty? Do the authors include references in the text and a detailed reference list? Can you identify the research method?

CASE STUDY

Sarah has to write a report looking at the sponsorship of children's sport by junk food companies and will need to develop recommendations based on the research evidence to provide guidance to schools in her local area. She feels she has found some good information, and her sources include:

- Carter, M.A., Edwards, R., Signal, L. and Hoek, J. (2012) Availability and marketing of food and beverages to children through sports settings: a systematic review. *Public Health Nutrition*, 15(8): 1373–79.
- Kelly, B., Baur, L.A., Bauman, A.E., King, L., Chapman, K. and Smith. B.J. (2011) Food and drink sponsorship of children's sport in Australia: who pays? *Health Promotion International*, 26(2): 188–95.
- Macniven, R. and Kelly, B. (2012) Sports sponsorship and kids' health: who are the real winners? *The Conversation*. Available at: http://theconversation. edu.au/sports-sponsorship-and-kids-health-who-are-the-real-winners-9845
- Mersiades, B. (2012) Junk bonds: close ties between fast food sponsorship and junior sport 'barrier to obesity fight'. *Sports Business Insider*, 4 December.

→ Use the checklist above to determine which of Sarah's sources you think will be acceptable for a research report at university.

→ If any sources are not appropriate, explain why they are unsuitable for a college research paper.

STARTING AN ASSIGNMENT

One of the hardest parts of writing an assignment is knowing how and where to start. It can be quite overwhelming if you are not sure what is expected of you, the standard that is required or even what you need to do to get started. Nevertheless, beginning an assignment can be as simple as following three easy steps:

Step 1 *Analyse the question*: This might seem to be the most logical thing to do, but many students glance at the topic, think they know what is being asked and never look at it carefully again.

Step 2 *Brainstorm the topic*: Think of all the ideas, terms and concepts that could be relevant or related to the topic.

Step 3 *Locate research sources*: Use the catalogue and databases in the library to find journal articles, academic books, edited books and other resources that will help you build a picture of the topic.

Each of these steps can be completed individually or together with your study group. It does not matter if you each have a different topic; you can still help each other dissect the question and brainstorm some initial ideas. It is also worth noting that the first two steps are reasonably quick and can be completed anywhere: standing in line for a coffee, walking between classes or lying on the grass. Use a small notepad or even your phone to record your ideas.

STEP 1: ANALYSE THE QUESTION

Understanding the question is the most important first step of any assignment. Start by breaking down the topic into its various components to ensure you understand exactly what is being asked. This is a critical step, as misunderstanding the question now means that you may focus your attention in the wrong area or write a paper that misses the point. No lecturer likes to receive a well-researched, well-written paper that does not address the research question. If it does not fulfil the criteria and respond appropriately to the topic, it cannot be awarded a high grade, no matter how good the piece of work is.

Start thinking about the research topic as soon as it becomes available. The more familiar your brain is with the ideas and concepts underpinning the assignment, the more likely you will recognize relevant content in your lectures. It would be disappointing to select a research topic only to realize it was covered in class weeks ago and you did not benefit from the discussion.

Research topics are generally structured to include task words, content words and limiting words, each of which provide direction about how the topic should be addressed:

- *Task words* outline the action you must take or, in other words, what you need to do. Also known as 'instructional' or 'directive' words, they are typically verbs and state clearly whether you need to describe an issue, evaluate an outcome, compare and contrast two or more perspectives or examples, and so on. There is a comprehensive list of task words with explanations of their meanings in Appendix 1.

- *Content words* confirm the overall topic under consideration. It is the general subject matter to be examined by your paper.
- *Limiting words* limit or narrow the subject matter specifically so that you focus on relevant issues. It is easy to overlook the limiting words and concentrate on broader issues rather than the specific area suggested by the research topic.

SAMPLE ESSAY TOPIC

As the writing process is explained over the next few chapters, a sample research topic will be used to work through the various techniques, so that you can see the abstract concepts 'in action'. The research topic is:

Discuss three reasons children drop out of sport in their teenage years.

The first step, as noted above, is to break down the research topic into its task, content and limiting words:

- *Task word – Discuss*: this means to consider and offer some interpretation or evaluation of the topic, which is how we are being instructed to respond to this question.
- *Content words – drop out of sport*: the phenomenon of attrition from sports participation is the broad area that is under investigation in this paper.
- *Limiting words – children, teenage, three reasons*: by understanding the limitations placed on this question, we will know to focus our attention on teenagers, not young children, adults or the elderly. To do so would move the paper away from the specific topic and would mean we are not fulfilling the requirements of the assignment. We also know that only three reasons are needed for this paper.

STEP 2: BRAINSTORM THE TOPIC

Once you have a clear understanding of what is required, think about everything you might already know about the topic. You will be able to develop some key words that will be used to start the research process. Prior knowledge might come from some of the course readings or lectures you have attended, or from your own personal experiences or general knowledge. It is simply a starting point, and as you locate relevant sources, you will be able to develop more sophisticated searches based on the key words and ideas you read in the literature.

Spend some time writing down every word or idea you can think of that relates to the limiting and content words. Let your mind flow freely with ideas and do not restrict your creativity. Brainstorming with your study group will return more suggestions. Sort through your ideas and group together similar ideas to create a list of key words to guide your literature search. Pictures or diagrams can help you visualize the relationships between ideas, and columns or tables can help organize your thoughts.

The next step is to find synonyms for your key words to increase the chances of locating relevant research. Use a thesaurus if necessary, such as www.thesaurus.com. Table 4.3 shows the synonyms for the key words of our research topic and reveals how critical synonyms can be. When searching for research, using key terms from the first column yielded only two relevant sources on the first page of results, whereas a combination of terms from the second column returned eight useful sources on the first page. As you access appropriate literature, you will find new phrases to refine your search terms.

STEP 3: LOCATE RESEARCH SOURCES

Once you have decided on your list of key words and synonyms, head to the library either physically or virtually. Libraries can be overwhelming, but a lot less daunting once you understand the kinds of materials available to you and the way that these are organized. Take a comprehensive library tour when you first start college, especially if it includes a practical introduction to show you how to search the library's holdings. If this is not available to you, then you should look for online tutorials or approach a librarian to assist you until you have the skills and confidence to conduct searches yourself.

Everything in the library is catalogued electronically, so the entire library – or library system if your campus has more than one library – is searchable at the click of a mouse. The main ways to find information will be to search:

- the catalogue – to find printed books, journals, videos and other physical materials;
- e-Journals – to find electronic journals to which your library subscribes;
- databases – to find a large range of electronic materials (not all of which might actually be available to you).

Table 4.3 Key words and synonyms for the sample research topic

Key words	Synonyms
Main reasons	issues, factors, motives, causes
Children	kids, young people, young adults
Drop out	cease, attrition, finish, stop, end, quit
Sport	physical activity, team/individual sports
Teenage	adolescence/adolescents, young adults

Your university library might have specific resources for sports studies, or you might need to use some of the broader databases. A good starting point for sports studies students is to consult a sports-related database, such as SPORTDiscus, which collects information on publications on sport from all over the world. Please note, however, that just because a resource is included in SPORTDiscus does not mean that your library will automatically have access to it, and it can be frustrating to know about relevant sources but not be able to read them. Depending on your subject area or assignment topic, there might be more specific databases that will help you. Again, reference librarians can help familiarize you with your university library's holdings.

Some libraries will allow you to log in and create your own personal library, with a record of your favourite articles, journals, books and databases. It can set up alerts to let you know when new publications in your area arrive. This is a terrific way to build your resources that will not only help your written paper but also provide background material for you to review when preparing for exams. At the very least you should be able to save your search results to either email or print. Keeping a record of your research will stop you doubling up on resources that you have already found and is particularly useful if you conduct your literature search over a few days or weeks.

Although the library might have extensive holdings, not all material is equally useful and you need to focus on finding appropriate, relevant sources, as a good-quality argument can only be built on good-quality research. As noted above, preparation before you start searching is critical, and you need to have an objective in mind before you begin:

- What kinds of materials will be appropriate?
- What kinds of issues should they focus on?
- Do I know any authors in this field already?
- Have I covered a similar topic in another module?
- Will any of the recommended readings help me?

SEARCHING THE LIBRARY

Searching for relevant materials is certainly a lot faster with electronic resources available at the click of a mouse, but it is still not necessarily a quick process. It will take time to build confidence in your ability to locate the most appropriate sources, and it will always take several sessions to find the best selection of research for each assignment. One search can certainly yield useful materials, but as you examine them, you will identify new ideas and search terms, prompting you to repeat the search process a few more times. Research is always a diligent and methodical process, and searching the library is no different from gathering your own raw data. You need to be systematic and organized, which will take time.

When searching the catalogue and databases, begin with basic or general search terms and gradually incorporate more complex key word combinations to find more specific materials. Remember that computers are poor at mind-reading, so you need to spend time developing terms that will return you the most relevant resources. There are different methods to ensure you make the most out of your searches:

- *Key word searches*: This is the most common method of searching and allows you to define the terms you want to use in your search. Use the key words and synonyms you developed in your brainstorming session to find useful research. If your search terms are quite broad, you may find the results contain a lot of irrelevant items, in which case it is time to be more strategic about how you search for resources.
- *Boolean logic*: To give yourself more control over your searches, you can employ Boolean logic, which allows you to either broaden or narrow a search with the use of AND, OR, NOT. If you include AND between two (or more) terms, the search will be narrowed so that the results contain both (or all) terms; using OR broadens the search, so that the results will contain either term you have included; and if you use NOT, unhelpful terms can be excluded from the results. Figure 4.3 represents the relationship between search terms as Venn diagrams.

  If you wanted to search for material on football in Canada, you could conduct the following searches using Boolean logic, depending on the kind of football you are researching:

  football AND soccer AND Canada
  football OR soccer AND Canada
  football NOT soccer AND Canada

  You can use Boolean logic to create sophisticated search terms using parentheses as a way of keeping the logic organized. If we are searching for terms to support our sample research topic, the following might useful:

  (Sport OR physical activity) AND (teenagers OR adolescents) AND (drop out OR attrition)

- *Parentheses*: Enclosing some terms within parentheses will create additional relationships between search terms. For example, (injury OR accident) rugby will search for results containing injury and rugby or accident and rugby.

Figure 4.3 Boolean logic depicted as Venn diagrams

- *Proximity search*: NEAR or NEXT can be used to look for materials that have particular terms close to each other without necessarily being directly next to each other. Use NEAR/ with a number to indicate how close the second term needs to be. To search for materials dealing with rugby injuries, type in 'rugby NEAR/5 injury' (to search for places where the word injury is within five words of the term rugby) or 'rugby NEXT injury' (to search for places where the word injury directly follows rugby).
- *Truncation*: Placing an asterisk (*) at the end of a word stem allows the search to find all terms with this common stem, thus broadening your search to encompass a wider selection of relevant terms without you having to think of, and type in, every variation. Typing in sport* will find sport, sporting, sporty, sports. Please note that some databases require a question mark (?) rather than an asterisk.
- *Wildcard*: Using a question mark replaces a single variable character that could be replaced with anything. If searching for materials on women in sport, use wom?n, as this will return results for both 'women' and 'woman'. This is also a useful way of picking up differences in British and US spelling, as in the case of behaviour/behavior.
- *Specific phrases*: Enclosing a phrase within inverted commas, such as "sports studies" will return results that contain that specific order of words.

Before looking up these sources, examine your initial results. How do these results compare to your 'aims' for this stage of research? Do all your key areas appear to be covered? If not, what is missing?

STUDENT VIEWPOINT

I absolutely recommend doing a library tutorial because it showed me the basic steps to find research in the databases and how to narrow my search to find only the articles of the highest quality. Before the tutorial I found this process very confusing, but once they showed me how and where to find sources I quickly got the hang of it and I'm now much more confident. It also gave me an understanding of how to begin with broad search terms and gradually find detailed and more suitable academic material to use in my assignments. The quality of research papers used is important because not all work published is academic or reviewed by a respected peer in that particular field. Peer-reviewed articles serve as a good quality control tool, but you still need to look at it yourself to make sure it is suitable for your assignment. Although this task was somewhat time consuming, it was well worth the effort when it came to writing the assignment.—Zac.

FILTERING SEARCH RESULTS

Although using the above techniques will help you find good research, please note that search functions are limited, and even though the papers you found contain the key words, they may not be the most useful or the best quality. Indeed, the search results essentially only tell you what is available, not what is relevant for your assignment. At this point, you need to start filtering the search results so that you do not waste time reading irrelevant papers.

- *Be highly selective*: Create an 'A' and 'B' list of research. Only place on the 'A' list materials that are extremely relevant to the topic. Those relegated to the 'B' list are not quite relevant to the entire topic but may be useful for background information on one or two sub-issues. You should concentrate on finding sources that can be placed on the 'A' list.
- *Research your research*: If you are not sure about the quality of a source, then research the research. Look at the author – what are their qualifications? Are they an expert in this field? Have they written on other, similar topics or published in this area before? Is the journal academic, trade or industry focused? Are the articles blind peer-reviewed? If you are not sure about the answer to any of these questions, you can always Google the name of the journal or author to find out more about them.
- *Check how old the source is*: It might be worth considering the age of the article/book when trying to determine its relevance. While some might suggest that anything published in the last ten years is considered 'up to date', this will entirely depend on the topic. If you are researching sport and amateurism in the Victorian era, a book that is twenty or thirty years old might still be useful, whereas if you are examining the impact of social media on athletes, a paper published on 'sport and the internet' in 2005 might be entirely irrelevant.

SUMMARY

1   Research papers are a widespread assessment strategy used in sports studies courses and require students to develop an argument based on research rather than presenting their personal opinion.
2   Academic research is the systematic and meticulous process of collecting and interpreting data. It relies on accepted methods and is published only after undergoing stringent peer-review.
3   Good-quality papers are only based on good-quality research, and it is incumbent on students to learn how to distinguish appropriate from unacceptable sources of evidence.
4   Every research paper begins with a careful analysis of the topic, the development of suitable search terms and a literature search.
5   The university library has extensive holdings in electronic databases that house tens of thousands of sources. Learning how to navigate the electronic collections by using Boolean logic is critical for research success.

EXERCISES

1   Register for a library workshop or seminar that introduces you to electronic databases and search techniques. Spend some time familiarizing yourself with the various systems, using online tutorials to guide you.
2   Use a research topic from one of your classes and identify the key elements of the question. Brainstorm the topic to come up with some suitable search terms and then visit your library to find relevant research materials from their physical or electronic collections by applying Boolean logic.
3   Read one of the research sources you find, and determine what kind of publication it is, the type of research that has been conducted (qualitative or quantitative) and the type of evidence used (primary/secondary).

REFLECTION

What might be the hardest part of starting an assignment? Are you concerned about addressing the question appropriately? What might you do to ensure your research is relevant to the research topic? Why is it important to assess the quality of research sources? Why are peer-reviewed journal articles considered a good standard for research? Do you think you will be able to recognize good-quality research sources when searching for materials? Will you have any challenges finding research materials in the library in the future?

FURTHER READING

Gratton, C. and Jones, I. (2010) *Research methods for sports studies,* 2nd edn. Abingdon: Routledge.
Smith, M.F. (2010) *Research methods in sport.* London: Sage.

5

LEARNING TO READ

Understanding academic readings and research

OVERVIEW

This chapter outlines:
- the purpose and structure of academic readings;
- how to scan academic research efficiently to locate relevant information;
- how to summarize readings into a usable format.

INTRODUCTION

If there is one guarantee at university, it is that you will read, read and read some more. You will read as you study; you will read as you write assignments; and you will read as you prepare for exams. Learning to decipher the complexities of academic research can, however, take time, and many students find the idea of reading a ten- or twenty-page article frustrating and difficult. Reading for academic purposes is not the same as settling down with a good novel or even skimming through a textbook. The language is more complex and not usually creative; the subject-specific jargon seems inaccessible; there is an assumption that you already have a background in the field; it is not always clear what the main point is; and, quite frankly, the turgid style can send you to sleep before the first page is turned. Indeed, titles such as 'One lesbian feminist epistemology: integrating feminist standpoint, queer theory, and feminist cultural studies' or 'beta-endorphin immunoreactive material and authentic beta-endorphin in the plasma of males undergoing anaerobic exercise on a rowing ergometer' are as easily understood as an obscure foreign language to students entering college. Although it can be a challenge to penetrate an academic article, there are techniques to help you make sense of the seemingly incomprehensible, and, like all skills, practice makes perfect. The more you employ these strategies, the more accessible academic research will become.

PURPOSE OF READINGS

Whereas lectures deliver a basic framework for understanding a topic, academic readings fill in the detail, offer different viewpoints, provide examples or case studies of ideas discussed in class, introduce or debate the merits of various theoretical approaches and are the basis for your research assignments. There are many kinds of academic readings, and each is used in a different context. Your lecturer might set required readings that should be completed ahead of lectures. These are not simply to use up your valuable study time but are intended to familiarize you with the lecture content. It is difficult in two or three hours to communicate all the relevant issues on a topic, so readings are used to reinforce key points and extend your knowledge beyond what was presented in class. These readings might be discussed in detail during a tutorial, or they may simply be left as support materials for your own learning.

In addition to required readings, a professor might list supplementary, recommended or optional readings. It is up to you whether or not you would like to read them, but they are particularly useful if you are struggling with a topic or are seeking further depth or clarification. Additional readings are best read after the lecture once you have a basic understanding of the main issues. There are also readings that are used specifically for assignments. Your professor may provide an indicative list of articles or you may be expected to find them all yourself. Finally, there are readings that will help you study and prepare for exams. It is good practice to get into the habit of finding one or two articles on each lecture topic yourself. Not only does it help develop your search skills but finding additional materials and alternative perspectives also deepens your understanding of a topic and provides you with more background to include in either your written papers or exams.

STRUCTURE OF ACADEMIC RESEARCH PAPERS

Successfully navigating around an academic research paper is the first step towards learning how to read it. While there will be variations depending on subject area and publication, the overall structure of academic research is reasonably consistent. In many cases, subheadings are used to highlight the various sub-sections, and these signposts help us find our way around the paper quickly. These sections are outlined in Figure 5.1 and discussed in more detail below.

ABSTRACT

The abstract is a short paragraph found at the beginning of most journal articles and is essentially a brief summary or the entire article 'in miniature'. It tells the reader the 'who', 'what', 'where', 'why' and 'how' of the paper, and is an instant snapshot of the objectives, method and findings (see Figure 5.2

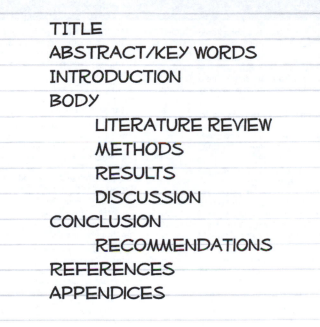

TITLE
ABSTRACT/KEY WORDS
INTRODUCTION
BODY
    LITERATURE REVIEW
    METHODS
    RESULTS
    DISCUSSION
CONCLUSION
    RECOMMENDATIONS
REFERENCES
APPENDICES

Figure 5.1 Typical structure of academic research

for examples). Reading the abstract will let you know whether it is worth delving into more detail. In many journals, key words are listed after the abstract, and it makes sense to compare these to your own as you may find one or two to help your next literature search.

INTRODUCTION

The introduction draws the reader from the broader context of the research towards the main purpose and objectives of the paper. It establishes the foundation for the study and takes the reader from the overall 'big picture' and leads them to the specific issue under investigation. The introduction outlines the reasons why the study was needed and may make some comment about how the paper fills a gap or provides additional insight into an issue. Even though the introduction to a journal article might be only a paragraph or two, the introduction to a book will be an entire chapter. It is not uncommon for the introduction to point to additional research that is related to the topic under discussion, which might also be relevant for your assignment.

When reading the introduction, look for the 'statement of purpose', also known as the 'thesis statement'. This is a specific declaration that explains in

Whitehead, S. & Biddle, S. (2008) Adolescent girls' perceptions of physical activity: A focus group study. *European Physical Education Review*, 14(2): 243–62.		Wisløff, U., Castagna, C., Helgerud, J., Jones, R. & Hoff, J. (2004) Strong correlation of maximal squat strength with sprint performance and vertical jump height in elite soccer players. *British Journal of Sports Medicine*, 38(3): 285–8.
Low levels of physical activity among adolescent girls are a cause for concern.	CONTEXT	BACKGROUND: A high level of strength is inherent in elite soccer play, but the relation between maximal strength and sprint and jumping performance has not been studied thoroughly.
Examining girls' physical activity perceptions and motivations through in-depth qualitative research allows for greater understanding of the reasons behind their physical activity-related choices.	PURPOSE	OBJECTIVE: To determine whether maximal strength correlates with sprint and vertical jump height in elite male soccer players.
Forty-seven girls aged 14 to 16 years participated in exploratory focus group discussions. Thematic analysis was carried out in which data were analysed inductively using a constant comparison method.	METHOD	METHODS: Seventeen international male soccer players (mean (SD) age 25.8 (2.9) years, height 177.3 (4.1) cm, weight 76.5 (7.6) kg, and maximal oxygen uptake 65.7 (4.3) ml/kg/min) were tested for maximal strength in half squats and sprinting ability (0–30 m and 10 m shuttle run sprint) and vertical jumping height.
The findings illustrate the extent to which adolescent girls' physical activity participation is affected by social influences and perceived societal norms. Furthermore, changing priorities throughout adolescence mean that physical activity is deprioritized, with many girls stating that they cannot be bothered to take part.	RESULTS	RESULT: There was a strong correlation between maximal strength in half squats and sprint performance and jumping height.
Recommendations to increase participation include encouraging parental support, introducing peer mentoring schemes involving girls who enjoy and regularly participate in physical activity and providing activities for adolescent girls that are fun, informal in nature and involve participation with friends.	RECOM- MENDA- TIONS	CONCLUSIONS: Maximal strength in half squats determines sprint performance and jumping height in high level soccer players. High squat strength did not imply reduced maximal oxygen consumption. Elite soccer players should focus on maximal strength training, with emphasis on maximal mobilisation of concentric movements, which may improve their sprinting and jumping performance.

Figure 5.2 The structure of an abstract

no uncertain terms what the paper is about. Even though it may not be obviously stated, every piece of good writing will identify the purpose of the article, book or chapter, and locating the thesis statement will help you determine if the paper is going to be relevant for your purposes.

Examples of thesis statements include:

The purpose of this study was to determine the validity of a novel subjective estimated-repetitions-to failure scale for predicting muscular failure during resistance exercise.

(Hackett *et al.* 2012: 1405).

This chapter discusses the production and reproduction of a cultural distaste for fat in fitness gyms.

(Mansfield 2011: 82)

This book aims to explore the multi-faceted relationship between alcohol in all its aspects and sport at all levels.

(Collins and Vamplew 2002: 1)

The thesis statement is usually supported by additional detail about the objectives of the research, and these provide more specific detail about the reasons for the study and the intended outcomes. Look for the objectives so that you understand the authors' expectations for their study:

> This chapter discusses the production and reproduction of a cultural distaste for fat in fitness gyms. It recognizes the relevance of the concept of stigma and explores in more detail the socio-dynamics of stigmatization for understanding how the appearance and display of fat in fitness cultures is denigrated and devalued, serving to classify fat women as the stigmatized 'other' in the gym environment and wider social life.
>
> (Mansfield 2011: 82)

BODY

The body of an article, book or chapter contains the authors' main argument, supported by the evidence that they have collected. The body contains several different sections that may be structured with subheadings (or chapter titles in the case of a book), and these can guide your analysis of the paper.

The first section is often a *literature review*, which is a detailed discussion of previous research on the topic. It summarizes the main findings to date and reiterates how the study adds to what is currently known. You will recognize the literature review by the many references to other studies. Please note that sometimes the introduction and literature review blend together, so that they are not always distinctive sections.

The next part is typically on *research methods*, and outlines in detail how the study has been conducted. It explains the research design, justifies the data collection process, confirms how the sample was determined and outlines the type of analysis that was conducted. These components are needed so the reader can be confident that the data were collected scientifically and the results are trustworthy. As you become more familiar with research, you will become skilled at interpreting research methods so that you can assess the quality of a study based on the information presented in this section.

Next comes the *results* section, which simply presents the study's findings. Depending on the kind of research being conducted, the results might be presented as graphs or tables, quotes from participants, or images or extracts from other documents. The results section only ever presents data; there is no interpretation or analysis at this point.

The last part of the body is the *discussion* (or analysis), where the authors interpret the results and outline what their findings might mean for future research. The discussion also links the results to previously published literature, so that they are contexualized within the broader subject area. In some disciplines, the results and discussion might be presented together. In qualitative studies, for example, it can be difficult to report 'results' such as excerpts from interviews and field observations independently of the analysis.

CONCLUSION

The final part of a research paper is the conclusion, which summarizes the main findings of the research and the authors' interpretations of the results, draws together the argument, reiterates the broader context and need for the study, and explains how the research contributes to the field. A conclusion might also identify limitations to the study as well as suggestions for future research directions. Depending on the nature of the research, there might be a list of recommendations or a call to action.

REFERENCES/APPENDICES

A list of the resources cited in the paper is placed after the conclusion. The reference list provides the bibliographic detail of the sources that informed the study and enables a reader to search for these materials themselves. Any information that is useful for the reader to see but is not absolutely central to the argument might be placed in an appendix at the end of the paper. Appendices might include a copy of the survey instrument or raw data, but are only ever used if there is direct mention of them in the paper.

HOW TO 'READ' A RESEARCH PAPER

Reading a research paper is like attending a lecture. Preparation is critical, and you need to be on the lookout for important points and ideas. Reading a research paper is not, however, like reading a book or magazine article, and instead of 'reading' it might be better to think of your task as 'processing'. Reading from start to finish wastes time and ultimately yields little return on invested effort. 'Processing', on the other hand, is a non-linear method of working through the paper to extract only the information that you need for your paper. Indeed, replacing 'reading' with 'processing' may liberate you from the obligation to start on page one and read every word until the end.

Before you start processing the paper, make sure you have a copy of your assignment topic in front of you, so that you can remind yourself about the kind of information that will support your argument. You should then organize your research into a logical order. Begin with the more general pieces and gradually build up to complex, detailed or technical papers. If this is a new area for you, then you might want to start with a textbook for a general introduction before delving into more sophisticated research papers.

TIP

NEVER sit down and read an article from start to finish with no specific purpose in mind. It is a waste of time and returns very little usable information.

Before turning to the first page, you need to establish your objectives for reading the paper by asking yourself some straightforward questions:

- Why am I reading this paper?
- What do I already know? What gaps in my knowledge are there?
- What ideas, terms or concepts might I come across in this paper?
- What do I need to learn from this material?
- What specific questions do I need answered by reading this paper?
- What sort of ideas will be relevant for my paper?

You will have a clearer sense of what to look for if you focus your attention on identifying relevant information rather than simply noticing interesting information or recognizing familiar ideas. Bear in mind that not every question will be answered in one reading, and it is not uncommon to need to engage with the text on a few occasions to really grasp the content and understand its potential contribution to your assignment. Indeed, each time you process the article, you might have different objectives and so be looking for different points.

When processing a paper, the overall goal is to focus on information that is directly relevant to your assignment. Not every single detail in every paper will be useful, so there is no point recording information that is irrelevant. Essentially, you need to process only as much of the paper as is needed to achieve your objectives. It may require you to read every word, or you may need to read only one or two sections to extract the necessary ideas. But the rule of thumb is: only read as much as you need to answer your questions. This is why it is so important to identify what you need from the paper before you start to read it.

STUDENT VIEWPOINT

It was a complete revelation to learn that I only need to read as much as I need to find the information for my assignment. Also, thinking of two or three questions I need answered makes reading articles so much quicker and easier. I always ploughed through academic papers, even though it made me so drowsy, and it just felt like a waste of time because I could never find anything relevant to my paper. But it makes so much more sense now. Why keep on reading when I've already found the answers I was looking for?—Elizabeth.

WHAT DO I 'READ' FIRST?

Once you have established your objectives for the article, you should set yourself a timeframe to process it. You will have a lot of research to examine, so it is important to be efficient. You might decide that twenty or thirty minutes is sufficient time to process the article, though some may need more and others may take less time. The next step is to preview the reading in three quick steps to familiarize yourself with the structure and general content of the paper. This should take no more than a few minutes.

Step 1: Scan

- Read the title of the paper carefully. Academic titles are usually quite specific and reveal a lot about the content of the paper. Look at your research topic again. Do the two seem related?
- Familiarize yourself with the structure of the paper. Can you see the sections outlined earlier in the chapter?

Step 2: Identify

- Find the thesis statement. Does the author clearly state the purpose of the paper? Look back at your research topic. Is the relationship between the thesis statement and topic still clear?
- What subheadings are there? In the biophysical sciences, these will be fairly standard, but in socio-cultural research papers, they may be a little more creative. Make sure you understand the subheadings and how each section might be useful for your paper.

Step 3: Read

- The final part of the initial preview is to read the abstract, even if you have already looked at it. This will remind you of the main findings of the paper. Then look at your research topic again to determine if the two are still nicely aligned.

The preview should enable you to make a decision about whether or not you should proceed with a more detailed examination. If the preview is promising, then you should print the paper so you can make notes on the hardcopy. If you do not think the article is suitable, put it to one side for now, but do not discard it entirely. There still may be useful and usable information buried in its pages, as will be discussed later in the chapter.

AFTER A POSITIVE PREVIEW

If you have decided to examine the paper in more detail, return to the thesis statement and underline or highlight it. Read the entire paragraph in which the thesis statement is found to gain more insight into the article's specific objectives and to establish what the paper does not cover. Being aware of the authors' stated aims is important so that you do not continue reading in the expectation of finding ideas that were never there to begin with.

The next step is to read the conclusion to know immediately whether the authors achieved their objectives and the significance of their results. If the conclusion is not identified by a subheading, then look at the last couple of paragraphs. Conclusions typically do not refer to other sources, as it is the summary of the paper, and the tone is normally slightly different from the discussion section.

It may seem back to front, but once you have a grasp of the overall findings of the paper, it is time to return to the beginning to examine the introduction and literature review in more detail. These sections provide the foundation for the study and will contain a lot of references to other studies, some of which might be useful for your assignment. Scan the sections by reading the first sentence of each paragraph. This is known as the topic sentence and is usually a clear statement of a main point. Reading the topic sentences will give you a reasonable overview of the argument without getting too caught up in detail that might not be relevant to your paper. Depending on how much detail you need to extract, you may need to delve deeper into the methods, results and discussion sections, though the important findings will be summarized in the conclusion.

NOTE TAKING

There is no point reading an article without recording what you have found. This might mean jotting a few notes in the margin, underlining or highlighting key points or writing down useful ideas. While all of these strategies are better than doing nothing at all, taking down notes that are meaningful when you look at them in a day, a week or a month's time requires planning and skill.

HOW DO I TAKE NOTES?

When taking notes from readings, it is strongly advised that you write them down by hand rather than simply underlining/highlighting, cutting and pasting or typing them out. The process of writing is slower and requires more engagement by the brain. By recording your own notes on paper, you are allowing yourself and your brain to work with the ideas, rather than absent-mindedly highlighting text that you are unlikely to remember as you turn the last page. Because writing takes more time, it forces you to think about whether you really need to write down what you have just read or whether you are just responding to an idea because it is interesting. Stay focused on the main findings of the paper and do not be swayed by interesting snippets.

Good note taking requires organization and a systematic approach:

- Where possible, use a separate notepad for each assignment. This keeps your research in one place and allows you to look back at the previous research to remind yourself of the material you have already covered.
- Use the first page or two of the notepad as a table of contents. As you start processing a new article, record the bibliographic details here as well as on the page where you will start writing notes.

- Always start processing a new article on a new page.
- The first things you should record are the full bibliographic details of the research source. Referencing will be discussed in detail in Chapter 8, but for now you should familiarize yourself with the essential information required to construct a complete reference:

  - author(s) (of an article, book or chapter in an edited book);
  - year of publication;
  - title of article (or chapter if it is an edited book);
  - names of editors (only for edited books);
  - name of journal (or book – edited or monograph);
  - volume/issue (not relevant for an edited book or monograph);
  - page numbers (not relevant for a monograph);
  - publisher (only for books);
  - place of publication (only for books).

  If you do not record these details, you may not remember the source of the notes, which will mean that the information cannot be included in your assignment.
- Leave plenty of room around each note so you have space to edit, annotate and revise later on.

WHAT SHOULD I WRITE DOWN?

When confronted with a lengthy research article, it is hard to know what to write down, so students often try to record as much detail as possible, worried that they might miss an important fact. This translates into furious highlighting or even writing out much of the article. It is worth bearing in mind why academics publish their research. They may be: offering new insights into an established topic; reformulating a theory to better suit the evidence; or offering a different application of an accepted experimental protocol. In short, every academic publication offers at least one new idea, and identifying the key findings of a paper is the purpose of your reading.

It is also important to consider the process of note taking, because writing without thinking means you may copy a lot of material without regard for the context, content or argument. This is not an efficient or effective use of your time. A good note-taking technique is to focus less on the words you write down and more on the reasons why you feel the passage is significant enough to record. Use contrasting coloured pens so that you copy quotes in blue and record your thoughts about the quote in red. Being consistent with this strategy means that whenever you see anything written in blue in any notebook you own, you will know that the material is copied directly from the source and is not written in your own words. Conversely, anything written in red is in your own words and can be rightfully included in your assignment. This technique helps you to avoid inadvertent plagiarism, which is discussed in Chapter 8.

Recording why you write something down is a form of reflective note taking, and the kinds of thoughts you might record in red include:

- why this quote will help your argument;
- where this piece of information might fit into your paper;
- how it relates to other papers you have read on the topic;
- any further ideas that this information inspires in you.

Essentially, you can write anything you like in red, but focus on explaining the relevance of the quoted passage to your assignment so that you capture your 'moment of genius'.

Here is how your mind works when you research. As you start to process a research source, a line, an idea, a sentence, a quote will suddenly stand out from the rest. 'Eureka!' you think to yourself. 'This is precisely the information I need for my assignment.' Normally, you might hastily scribble down the idea and move on to the next concept that attracts your attention, but when you open your notepad days or weeks later in preparation for writing your assignment, you suddenly realize that your notes no longer make any sense. 'Why did I write this down?' you wonder. 'What does this even mean?' Because the passage no longer has any meaning, you just disregard it.

What has happened is that before you read the article, you prepped your mind by thinking about the ideas you were hoping to find as well as the gaps in your knowledge base. You previewed the article, read some of the introduction, literature review and conclusion, and had a good understanding of the overall context for this paper. In other words, your mind was well primed for recognizing information that was going to fulfil your research needs, so when you saw relevant ideas, they leapt off the page and you wrote them down. Your 'moment of genius' occurs when all the elements come together to provide that spark of inspiration that sends your mind off in a million different directions thinking of the possibilities for this concept and how it could be used in your paper. 'Wow,' you think. 'This idea is so different from what Smith said in his article. But you know, it sort of confirms what Anderson was writing about in her book. Hmm, I wonder which approach I should take. I'll need to look for some more evidence on each of these ideas to see if one perspective is more mainstream.' Sadly, the 'moment of genius' usually does not materialize when we are sitting in front of a blank computer screen trying to start our assignment, so it is important that we harness those moments of intellectual insight and write them down before we lose them.

Figure 5.3 is an example of a note for our sample essay topic. It seems perfectly reasonable. It outlines a reason why girls might be less interested in participating in sport. We could write a few lines about this issue in our assignment, and attribute the idea to the author. But the note is pretty limited in value. By comparison, look at the example in Figure 5.4 and see how just recording the 'moment of genius' offers some great insights and further research ideas that will allow us to write an entire paragraph about this very issue.

By shifting the emphasis from the quote to your response to the quote, we are no longer restricted to one simple idea and instead have three, four or five ideas to explore, which ultimately inspire a more comprehensive treatment of

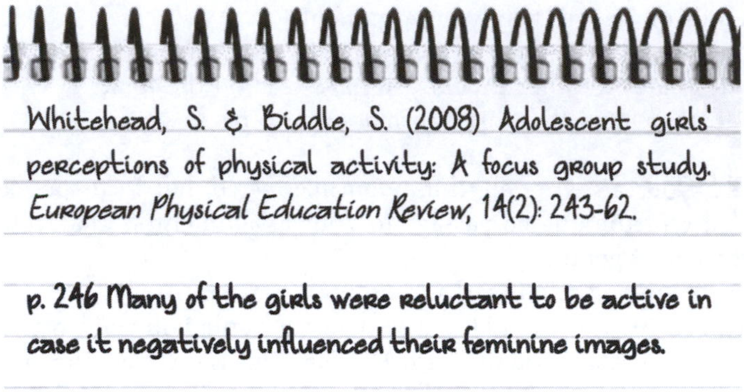

Whitehead, S. & Biddle, S. (2008) Adolescent girls' perceptions of physical activity: A focus group study. European Physical Education Review, 14(2): 243-62.

p. 246 Many of the girls were reluctant to be active in case it negatively influenced their feminine images.

Figure 5.3 Taking notes from readings without annotation

the concept. And remember, whatever is written in red is your work, so you can add any particularly useful or brilliantly written phrases or sentences into your assignment, though the idea may still need to be referenced.

TO HIGHLIGHT OR NOT TO HIGHLIGHT?

When reading a printed copy of a reading, many students avidly highlight any and every term, sentence or quote that they see. The result is a page covered in highlighter pen that is distracting and meaningless. In essence, they are highlighting the wrong things. Instead of making a note of the key points or critical ideas, students are highlighting anything that seems familiar (it can be a relief to see at least something that you already know) or anything that is simply interesting. Neither of these approaches will help you identify relevant information because highlighting is not the same as understanding. Simply noting an idea does not confirm that you have comprehended the information or thought about how it could be incorporated into your paper. In short, you should avoid overusing a highlighter, but if you feel compelled to highlight, use different colours and be selective of what you are highlighting:

• Identify the thesis statement and highlight in green.
• Identify the topic sentence of each paragraph and highlight in blue.
• Identify the main findings and highlight in pink.

WHAT IF AN ARTICLE IS NOT RELEVANT?

Your searches will return many hits, and the titles of most of these may seem pertinent, but after the initial preview, you may find that one of the articles appears less than suitable for your assignment. Rather than discarding it altogether, check whether the paper might still have some usable information. Even if the actual study does not align with your argument, the overall

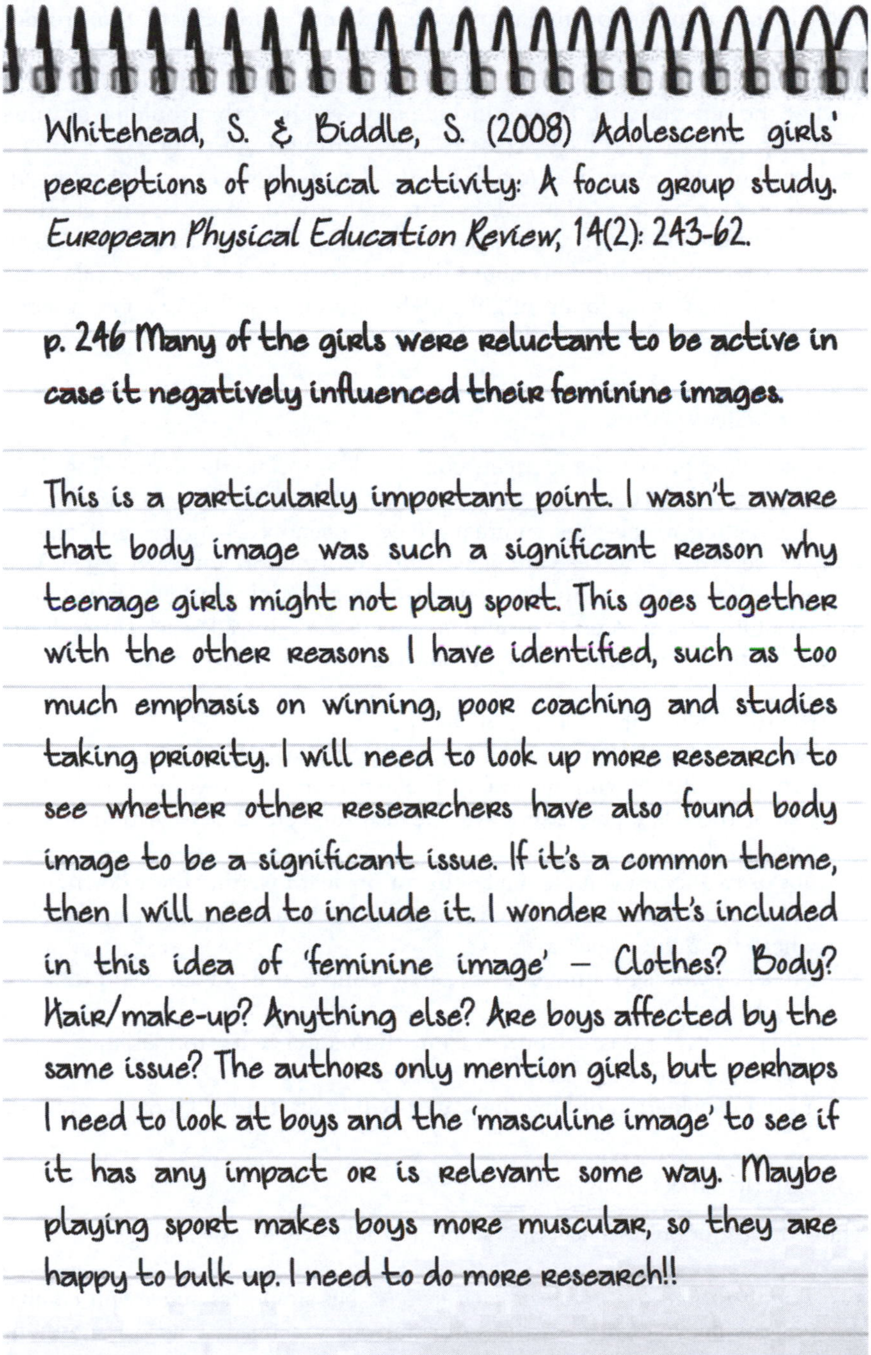

Whitehead, S. & Biddle, S. (2008) Adolescent girls' perceptions of physical activity: A focus group study. European Physical Education Review, 14(2): 243-62.

p. 246 Many of the girls were reluctant to be active in case it negatively influenced their feminine images.

This is a particularly important point. I wasn't aware that body image was such a significant reason why teenage girls might not play sport. This goes together with the other reasons I have identified, such as too much emphasis on winning, poor coaching and studies taking priority. I will need to look up more research to see whether other researchers have also found body image to be a significant issue. If it's a common theme, then I will need to include it. I wonder what's included in this idea of 'feminine image' — Clothes? Body? Hair/make-up? Anything else? Are boys affected by the same issue? The authors only mention girls, but perhaps I need to look at boys and the 'masculine image' to see if it has any impact or is relevant some way. Maybe playing sport makes boys more muscular, so they are happy to bulk up. I need to do more research!!

Figure 5.4 Taking notes from readings with annotation

'big picture' information might provide a decent summary of the broader issues, so read the introduction and literature review for some inspiration. They might identify some additional themes or ideas that you had not considered. Review the reference list. Does it include any resources that could be of value to your paper? Do you have access to them through your library? This is a great way to add to your research, but only if you can read them for yourself. Even though this paper is limited, has the author written something else that might be more relevant to your topic? Look them up in the databases or do an online search to find out more about their research. Just remember that even though the paper you found might not be useful, it still may contain some valuable leads to other research.

REVIEWING/SUMMARIZING

After you have processed the paper, you should translate the key findings into your own words to determine the extent to which you have understood the study. Creating a one-page summary (see Appendix 2) means you have a succinct record of the relevant ideas and information for each paper you examine. When it comes to working with the material you have gathered, it will be a lot easier to refer to a summary page than to wade back through the original article. The summary should include:

- the full bibliographic details of the source;
- two questions that you need answered by the paper;
- summary of the main purpose of the article in your own words;
- two or three key points that are relevant for your paper, written in your own words;
- one or two accurate quotes and your rationale for writing these down using the red/blue note-taking system, making sure you include the page number where the quote appears;
- three key words to summarize the article and to use in your next literature search;
- three relevant research sources from the reference list to look up;
- a star rating for how useful the paper is;
- a brief explanation of how this paper will be useful for your assignment.

COMMON NOTE-TAKING MISTAKES

There are common mistakes that students make when researching:

- *Trying to find too much in each article*: No single reference will be able to provide you with all the information you need. Every assignment requires you to gather evidence from a range of sources to piece together your argument. Each relevant resource should yield a handful of ideas, usually between two and four useful points, that can be incorporated into your paper.

CASE STUDY

Seamus is writing a paper using the sample essay question noted above. He has located some relevant research and has started the process of summarizing it. Examine his first attempt at a summary sheet below:

ADOLESCENT GIRLS' PERCEPTIONS OF PHYSICAL ACTIVITY: A FOCUS GROUP STUDY

The purpose of this study, therefore, was to start to build a comprehensive picture of physical activity as it relates to adolescent girls.

Key points:

1   Girls play less sport and tend to drop out more, which is a concern.
2   They surveyed 47 girls (14–16 years) to find out if they played sport.
3   They recommend increasing participation by making it fun.

Quote: 'Many of the girls were reluctant to be active in case it negatively influenced their feminine images.'

Value of this paper: this paper is very useful because it outlines five main reasons why girls stop participating in sport.

→   How effective do you think Seamus will find this summary sheet?

→   What critical information is missing?

→   How would you improve this summary?

Refer to Appendix 2 to see an example of a completed summary sheet.

• *Getting stuck in the 'nitty-gritty' detail*: Research papers can be quite lengthy, especially those in the socio-cultural areas. A common mistake is to get stuck in the 'nitty-gritty' of the research paper. Essentially, you are looking for 'big picture' ideas, not the minutiae of evidence that the authors needed to provide to substantiate their argument. Avoid writing down their detailed explanations and focus instead on the overarching concepts they are contributing to the field.

SUMMARY

1   Academic research sources are not meant to be 'read' as much as they should be 'processed' to extract as much relevant information as possible.

2   The basic structure of most research papers follows a standard format, making it quite straightforward to identify the objectives and outcomes of any source.

3   Avoid mindless highlighting in favour of creating meaningful and usable notes tailored to the specific research topic. Condense lengthy research papers into concise summary sheets that can be used to build the structure of your paper.

4   Develop a systematic approach to taking notes that records not just direct quotes but a critical interpretation and response to the original passage.

5   Focus on the 'big picture' ideas of each research source, rather than detailed evidence that is not usually relevant for student papers.

EXERCISES

1   Look at some research sources across several sports studies disciplines. Can you recognize the basic structure outlined in this chapter?

2   Review notes that you have taken for previous assignments. Are the notes clear and meaningful? Do you understand why you recorded these ideas? Could they be used for an assignment today or do they no longer make much sense?

3   Condense two of the research sources you found for Chapter 4, Exercise 1 into individual summary sheets using the template in Appendix 2.

4   Take notes electronically by either typing or cutting and pasting from the source, and then practise taking notes by hand. Note the difference in the amount of text you record. Review the two strategies and see which one produces the more valuable notes.

REFLECTION

Think about your current note-taking habits. Do you focus on key ideas or do you tend to be swayed by detailed evidence? Are your notes typically meaningful when you return to them or are they a jumbled mess, forcing you to go back to the original sources? Consider strategies from this chapter to make the process more efficient. Which tips and techniques might be the most beneficial for you?

FURTHER READING

Fairbairn, G.J. and Fairbairn, S.A. (2001) *Reading at university: a guide for students.* Basingstoke: Open University Press.

Locke, L.F., Silverman, S.J. and Spirduso, W.W. (2009) *Reading and understanding research*, 3rd edn. London: Sage.

6

ACADEMIC WRITING

How to write research essays

OVERVIEW

This chapter outlines:
- how to construct evidence-based research assignments;
- the Academic Writing Formula and associated formulae to build an effective introduction, body and conclusion;
- the process of editing and proofreading assignments to create high-quality papers that address the research topic.

INTRODUCTION

Your undergraduate studies are like an apprenticeship: you are trained in various aspects of intellectual engagement, including the conventions of academic writing. Throughout your degree you will contend with many kinds of writing, each with its own style and standards. For example, you may be asked to write a formal research paper or to produce a lab report. You might be required to reflect personally on your experience of playing sport or to blog your thoughts about Olympism. However, the form that academic writing takes differs significantly from the kinds of sports writing that we see every day. The headlines, anecdotes, superlatives and clichés that are used to generate suspense and excitement or evoke a sense of being there are not appropriate in the academic context.

No one begins with perfect writing skills, so the mechanics of producing quality written work needs to be learned and refined over time. This chapter outlines techniques to assist you as you start to write papers to an appropriate academic standard. It focuses specifically on formal essay writing, utilizing the research collected in Chapter 5, and introduces easy 'formulae' as a practical strategy for building effective evidence-based papers. It outlines how to edit and proofread assignments to ensure the final version is of a high standard.

ACADEMIC WRITING

For many, academic writing seems quite bland and certainly not as exciting as fiction, feature articles or other more creative formats. Academic writing requires a certain formality in terms of style, content and presentation because its purpose is not to entertain the reader or express the author's personal thoughts but to present a cogent argument drawn from the research literature. This is probably the singularly most important characteristic of academic writing: the presentation of an evidence-based argument.

In order to construct an evidence-based argument, you need evidence. As the name suggests, no *research* paper can be written off the top of your head or simply from your personal perspective. Instead, it must be based on the ideas and theories that have been generated by researchers over decades or centuries. A research assignment is your evaluation of previously published materials, and your tutors or professors are assessing your ability to locate and draw together research and synthesize the key points from that research into a coherent and logical argument. They are not assessing your opinion.

OPINION VERSUS ARGUMENT

One of the hardest aspects of learning to write at university is appreciating the difference between opinion and argument. An opinion is an anecdotal and personal position on a particular topic. You might have an opinion on the salaries that athletes are paid or personal experience that leads you to prefer one type of fitness training over others. When you are chatting with friends about the merits of athlete salaries or training regimes, you are free to express your opinion, listen to theirs and perhaps debate passionately who is right. An argument, on the other hand, is a reasoned claim that is justified by supporting evidence that is used to persuade the reader about a particular position. Arguments are used all the time in daily life – indeed, you may present quite persuasive arguments to your friends about why athletes are paid too much. In an academic argument, however, the standard of evidence required to support a claim is much higher than the standard your friends might accept. Arguments need to be founded on high-quality evidence, and the conclusions must be logical and reasonable.

The argument you present does not need to conform to your opinion on a topic, although they may coincidentally overlap from time to time. You may find yourself arguing a position that you personally disagree with – for example, responding to an essay topic that asks you to explain 'why blood doping should not be considered cheating'. You may believe that blood doping fundamentally represents a clear case of cheating and is one of the most despicable things an athlete can do, but sadly, your opinion is immaterial in the context of the research topic. You need to argue, based on research, why blood doping is *not* cheating, regardless of your personal stance. Personal opinion is encouraged in some forms of writing, such as reflective journals, but even then you should offer considered and informed opinion, rather than uneducated assertions, and focus on understanding how or why you might hold the opinions that you do.

BUT WHAT ABOUT ME?

It can be confronting to learn that your opinions 'do not matter' or that your perspective on a particular issue is 'irrelevant' to a college essay. Many students wonder 'Do I count for nothing? Am I just supposed to repeat what everyone else has said? What about me?' It is important to understand that there are many opportunities for you to express your personal standpoint, such as in tutorials or class discussions, in online discussion groups and with your study group. If you remember what is being evaluated in a research paper, it is not what you *think*, but what you have *researched*. Bear in mind that your name is on the cover, so while the paper may not reflect your *opinion* on the topic, it most definitely represents *you*: your research, your evaluation of the research, your decisions about the ideas to include, your understanding of how the various pieces of evidence fit together and your final argument. From start to finish, this paper is an individual product that reflects your thought processes and powers of argumentation. When you think about it, is it not preferable at university to be judged on your academic argument than on your personal beliefs?

STUDENT VIEWPOINT

Once I let go of feeling like I had to express my opinion in my assignment, I found it much easier to focus on summarizing the research and building an argument based on those ideas. I mean, it is actually a relief not to have to defend my opinion and then find research that supports it. I actually feel like I learn more by letting the evidence speak rather than imposing myself on the paper.—Jess.

WRITING RESEARCH ASSIGNMENTS

When it comes to writing papers, many students tend to make the same error that they make when they read research articles: they start with the opening line and end on the final word. Writing linearly from start to finish is difficult and does not allow for the fact that essays need to be carefully constructed around main points and supporting evidence. Just as readings are not supposed to be 'read', assignments are not supposed to be 'written'. Instead, they are 'built' or even 'assembled' from raw research materials. This analogy suggests that an assignment is planned, developed, slowly crafted and embellished, and we can even compare writing a paper to building a house as per Table 6.1.

Table 6.1 Comparing the process of 'building' an essay with building a house

Building a house	Constructing an essay
Consult with the client	Break down the question
Find inspiration	Brainstorm
Gather the materials	Locate your research sources
Develop the framework	Develop the essay plan or outline
Fill in the walls	Draft the content
Add in the fittings, decorate, embellish	Review, revise, edit, proofread

WHERE TO START?

At one time or another, most of us will have sat in front of a blank computer screen, wondering how to start an assignment or what to write next. Writer's block affects even the most confident author, so having defined steps in place will alleviate the panic of not knowing what to do. As discussed in Chapter 5, to avoid writing a paper that does not address the question, you must understand what is required before you begin. Your first task, therefore, is to read the research topic carefully and ensure you are fully aware of the various components of the question and how you are being asked to approach it. Discuss the research topic with your study group or ask your professor for clarification if you are not sure. Do not disregard elements of the question that you do not understand, and do not produce an essay on a version of the question that you *want* to answer. The argument you produce needs to relate explicitly to the research topic.

BASIC STRUCTURE OF AN ESSAY

Before conducting any research or brainstorming the topic, an essay needs to start with a blueprint to give yourself a holistic or 'big picture' overview of what you need to produce and to ensure you consider the various components that comprise a university standard essay. All forms of writing have the same basic structure:

- *Introduction*: tell them what you are going to say.
- *Body*: say it.
- *Conclusion*: remind them what you just said.

These three components form the basis of the Academic Writing Formula, which is a simple tool to create an essay plan. It works for a paper of 500 words or a dissertation of 50,000 or 100,000 words, and applying the basic formula should be your first step as you start your paper.

ACADEMIC WRITING FORMULA

The Academic Writing Formula, which is unique to this book, breaks down any written paper into manageable parts and provides a simple formula to help write each one (see Table 6.2).

Once you have used the Academic Writing Formula to develop a basic outline and have established how many main points you will need, it is time to start building the argument. Take the one-page summary of each source, developed in Chapter 5, and arrange them physically or electronically in front of you so that you can review the key points from each paper. For the purposes of this exercise, assume you have five sources to consider and have identified three key points in each one. This means that you have fifteen key points to work with. List all the key points from your summary sheets on a new page, keeping the authors' names next to each one so that you remember the source of each idea.

The next step is to ascertain the main themes that emerge from the list of key points. Look for commonalities or points of difference, and group similar key points together. If you are working electronically, it is easy to shift these points around so that you create groups of related key points. If you are working on paper, you can use a highlighter pen or even write the ideas on Post-it notes to arrange them into groups easily. Organizing the material you have collected is much easier when working with summary sheets and key points rather than searching through unwieldy and lengthy research papers for ideas.

Use a mind map or diagram at this point to illustrate the perspectives that are starting to emerge from the literature. You will have quite a few different categories, so, depending on how long your paper is, you will need to select

Table 6.2 The Academic Writing Formula

Component	Description	
Introduction	~10–15% of total word count	
Main point	Claim/ explanation/ evidence/ link	The number of main points will vary according to assignment length, but allocate around 200–250 words to each main point
Main point	Claim/ explanation/ evidence/ link	
Main point	Claim/ explanation/ evidence/ link	
Conclusion	~10–15% of total word count	

Table 6.3 Developing main points from key points

STEP 1 List all key points from the research summary sheets (identify the authors)	STEP 2 Group them under overarching headings to create main points
Body image (Whitehead and Biddle)	✓ Body image (W&B, Guillet et al., Alley et al., Allender et al.)
Friends (Yungblut et al.)	Femininity
Fun (W&B; Young et al., Yungblut et al.)	Uniform
Femininity (Guillet et al.; W&B, Alley et al.)	✓ Competing interests (B&S, Yungblut et al., W&B)
Study (Boiche and Sarrazin)	Study
School (B&S)	School
	Friends
Uniform (Allender et al.)	No time
Too competitive (Wells et al.)	✓ Fun (W&B, Young et al., Yungblut et al., Wells et al.)
No time (W&B, B&S)	Too competitive
Friends don't play (Yungblut et al.)	✗ Other issues (Yungblut et al., Berger et al., Fraser-Thomas et al.)
Parents can't take me (Berger et al.)	Friends don't play
Poor programmes offered (Fraser-Thomas et al.)	Parents can't take me
	Poor programmes offered

the main themes that are the most relevant, work well together and have the most support. Choosing ideas that come from at least two or three different sources means that you are more likely to be representing the main perspectives in the literature, which suggests to your professor that your research has been broad. Selecting obscure topics suggests, conversely, that you do not have a comprehensive understanding of the field because you did not read widely enough to find the most critical points. Put to one side the ideas that have little support or that seem 'offbeat', and then give each of the main groups a thematic heading.

After establishing the key themes, you should be able to identify if there is anything missing from your research or areas that need some more support. This will prompt you to conduct a further literature search or revisit the papers you have already collected to process them for new information. It is not uncommon to conduct several literature searches as you begin the writing process, and you will find that the more familiar you are with the material and the key ideas, the more efficient your literature searches become.

Table 6.3 demonstrates the process of developing main themes based on individual key points, using the sample research topic. Note how the authors' names remain attached to the ideas throughout the process to assist with accurate referencing.

Table 6.4 Arranging main points according to the Academic Writing Formula

STEP 1 Allocate words to each paragraph		STEP 2 Arrange the order of the main points
Introduction	150 words	Introduction
Main point 1	250 words	Sport is no longer fun/ too serious/ too competitive
Main point 2	250 words	Body image/ femininity (not often discussed)
Main point 3	250 words	Other/ competing interests: school, friends, work
Conclusion	100 words	Conclusion

APPLYING THE ACADEMIC WRITING FORMULA

Now that you have identified the main ideas that will be included in your paper, the next step is to work on the framework by applying the Academic Writing Formula to guide you. This process is outlined in Table 6.4 using the example of a 1,000-word paper that addresses the sample research topic. Note that each main point is allocated a number of words so we know how much 'room' there is for each one. The next step is to arrange the main points in the most logical order, beginning with the most important ideas. You should also start to think about how main points will transition from one to the other so that the paper flows clearly from idea to idea.

After you populate the basic framework, the next step is to start building your argument by transforming the generic main points into strong assertions that are aligned with the research topic. The resulting statements are topic sentences, which are assertions or claims that state a position supported by the evidence. A topic sentence must be able to stand on its own, so that a reader understands the main point without having to read further. Indeed, if the reader reads *only* the topic sentences in your paper, they should have a reasonable overview of your argument. Importantly, a topic sentence does not 'look backwards' or rely on the preceding paragraph in order for it to make sense. There should be a clear relationship between the research topic and the topic sentence, and you can test its strength by reading the research topic and then the topic sentence to see whether the latter relates to the former.

Converting the first main point of our sample essay into a claim that reflects the research topic results in the following:

> *Research topic*: Outline three reasons children drop out of sport in their teenage years.

Main point: Sport is no longer fun/too serious/too competitive

Topic sentence: A significant reason teenagers drop out of sport is that organized sport becomes too competitive and is no longer perceived as a fun activity.

Once you have rewritten each main point as a topic sentence, consider their order again to determine if they still are sensibly organized. Read them aloud to hear if the sequence is logical and ask yourself whether the reader will understand the relationship between the points. If not, think about how you might be able to better arrange the topic sentences to create a more coherent structure.

The next step is to consider the introduction and conclusion, and to create both your thesis statement and a summary statement. A thesis statement is an unequivocal statement of the purpose of the essay, whereas the summary statement summarizes the main point of the entire paper, and often closely mirrors the thesis statement. The easiest way to write both the thesis statement and summary statement is to incorporate the research topic:

Research topic: Outline three reasons children drop out of sport in their teenage years.

Thesis statement: This essay examines three main reasons children drop out of sport in their teenage years.

Summary sentence: This paper has outlined three reasons why children drop out of sport in their teenage years.

It might seem a little crude to rewrite the research topic, but it is the safest approach to ensure your paper is focused appropriately. The thesis statement should not add additional promises about what the paper covers or leave anything out from the original topic. You are asked to deliver a paper on a specific topic, and your statement of purpose needs to accurately reflect that request.

Table 6.5 contains a thesis statement, three topic sentences and a summary sentence for the sample question to demonstrate how the basic essay plan has been developed into the rudiments of an argument.

With a framework in place, it is time to start working on the specific sections. You will need to consider how to build your argument and decide the evidence that will be most useful. A simple way to develop your paper is to use some easy 'formulae' that show you how to construct effective introductions, paragraphs and conclusions.

INTRODUCTION: YOUR OPENING STATEMENT

The introduction is your first contact with the reader, as well as your one opportunity to state the purpose of your paper and provide some background about the general topic area. If the research topic is quite broad, the introduction

Table 6.5 Developing an essay plan based on the Academic Writing Formula

Research topic	Thesis statement
Outline three reasons children drop out of sport in their teenage years	This essay examines three main reasons children drop out of organized sport in their teenage years.

Main points	Topic sentences
Sport is no longer fun/too serious/ too competitive	A significant reason teenagers drop out of sport is that organized sport becomes too competitive and is no longer perceived as a fun activity.
Body image/femininity (not often talked about)	One of the main reasons that teenagers drop out of organized sport is body image.
Other interests, e.g. school, friends	Children in their mid-teens often have a series of demands that compete for their attention and time.

Research topic	Summary statement
Outline three reasons children drop out of sport in their teenage years	This paper has outlined three reasons why children drop out of sport in their teenage years.

will clarify the areas that you have chosen to focus on. If you think of a research paper like a TV courtroom drama, then the introduction is like your opening statement to the jury. During an opening statement, prosecutors will provide an overview, assert the purpose of their case and give the jury a sense of the evidence they will present during the trial. Similarly, the introduction to an essay establishes the context for the paper, states the purpose of the paper in a thesis statement and previews the evidence so the reader knows what to expect. Above all, an introduction is specific to *your paper*. It would, for example, be unusual to use quotes in an introduction, because no one else's words can explain to the reader what your essay is about. Keep your 'witnesses' for the body of the paper.

Introduction Formula

The Introduction Formula breaks down the first part of your paper into its constituent parts and helps you construct an effective entry point to any argument. An effective introduction has four components:

- *'Big picture'*: The first part of the introduction provides the overall context for the assignment by situating the paper within the broader area. This eases the reader into the paper rather than hitting them over the head immediately with your argument and evidence.

- *'Little picture'*: The second part of the introduction focuses directly on the topic you are examining. It adds a little more relevant detail to narrow the 'big picture' and guides the reader towards your argument.
- *Thesis statement*: The thesis statement states the specific purpose of the paper. A good thesis statement incorporates the essay question or summarizes the research topic. If you choose not to restate the essay topic, please make sure you are accurately reflecting the stated content and are not adding to or subtracting from the research topic.
- *'Roadmap'*: The final element of the Introduction Formula is a roadmap, which previews the actual points that the reader can expect to see in the essay, presented in the order that they appear in the assignment. Write this part of the introduction only when the structure of the paper is confirmed.

A common error that students make is to begin the introduction with a conclusion, which makes little sense as it is impossible to state your findings before you actually present your case. Consider the following example:

> There are many reasons why resistance training is important to athletes, including developing strength, decreasing the risk of injury and burning more fat. These form the fundamental rationale for including resistance training in any balanced programme. This paper examines the benefits of resistance training for athletes.

The first sentence provides the 'answer' to the topic so the thesis statement looks repetitive and, ultimately, redundant. There is no point in reading the rest of the paper if results are already stated in the first line.

TIP

Many people suggest writing the introduction once you have written the rest of your paper, whereas others feel they need to have an introduction in place from the start. Using the Introduction Formula means you can easily write an introduction at any point after you have selected the main points of your argument.

Sample introduction

The sample introduction in Figure 6.1 demonstrates how the Introduction Formula helps to create a clear, straightforward and, above all, relevant introduction to the paper.

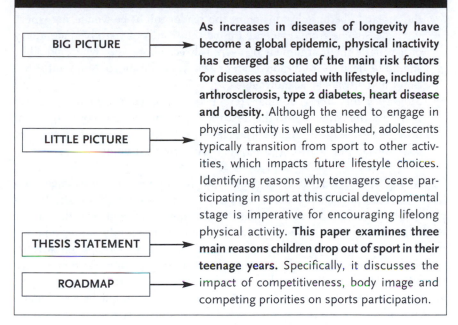

Figure 6.1 Sample introduction based on the Introduction Formula

BODY: PRESENTING EVIDENCE/INTERROGATING WITNESSES

If we continue the courtroom analogy, the body of the paper is akin to the prosecutor presenting physical evidence and interrogating witnesses in order to convince a jury that their argument is conclusive. It is a meticulous process that requires each piece of evidence to be presented in logical order and explained so that it supports the overall case. A research essay also relies on a rational argument that is supported by evidence and 'witnesses'. While it would be terrific to convince experts to come along and support your case verbally, in reality you will need to incorporate their testimony by referring to their published works.

Paragraph Formula

The body of the paper consists of a series of carefully sequenced paragraphs, each one a single, self-contained idea that is asserted in the topic sentence. The formula below outlines the four components of a paragraph:

- *Topic sentence*: Typically the first line of a paragraph, the topic sentence communicates a main idea or claim based on research and links it back to the research topic.

- *Further explanation*: The next step is to further explain the topic sentence, adding more detail and depth to the initial assertion.
- *Evidence*: The third part of the paragraph requires specific evidence from the research, because by this point the reader might be wondering where your ideas come from. Evidence can be the results of a study, a summary of a paper's main argument or even a direct quote and, where possible, should be derived from more than one source. The source of the information must always be acknowledged.
- *Summary and link:* The final step is to summarize the main point and then link the paragraph to the next topic sentence so that your argument flows effortlessly throughout the paper. A simple link creates a sense of cohesion by not 'startling' the reader with the next point.

Depending on the length of the paper and the number of words/pages you have allocated to each key point, paragraphs can vary in length. For longer paragraphs, you could add in further explanation and evidence, then more explanation and more evidence. Be careful that you are only explicating *one* main point and not trying to add so much detail into a single paragraph that you start to raise other areas. Equally, avoid writing paragraphs that are too brief. From the formula, it is clear that the most basic paragraph needs to be at least four sentences, though in most cases the paragraph will be longer. Effective paragraphs certainly can never be only one or two sentences long.

Sample paragraph

The sample paragraph in Figure 6.2 demonstrates how the Paragraph Formula helps to create a strong paragraph with a single main point that is explained and supported by evidence.

CONCLUSION: YOUR CLOSING ARGUMENT

The final part of the paper is the conclusion, which summarizes the main points and links these back to both the research topic and the broader context. The conclusion is the last opportunity you have to 'appeal to the jury' or, in your case, the person assessing your paper, so make sure the paper ends on a strong point. Try to avoid ending on pithy witticisms or casual anecdotes, as these just lower the scholarly tone of your paper and undo all the hard work of your argument. A conclusion is only ever a summary, so avoid introducing new ideas or using quotes in your conclusion. Like the introduction, the conclusion is specific to your paper, and no one else's words can conclude your essay. If the material is important enough to mention in the conclusion, it is important enough to include in the text of your paper. There is no need to begin with 'in conclusion', as it is usually evident that this is your final comment.

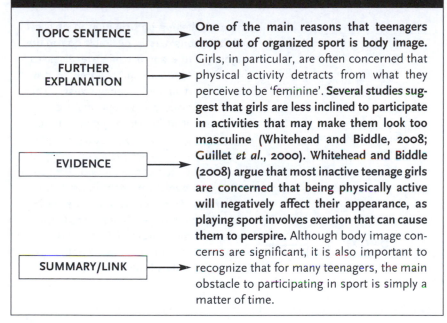

Figure 6.2 Sample paragraph based on the Paragraph Formula

Conclusion Formula

The conclusion draws together and restates the main points and relates these to the research topic and the broader context. In many respects, it mirrors the introduction, as evidenced by the three components in the Conclusion Formula:

- *Link*: Link your conclusion and overall paper back to the specific question. Like the thesis statement, incorporating the research topic into your conclusion reminds the reader that you have addressed the specific issue and have not deviated from the main task.
- *Summary*: Restate and summarize the main points raised in the paper. You do not need to explain all of these again in detail, but a brief indication of how the ideas link to the topic is important.
- *Context*: Relate your summary back to the big and little pictures. If the topic asks for recommendations or solutions, they can be included at this point.

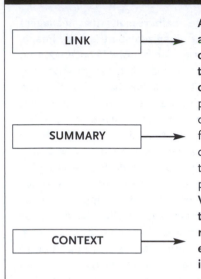

SAMPLE CONCLUSION
Outline three reasons children drop out of sport in their teenage years.

LINK

SUMMARY

CONTEXT

Although lifelong participation in physical activity is considered a desirable goal in the ongoing battle against lifestyle diseases, there is a tendency for children to drop out of sport in their teenage years. This paper has discussed several main causes of adolescent attrition from organized sport, focusing specifically on young people's distain for the overemphasis on competition, body image concerns and the competing demands on their limited time. **Withdrawal from physical activity during this important stage hinders the development of a long-term commitment to healthy exercise and can instil behaviours that impact the child's future health.**

Figure 6.3 Sample conclusion based on the Conclusion Formula

Sample conclusion

The sample conclusion in Figure 6.3 outlines how the Conclusion Formula summarizes the key ideas presented in the paper while reiterating the research topic and situating the argument within the broader context raised in the introduction.

EDITING AND PROOFREADING

Every assignment must be revised a number of times to ensure the paper is as effective as it can be. Although many people conflate editing and proofreading, they are two different processes. Editing focuses on the structural elements of a paper to determine whether the research topic is addressed, the argument is logical and flows clearly from point to point, the main claims are supported by sufficient evidence and the conclusion draws the main points together. Proofreading, on the other hand, focuses on the accuracy of language, including spelling, grammar and punctuation, as well as formatting and presentation.

The review process is a good time to familiarize yourself with the grading system at your institution. Most colleges and universities publish a detailed explanation of the level of competency expected for each letter grade (A, B, C) to achieve a High Distinction or to receive various percentage bands. Institutional expectations are translated into specific grading criteria, which are aligned

CASE STUDY

Lucas has written an assignment using the sample research topic and has asked you to review it for him. You can read his introduction and first two paragraphs below:

OUTLINE THREE REASONS CHILDREN DROP OUT OF SPORT IN THEIR TEENAGE YEARS.

This paper looks at the reasons why teenagers stop playing sport and lead sedentary lives. It tries to find ways to encourage these young people to play more sport so that they do not become obese and keep up an active lifestyle as adults. It is well known that most teenagers drop out of sport, so this paper examines why.

One of the main reasons teenagers drop out of organized sport is because of body image. Girls are especially worried that physical activity will not make them feel as feminine as they want to be. Whitehead and Biddle (2008) think that too many young ladies do not exercise very much because they worry that physical activity will make them look ugly. In my opinion, I feel that teenage girls are led to believe what they should look like by what their friends think, rather than doing what they would like to do.

Not having enough parental support is another reason why teenagers drop out. Perhaps their parents want them to focus on their studies or will not take them to practice. Either way, it is important that parents get behind their kids and encourage them to stay in sport so that they develop a healthy lifestyle that will prevent obesity. Parents' attitudes are therefore very important in this area.

→ How effectively did Lucas apply the various formulae outlined in the chapter?

→ What aspects of the paper (if any) are well done?

→ What feedback (if any) would you give him to improve his paper?

with the learning outcomes for the module overall. The stated criteria outline the level of achievement for each assessment task and should be available to you before the submission date. If you cannot find an outline in your course materials or on the university website, ask for a copy.

It takes time to edit and proofread effectively, and most assignments will go through several versions before it is ready for submission. It is critical that you give yourself a sufficient break between drafts to clear your mind, so that you can return to the paper with fresh 'eyes' and a clear perspective.

It is typically the revision process that is abandoned when students are scrambling to write a paper the night before it is due, and the lack of polish is always apparent.

EDITING

Editing is not merely reading through your essay passively but also an active process that critically reviews your draft. *Processing* the paper requires you to step back and ask some 'big picture' questions:

- Have I done what was asked of me?
- Is the topic addressed appropriately?
- Have I met the stated criteria?

These questions are answered by looking closely at the various components and determining whether they work together to produce an effective argument that responds clearly to the research topic. Start with an overview of the entire paper and work down to the level of individual sentences to assess your work. Beginning with the overall structure, ask yourself the following questions: Do you have an introduction, body and conclusion? Are the main points presented in a logical order? Does the paper seem to relate well to the research topic?

Move down to the level of the paragraph and examine the introduction, body and conclusion individually. Does each one follow the relevant formula? Are all necessary components included? Is each paragraph focused around a single main point? Is that main point stated confidently in the topic sentence? Is the topic sentence linked to the research topic? Have you provided evidence to support the claims you are making? Are at least two different sources used to support each main point? Does each paragraph transition smoothly to the next point? Does the conclusion mirror the introduction? Finally, look at individual sentences. Does each one make sense? Is each one clearly written with no room for ambiguous interpretation? Are the sentences scholarly or chatty? Does each sentence follow the one that preceded it?

DID I ADDRESS THE TOPIC?

One of the main errors that students make is that they simply do not address the research topic. While the development of the essay structure outlined above builds in moments to check the paper against the research topic, there are also ways to ensure you have addressed the topic clearly and specifically during the editing process. The flow chart in Figure 6.4 outlines the steps to take to ensure the paper addresses the question, and these are explained in more detail below:

- *Check the thesis statement*: Start by looking at the topic and then reading your thesis statement. Is there a clear relationship? Does the thesis statement mirror the research topic? Or have you already deviated from it?

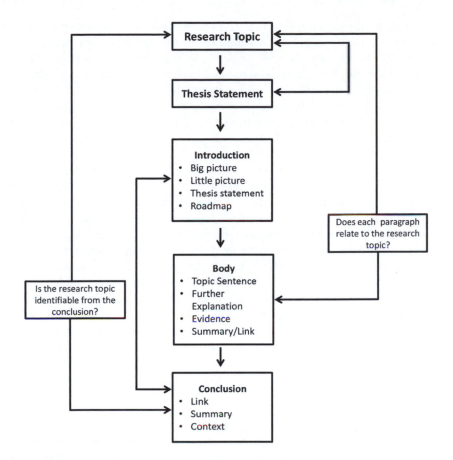

Figure 6.4 How to determine whether a research paper addresses the topic

Are you adding more to the topic than needs to be there or have you left out a key part of the question?

- *Examine the introduction*: Do the 'big' and 'little' pictures make sense in the context of the question? Are they providing sufficient background without diverting attention to irrelevant issues? Do these components lead the reader logically to the thesis statement? Does the roadmap support the thesis statement or have important details been subtracted or irrelevant ones added? Does your roadmap list the key points in the same order as they appear in the body of your paper? A quick scan through the topic sentences will confirm the order is correct. Do you actually deliver every-thing in the paper that you promise in the roadmap? If not, insert or remove points as required to ensure the roadmap conforms to what is discussed in the paper.

- *Scrutinize each paragraph*: Read the research question again and then read the first topic sentence. Do they relate to one another? Could someone read just the topic sentence and figure out what the research topic is?

Examine the paragraph in detail, glancing back at the research question every now and then. Does the paragraph explain the topic sentence in more detail? Does it provide good evidence to support your assertion? Is the evidence relevant to the research topic? Look at each sentence individually. Is it complete? Does it flow logically to the next sentence or have you presented a series of disconnected statements? Does the paragraph link from one point to the next topic sentence so that the reader is taken through neatly to the next idea? Once you have repeated this process for all paragraphs, move on to your conclusion.

- *Check the conclusion*: Have you summarized the key points mentioned in the body of your paper? Have these been linked effectively to the research topic? Has the topic then been resituated in the broader context? Do you end on a strong, relevant point, or have you floated off on a fluffy, meaningless comment? Assess whether someone who reads only your conclusion will be able to understand what the paper was about and what your research revealed. This is an excellent test of an effective conclusion.

- *So what?* Finally, to test the relevance of all the material included in the paper, apply the 'so what?' standard to every sentence. After you read a topic sentence or explanation, ask yourself 'So what?' If you can justify why the information is relevant or belongs in the paper, you can be confident it fits in. Occasionally, however, random statements appear in our work that do not seem to contribute much to the argument. In those instances, asking 'So what?' will confirm that the sentence or passage needs to be deleted in order to clarify your argument.

'GRADE' YOUR PAPER

The final step is to critically appraise your paper to identify any remaining weaknesses and areas for improvement. Use the available marking guidelines to 'grade' your essay, applying the criteria honestly and ruthlessly. Sugar-coating the shortcomings of an assignment does not help you produce a better piece of writing. If you are working in a study group, offer to 'grade' each other's papers. Your peers will bring a fresh perspective to your assignment and will be able to offer feedback that is difficult to see or easy to overlook when you are close to the work. The sample criteria sheet in Figure 6.5 gives you the option of rating the quality of each component of the paper and covers the main areas that typically contribute to the overall grade. Ask your professor for a copy of the criteria sheet that will be used to grade your work.

PROOFREADING

Editing focuses on the overall structure and quality of the argument, whereas proofreading is more concerned with identifying technical and presentation errors that detract from the quality of the paper. Although your professor will be mostly concerned with the argument presented and the evidence you use to support it, a paper replete with spelling, punctuation and grammatical errors

SAMPLE CRITERIA MARKING SHEET

Overall Presentation	Good	Poor		
	Excellent	**Average**		**Poor**
Spelling/ Grammar	|------------|------------|------------|------------|------------|			
Expression/Style	|------------|------------|------------|------------|------------|			
Introduction adequately introduces topic	|------------|------------|------------|------------|------------|			
Major issues are considered	|------------|------------|------------|------------|------------|			
Explanation of key concepts/ideas	|------------|------------|------------|------------|------------|			
Logical development of argument	|------------|------------|------------|------------|------------|			
Evidence supports argument	|------------|------------|------------|------------|------------|			
Conclusion wraps up main points	|------------|------------|------------|------------|------------|			
Quotations used effectively	|------------|------------|------------|------------|------------|			
Ideas correctly accredited to source	|------------|------------|------------|------------|------------|			
Relevance of sources to topic	|------------|------------|------------|------------|------------|			
Adequacy of reference list	|------------|------------|------------|------------|------------|			
References correctly formatted	|------------|------------|------------|------------|------------|			

Other Comments:

FINAL GRADE:

Figure 6.5 Sample criteria marking sheet

will seem careless and poorly constructed. Given the work you have put into the paper, it is worth setting aside time to give your paper a final polish.

A common error in proofreading is to simply read through the paper expecting errors to stand out. However, after you have been working on the paper for some weeks, you will more than likely read what you think is on the page, rather than what is actually there. Our eyes tend to skip over our own errors, even if we are skilled at seeing them in other people's work. Proof-reading, therefore, needs to be conducted with purpose, focusing on specific problem areas. If you know that you are not good at spelling, or that your grammar can be weak, then proofread your paper to look only at spelling or grammatical errors. Sometimes it is easier to hand the paper to a friend, family member or classmate to review.

Most word processing packages will have inbuilt spelling and grammar checks, though these can only take you so far. Knowing the kinds of errors that normally appear in student work will make proofreading more effective and more efficient. In Appendix 3 there is a list of common student errors that will guide your proofreading efforts. The easiest way to use this list is to look specifically for each error, using a search or 'find' function on your computer. For example, the use of contractions (won't, don't, it's) is discouraged in formal academic writing, so simply check for apostrophes followed by a 't' in your paper. Similarly, where there are similar words that are used in different contexts (effect/affect; advice/advise), look for each one and make sure the correct variation is used. Add your own common mistakes to the list to remind yourself to look out for these when proofreading.

When it comes to identifying grammatical problems or even just awkward or poor phrasing, we tend to read what we thought we wrote. A useful technique to pick up these mistakes is to slowly read the paper aloud. Your ear will be better tuned to hearing grammatical errors and they will be more noticeable than in written format. Similarly, it will easier to hear a passage that sounds strange, awkward or incomprehensible.

LANGUAGE

Another aspect to the editing and proofreading process is ensuring that the language you use is appropriate for a college paper. Academic work is much more formal than other forms of writing, so the language should not be chatty or conversational. The best way to improve your writing is to read, read and read some more. The more you read, the more familiar you will become with suitable word choices, sentence structure and the overall clarity of expression needed to convey your argument. Improving your written work also needs as much practice as possible, so actively engage with your writing and examine each sentence to look for ways to improve your style and expression.

One of the basic requirements for academic writing is that you are dis-passionate in your approach. As you are not conveying your personal opinion, avoid using the 'first person' (I, me, my, we, us, our) and 'second person' (you, your). 'I think', 'I feel', 'I believe', 'In my opinion', 'We can examine', 'As you will see' are the sorts of phrases that do not belong in academic writing. If you look carefully at journal articles, academic books and textbooks, you will notice that it is rare to see 'I' in academic research. Because your name is on the cover, the reader knows that this is your argument, so there is no need to foreground yourself.

Compare the following thesis statements:

> This essay examines three main reasons children drop out of sport in their teenage years.

> I'm going to examine the three main reasons children drop out of sport in their teenage years.

The first version is authoritative and places the emphasis on the paper and the argument that is contained therein. In the second thesis statement, you are inserted into the paper and are placing yourself at the centre of the argument.

The latter is too informal and the emphasis is incorrectly placed. When editing, do a search for 'I'. In most cases, you will just need to remove the 'I think' or 'I believe' phrase, though for others, such as the thesis statement above, you might need to rewrite the sentence briefly.

The paper, including the thesis statement, is usually written in the present tense (this essay *examines* . . .). Students often write this in the future tense (this essay *will examine* . . .). This does not make sense because after the paper is written, the examination is occurring as someone reads it; it is not going to occur at some point in the future. Similarly, authors mentioned in the text are usually referred to in the present rather than the past tense, regardless of how old their research is. For example:

> Whitehead and Biddle (2008) *argue* that most inactive teenage girls are concerned that being physically active will negatively affect their appearance, as playing sport involves exertion that can cause them to perspire.

Another characteristic of academic writing is that it is usually quite concise, removing extraneous words and phrases so that meaning is not obscured. When proofreading, look at each sentence and see if it can be written more concisely or whether there are words or a phrase that can be deleted. In many cases, the use of 'flowery' descriptions, including a lot of adjectives, adverbs or qualifiers, clouds the point you are trying to make.

Finally, always look for higher-order words to create stronger and intellectually engaging sentences. Concerns around body image may have a 'massive' or 'huge' impact on young girls' motivations to play sport, but 'massive' and 'huge' are poor word choices in an academic context. Use a thesaurus to find more suitable words, such as 'notable', 'considerable', 'significant', though this is not a suggestion that you need to pepper your work with impressive words from the thesaurus. Sometimes it is powerful enough simply to state there was 'an impact' without needing to describe it in further detail. If you use a thesaurus, make sure you choose only words with which you are already familiar, because selecting words you do not understand can be disastrous.

Look at the following example of poor writing. It is not concise, is too informal and foregrounds the author's opinion rather than the research evidence:

> There are many, many reasons why teenagers drop out of organized sport, like not really getting into it, but a massive reason can be body image. Girls and boys, but especially girls, are really very worried that playing sport will not make them feel as pretty and girly as they want to be. Whitehead and Biddle (2008) think that loads of girls that do not exercise very much worry that physical activity will make them look ugly. In my opinion, I feel that teenage girls are led to believe what they should look like by what their friends think and this is a huge problem in sport and society today, which needs to be fixed. I kind of feel sorry for them, cause sport is really awesome and they are totally missing out by caring so much about being ladylike.

FORMATTING

The final part of editing and proofreading is ensuring the essay is formatted according to the specifications of your individual professor. Never assume you know what is required, and if specific formatting guidelines are not provided, you should ask for guidance. If no guidance is available, then follow these simple steps to present your assignments as neatly as possible (there is a more extensive formatting checklist in Appendix 4, which can be modified to suit your institution's or programme's specific formatting requirements):

- *Font, point size, colour*: An academic submission is not the time to go crazy with fonts and colours. Keep it formal. A paper presented in Times New Roman will look more scholarly than one presented in Comic Sans. The point size should be either 11pt or 12pt, and the text should be printed in black only.
- *Margins*: Ensure there is a decent margin all around the page. A standard margin is 2.5 cm/1 in, though some lecturers like more space in which to write comments.
- *Line spacing*: It is usual to space written assignments so that it is easier to read and there is room for corrections and comments. Double-line spacing is a good rule of thumb in the absence of specific guidelines. Use the line spacing function in your word processing programme rather than hitting enter at the end of each line.
- *Page numbers*: These should be placed consistently; the top right-hand side of the page is standard.
- *Title page*: Include your name and student number, the name of the class, the name of the assignment, the full research topic, the name of the professor and the date of submission on a separate title page. You may also be asked to attach a university cover sheet to your submissions.
- *Reference list*: The reference list should always start on a new page and be presented in alphabetical order according to the surname of the first author. Use the referencing guides to ensure the sources are formatted properly.
- *Printing*: Some professors will prefer you to print on one side of the page only whereas others will be happy for you to use the front and back. If you are not sure, then one side of the page should be the default position.
- *Binding*: Some institutions will expect you to submit everything in a plastic folder; others will only want the paper stapled with a single staple in the corner.

SUMMARY

1   Academic essays present carefully constructed arguments based on research evidence rather than personal opinions. The 'student' is central not because of what they 'think' but because of the research, decision-making and critical thinking processes they display through their final essay.

2   The Academic Writing Formula as well as the various formulae for
     components can be used as a starting point for those unfamiliar with
     academic writing conventions and as a checklist for those who are more
     confident.
3   Addressing the research topic is a fundamental part of the essay writing
     process, and one that is too often overlooked. Ensure that each part of the
     paper links clearly to the research topic and that the overall argument
     responds appropriately.
4   University papers are written more concisely and formally than other forms
     of writing. Dispense with unnecessary 'clutter' in favour of succinct
     sentences that articulate the main point clearly.
5   All papers must go through a series of drafts before submission. Ensure
     there is sufficient time to edit, proofread and format carefully, using the
     checklists provided.

EXERCISES

1   Examine a research article and look carefully at the structure of the
     introduction, paragraph and conclusion. Compare these to the various
     formulae presented in this chapter.
2   Look at the writing style in some print or online magazines and compare
     these to one or two academic papers that discuss a similar topic.
3   Select an essay you have written previously and try to rewrite the intro-
     duction, several paragraphs and the conclusion in line with the formulae.
     Try to use more formal language and omit 'flowery' words that obscure
     the point you are making.
4   Produce your own essay outline for the sample assignment. Utilize the
     Introduction Formula to write a preliminary introduction and then identify
     three topic sentences that will form the body of the paper.

REFLECTION

Reflect on the different requirements for academic writing compared with the
kinds of writing with which you may be more familiar. Do you have any
concerns about writing a research paper at the standard expected at university?
What challenges to writing a good-quality research paper do you think you
will have? What do you need to do to overcome these challenges? How might
the basic Academic Writing Formula be applied to other written assessments?
Did you feel your work was improved by utilizing the three 'formulae'?

FURTHER READING

Creme, P. and Lea, M.R. (2008) *Writing at university: a guide for students*. Maidenhead:
    McGraw-Hill.
Moore, K.M. and Cassel, S.L. (2011) *Techniques for college writing: the thesis statement
    and beyond*. Boston MA: Wadsworth.

7

ACADEMIC WRITING

How to write reports

OVERVIEW

This chapter outlines:
- the key differences between reports and essays;
- the structure and format of business, scientific and field reports;
- how to format and present reports using headings/subheadings and tables/figures.

INTRODUCTION

The type of assignment you will be asked to write will depend on the research question, the discipline you are studying and the expectations of your lecturers. In the previous chapter, the process of writing research essays was outlined. Essays are typically used in the socio-cultural disciplines, including sports history, philosophy and sociology, whereas the management field and bio-physical sciences more commonly communicate research findings in reports. Reports may also be used to present the outcomes of fieldwork, internships and work placements. This chapter outlines how to produce well-structured reports and examines the three main types that you may come across within the field of sports studies.

DIFFERENCE BETWEEN ESSAYS AND REPORTS

Essays and reports have many similarities. Both present material based on research and evidence; both rely on good quality sources that are referenced; both require analytical or critical thinking; and both are written in a formal, dispassionate style. There are, nevertheless, key differences, which are sum-marized in Table 7.1.

Table 7.1 Differences between reports and essays

Report	Essay
Investigates a specific problem or case study	Analyses a research topic
Is designed to be scanned	Is usually read carefully
Is usually written for a specific client or audience	Is typically only written in a university context
Focuses on presenting primary research	Evaluates and analyses secondary research
Structures information in a concise, logical manner	Presents a carefully structured argument in response to a specified research topic
Contains numbered sections with headings and subheadings	Contains a continuous argument that is not disrupted by sections, headings or sub-headings
Uses paragraphs that are usually brief and to the point	Provides paragraphs covering relevant background, explanation and evidence
May use bullet points to communicate key ideas	Uses paragraphs that flow from one to another to develop the argument – bullet points are never used
Makes the data collection method explicit	Research methods may be implicit
Typically summarizes information in graphics (tables, figures)	Rarely uses graphics
Usually has recommendations for future action based on the findings	Does not have recommendations

STUDENT VIEWPOINT

Having a clear structure to follow makes writing a report so much easier. I can organize my ideas, present the various sections for the client in a logical manner, and keep important recommendations to the end. I thought that writing the executive summary was repetitive but realized that this was the key section the reader refers too. Writing a strong executive summary that outlines all the key findings and recommendations is critical for a successful report.—Adam.

STRUCTURE AND FORMAT

Like essays, reports conform to the basic structure of introduction/body/ conclusion, but the material is presented in a more technical manner under specific sections, headings and subheadings. Different styles of reports have different peculiarities when it comes to format, and outlined below is a general structure for business reports, scientific or lab reports and field reports. You should always check with your lecturer to ensure that you are familiar with the specific requirements for reports in your course.

BUSINESS REPORTS

If you are studying sports management, it is likely that you will take subjects such as sport marketing, event management, strategic planning and operations management, which will require you to write business reports in preparation for employment in the industry. Business reports are typically designed to provide recommendations or solutions to specific problems and, in the business world, are used to support decision making or to take action. Within the context of university, you will be asked to apply management or business theories to practical or 'real world' problems to demonstrate your ability to identify relevant data as well as your capacity to analyse and problem-solve. There is rarely a 'right' or 'wrong' answer when it comes to business reports; your recommendations will depend on your evaluation of the available data framed by appropriate literature. For example, if you are examining the benefit of sponsoring a sporting event to a business, then you would need to provide a cost-benefit analysis as well as consider advantages and disadvantages of the potential investment. Your recommendations will be based on how you interpret the significance of the raw data in light of the client's strategy and objectives.

Business reports are typically written for clients who have commissioned the research. When writing such reports, it is important to keep the audience in mind. Although at college the only reader is likely to be your professor, it is still worth trying to write a report as if it was geared towards a specific client. Determining who the end recipient is will help you decide the kind of material you include, the level of detail you go into and the most appropriate recommendations. It would not, for example, be realistic to recommend large-scale revision of a firm's infrastructure if the report is only going to be read by the lower levels of management. Conversely, if you are presenting a report to the board of directors, it would not be appropriate to comment on changes that should be made to the management of an individual team.

Business reports typically include the following elements:

- *Title page*: The title of the report, your name, student number, course code and name of the course, date of submission and other details required by your professor are listed on the title page. Please note that the titles of reports are a concise summary of the main purpose, so they should closely reflect the content.

- *Executive summary*: Like an abstract, the executive summary provides a summary of the context, aims, main findings, conclusion and recommendations of the report. Include all pertinent information so that a reader will understand the report without having to read the entire document. In the business world, this may be the only part of the report that is actually read, so it needs to be comprehensive. The executive summary is always written after the report has been finalized.

- *Table of contents*: This lists all the sections and sub-sections of the report by page number. Any tables or figures that are included should be presented in separate lists on separate pages in the order they appear with their corresponding page number. Either create the table of contents after your report is completely finished, or use the table of contents function in your word processing programme to save time and avoid errors.

- *Abbreviations (if needed)*: Provide a list of abbreviations used throughout the report as well as the full terms to which the abbreviation refers. For example:

AIS	Australian Institute of Sport
FINA	Federation Internationale de Natation
IOC	International Olympic Committee
USOC	United States Olympic Committee

- *Introduction*: An introduction is typically brief and to the point, but contains some key details including a description of why the report was created, a statement of purpose, the scope of the report, the methods used to gather the research, any limitations to the study that you have identified and a brief overview of the various sections to follow. You may also have to provide a review of relevant literature. These components each appear under their own subheading.

- *Results/findings/discussion*: This is the critical substance of your report. This section contains a detailed explanation of the findings of your study, presented under subheadings according to the issues identified in the introduction. Results are presented visually in figures or tables, though some material will need to be explained in prose. The results section includes data only and does not interpret those data. An analysis of the results is contained in a separate discussion section, which links your results to those found in previous research. Alternatively, you can present the results of each part of your study followed immediately by a discussion, before moving on to the next set of results. If you are not collecting primary data and are simply reporting secondary sources, then you would organize your material thematically under a series of relevant subheadings.

- *Conclusion*: A conclusion draws together the results of the study and explains them in light of the hypothesis or statement of purpose. Essentially, you are trying to explain what your results mean and the main ideas that can be inferred from the data. You should also outline any limitations of the data and provide your final evaluation of the value of the study's findings. Do not introduce new material into the conclusion, and do not ignore results that do not match your expectations. A good conclusion will take these into account as they may lead to interesting recommendations about future decisions or strategy.

- *Recommendations*: The recommendations need to be closely related to the findings of your report and should be a logical and realistic extension of your conclusion. It is here that you can recommend future action, research directions or policy changes. Recommendations are normally listed in bullet points with the key recommendation forming a heading (which may be numbered) accompanied by a brief explanation underneath. Group similar or related recommendations together and order them logically. Use clear and direct language and provide sufficient detail so that a reader can understand the key recommendations without needing to read the entire report. A recommendation needs to include specific detail about how it can be achieved. For example, do not simply suggest 'Sponsor needs to increase their leverage of the sporting event'; indicate how they might do this by increasing their marketing activities, advertising or presence at the event. An improved recommendation would be 'Sponsor needs to increase their leverage of the sporting event by investing at least $50,000 into print and social media advertising prior to the event'.

- *References*: You will need to provide a full list of all literature that has been referred to in the report. The reference list starts on a new page and sources are listed alphabetically by the last name of the first author.

- *Appendices*: Appendices include any additional, relevant materials that support your study but are not integral to understanding the research. This section might include a copy of the survey, more detailed results, transcripts of interviews, copies of consent forms and information sheets and any other materials that have been referred to in the report. Each individual item should be labelled independently as 'Appendix A', 'Appendix B' and so on, and are referred to as such in the report – for example, 'Each participant was given an information sheet (see Appendix A).' Do not include anything in the appendices that is not mentioned in the text of the report.

SCIENTIFIC OR LAB REPORTS

Scientific reports are a record of practical experiments or studies, their results and your interpretation of those findings. Scientific papers carefully detail each step of the experiment and are published to alert others to your results and analysis and to contribute to the overall body of scientific knowledge. Lab reports are shorter than full scientific papers but no less important when it comes to detailing your research activities. The experiments you conduct at college are not usually original research, but are designed to introduce you to the scientific method and develop your skills as a scientist. Writing up your results teaches you how to record scientific experimentation and communicate your research findings. Lab reports describe why and how you have conducted the experiment, the results you found, what you think these results might mean and how they compare to the literature.

CASE STUDY

Josie has written a report outlining a proposed social media marketing strategy for a new personal training studio, Results. Read her executive summary below.

EXECUTIVE SUMMARY

The use of social media in marketing is increasing exponentially, particularly as the number of Facebook and Twitter users has grown rapidly. People are more connected than ever before, and the personalized nature of these online interactions makes them a useful site for direct marketing. Local businesses can utilize personal networks to develop awareness and a client base. By encouraging 'likers' and 'followers', companies have the opportunity to target an interested market with discounts and promotions. This report provides an overview of social media opportunities for Results Personal Training and suggests a range of marketing strategies to develop brand awareness and increase business among the target demographic. It highlights the mechanisms by which members of the consumer group interact online, reviews the most attractive and successful promotional activities, and suggests the right social media platforms for Results Personal Training. The cost–benefit analysis reveals the value of social media for this start-up business, and a month-by-month marketing plan and associated budget for the first year is presented. The report concludes with an analysis of the limitations to social media and recommendations for complementary marketing activities.

→ How effective do you think Josie's executive summary is?

→ Does it provide sufficient information for the reader to understand the report's findings?

→ Can you identify Josie's main recommendations for the client?

There are conventions when it comes to reporting scientific research, such as being objective in the reporting and providing sufficient detail so the study is reproducible, both of which are at the heart of the scientific method. Like business reports, scientific reports are formatted with headings and subheadings; however, the sections are slightly different from those described for business reports.

Scientific or lab reports include the following components:

• *Title page*: This notes the title of the report, your name, student number, course code and name of the course, date of submission and other details as required by your professor. Please note that the title of a report is a concise summary of the main purpose, and a reader should have a clear idea of what the report is about from the title.

- *Abstract*: An abstract is essentially the report in miniature and is written so that someone understands at a glance the key aspects of the study. In a single paragraph of around one hundred words, briefly outline the purpose of the study, method, results, key findings and your interpretation of those results.

- *Introduction*: The introduction contains a brief overview of the broad context for the study, a review of previous, relevant literature, a statement of purpose or hypothesis, and aims and objectives of the study. By starting broadly and becoming more specific through the introduction, you are providing a careful justification for your study. By the end of this section, the reader should: a) recognize the gap in the literature that these results fill; b) understand why this study is needed; and c) agree that the study will make a valuable contribution to the knowledge base.

- *Method*: While the methods section is often the least exciting part of a report to write, it is in many respects the most critical as it is the foundation upon which your results rest and are evaluated. The methods section confirms the experimental design and lists all the materials and equipment that was used in the study. If you are using human subjects, then you need to indicate the number of participants, how the sample was selected, and any relevant details about the group, such as gender, mean age and range of ages and/or level of fitness. You should also identify whether ethics approval was sought, though this is not normally required for a college lab report. The methods section also needs to describe the step-by-step process you followed to conduct the study, and it is important to strike a balance between providing too much and giving insufficient detail. A good rule of thumb is to write enough so that someone could easily reproduce the experiment just by reading your report. Familiarize yourself with the level of detail required by carefully reading the methods sections of scientific journal articles. The method is always written in the past tense, avoiding the use of 'I' and 'we'. For example: 'The subjects were asked to sprint between the two timing lights', rather than 'I asked the subjects to sprint between the two timing lights'.

- *Results*: The results section simply describes the results of the experiments, but does not interpret them. Results can be presented visually in figures or tables, and key findings should be identified and highlighted, though not explained or analysed. Raw data are not typically presented in their entirety, though if relevant, they could be included as an appendix. Instead, focus on presenting statistical or aggregated results. You need to provide an accurate representation of your findings and not simply include those results that support your hypothesis or research objectives.

- *Discussion*: The discussion explains the results of your experiment and outlines the significance of your findings in view of the related research presented in the review of literature. This section is often organized around the specific aims and objectives of your study, so that you can determine the degree to which each have been met. You can also discuss any unexpected results and try to determine why these were obtained, perhaps by referring to the methods or limitations of the study. Finally, you can identify areas for future research.

- *Conclusion*: The conclusion reiterates the main findings and explains their significance in a succinct, brief paragraph.
- *References*: Any sources cited in the report must be included in the reference list.

FIELD REPORTS

Field reports are used to record the results of practical work, such as observations, within the applied social sciences. These might include sports psychology, physical education, recreation studies, sports sociology and any other area that examines human behaviour – your own and/or that of participants. The purpose of a field report is to link your observations to established theories or to link your practice to the theory you have learned in college. In a field report you need to record your observations systematically, taking care to be as comprehensive as possible.

You should prepare well ahead of time with a defined plan of what will be observed, who the subjects are, how you will observe them, what you will note down and how you will interpret the results. Stay focused on your main objectives and keep the theory at the forefront of your mind so that you can ask yourself questions about what is happening along the way. At the same time, you should remain open to being flexible with the type of observations you record.

There are a number of ways of recording your observations, including taking field notes, either at the time of the activity or as soon as is practicable afterwards, and making video or audio recordings of the sessions. Writing down notes is the most common way of logging your observations, but it can be cumbersome, so try to develop a system of shorthand or symbols to help your efficiency. Divide your page in two and record actions on one side of the page and your initial thoughts and interpretation on the other side. This will help keep your thoughts independent of the raw data when it comes to writing up your results. Finally, leave sufficient space on each page to add in additional notes, links to the research and subsequent ideas so that when you revise your notes you can keep all relevant material together. Video and audio recordings can be a useful way of documenting the events so that you can review them later to ensure you have not missed any pertinent comments or actions. Depending on the nature of the research, these recordings might be quite intrusive, which may impact the way that participants interact, leading to an artificial record. Video and audio recordings also cannot capture the full range of activities, and for lengthy observations you may be creating a lot of additional material to examine.

Field reports tend to be a little less proscriptive in terms of their structure. You should always confirm the required format with your professor, as it will differ between courses and institutions, but generally they include sections to describe, record, reflect and analyse:

- *Introduction*: The introduction provides a clear rationale for the field research, a review of relevant literature, a comprehensive description of the setting, participants and activities under observation, and the methods you have used to gather the data. It might also be appropriate to reflect upon your own personal perspective or background as a way of recognizing how your experiences may influence your selection, interpretation and/or analysis of your observations.
- *Results/findings*: This section presents your findings. Depending on the nature of the observations, the data might be presented in tables or figures, or it may include other representations such as quotes, comments, extracts from your field notes, photographs, diagrams and sketches.
- *Analysis*: This is the place for you to discuss your observations and to interpret and analyse their significance. The analysis should also refer back to relevant theories and literature, so that you are not expressing simply an opinion but an informed and educated assessment of what has occurred. You can also critique the process you followed and identify whether it had any impact on your results. Please note that it may be easier to combine the results and analysis into one section.
- *Conclusion*: Here you need to briefly summarize the overall experience and draw your final conclusion about the significance or meaning of what you have observed. You can consider limitations to the study and identify any relevant recommendations. As with any conclusion, do not introduce new material.
- *References*: This is where you provide a full list of any resources used in the report.
- *Appendices*: The appendices should include any material that would be useful for the reader to see but would disrupt the flow of the report. This material might include extracts from your field notes, detailed information on the location or event, a transcript of interviews, a list of guidelines you prepared for your fieldwork or any other materials that contribute meaningfully to the overall report. Only include materials in an appendix if they are referred to in the text of the report.

PRESENTATION

Reports should always be professionally presented, taking into consideration any specific guidelines provided by your institution or professor and the principles of editing and proofreading discussed in Chapter 6. A professional standard of presentation will differ across disciplines, so a sports marketing report may look quite different from an exercise physiology lab report.

Regardless of the subject matter, there are some key presentation elements that will be common across all reports:

- Include a title page as outlined above.
- Start each part of the report on a new page.
- Use page numbers, starting with page 1 on the first page of the introduction. The front matter (title page, executive summary and so on) may be labelled with Roman numerals: i, ii, iii.
- Use numbered headings and subheadings (see below for more information).
- Do not be afraid of white space – in other words, avoid a cramped layout. White space gives a spacious, professional look to your report.
- Use a good-sized margin and appropriate spacing between each line.
- Use standard fonts – nothing intricate, fancy or 'fun'. Your report will not be taken seriously if it is presented in Comic Sans.
- Avoid decorating your report with clip art or images. Use photographs or illustrations only if they are part of your findings and are actually discussed in your report.
- Use figures and tables to present findings.
- Use bullet points to list and emphasize key points.
- Use formal language, avoiding the use of first/second person (I, we, you).
- Proofread and edit your report carefully.

HEADINGS, SUBHEADINGS AND NUMBERING

Each section of a report should be numbered in order and labelled with a concise, relevant heading or subheading. Your professor may have a preference about how the headings and subheadings are formatted, but if not, it is important to use bold, italics and/or underlining to highlight the different level of heading (see Table 7.2). You need to be consistent with the style and format that you choose.

Please note that the table of contents normally includes only headings and subheadings, and not levels below subheadings. Headings and subheadings should appear in the table of contents exactly as they appear in the text. Using the automated table of contents function of your word processing programme will ensure consistency between the headings/subheadings and the table of contents. See Figure 7.1 for an example of numbered headings and subheadings.

Table 7.2 Sample heading formats

Level 1 heading	**BOLD CAPS**
Level 2 subheading	**Bold, first word capitalized**
Level 3 sub-subheading	*No bold, italics, first word capitalized*

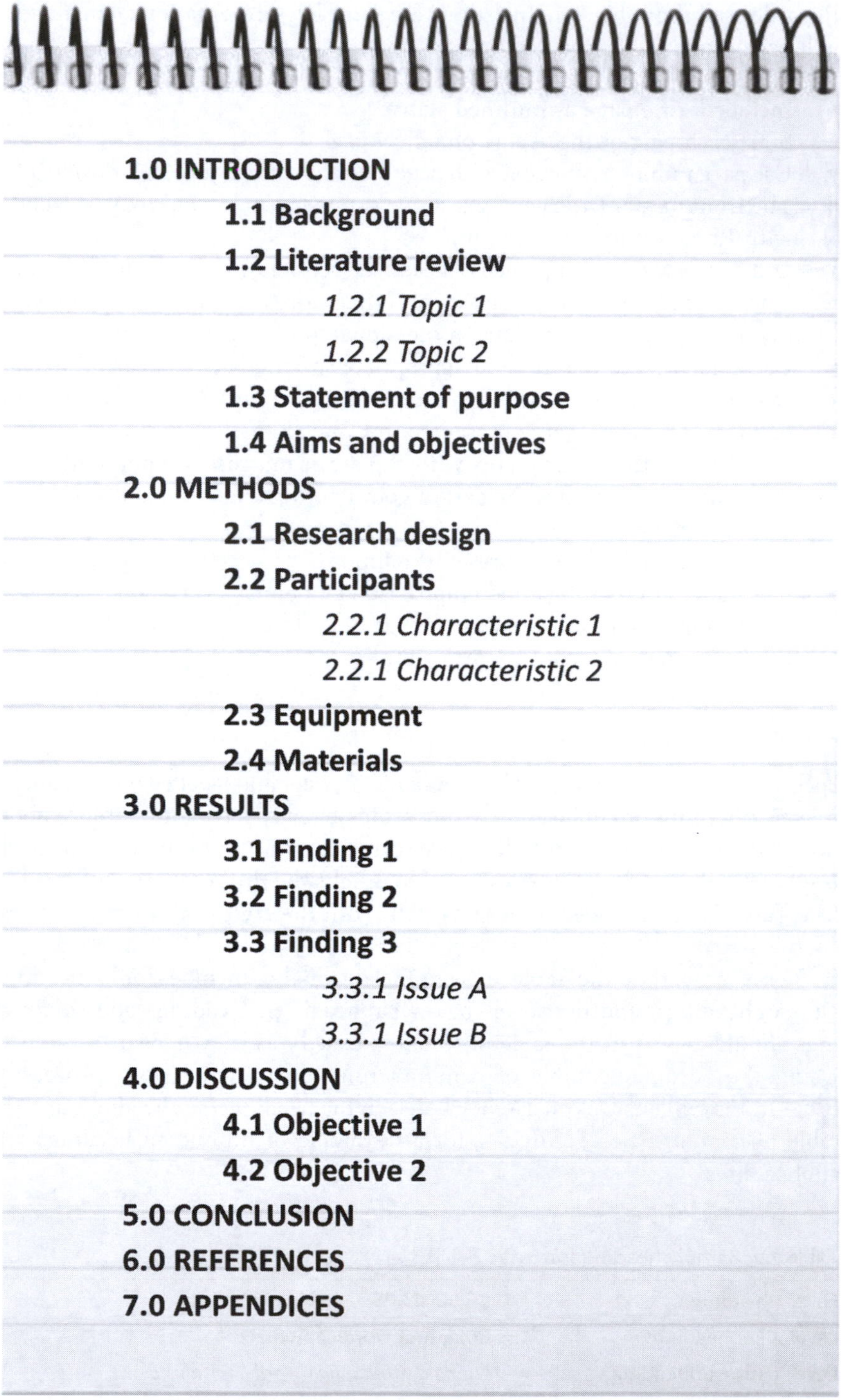

1.0 INTRODUCTION

    1.1 Background

    1.2 Literature review

        1.2.1 Topic 1

        1.2.2 Topic 2

    1.3 Statement of purpose

    1.4 Aims and objectives

2.0 METHODS

    2.1 Research design

    2.2 Participants

        2.2.1 Characteristic 1

        2.2.1 Characteristic 2

    2.3 Equipment

    2.4 Materials

3.0 RESULTS

    3.1 Finding 1

    3.2 Finding 2

    3.3 Finding 3

        3.3.1 Issue A

        3.3.1 Issue B

4.0 DISCUSSION

    4.1 Objective 1

    4.2 Objective 2

5.0 CONCLUSION

6.0 REFERENCES

7.0 APPENDICES

Figure 7.1 Numbered headings and subheadings

FIGURES AND TABLES

Figures and tables are used to present numerical data and to show relationships or trends. Tables structure data in columns and rows, whereas figures visually represent the results in graphs, charts or diagrams. Tables and figures should be included only if they are referred to in the results section. It is not appropriate to simply include tables and figures for illustrative purposes. As you describe particular findings, make reference to the specific table or figure where the reader can see the overall results for themselves. Be consistent in the style of table and figures you use:

- *Title/caption*: Figures and tables must be numbered and labelled with a title or caption. The title or caption should contain sufficient information for the table/figure to be self-explanatory. For example, a table labelled 'Female athletes' reveals little about the subject matter, whereas a table labelled 'Number of female athletes competing in the Summer Olympic Games, 1972–2012' explains the table's content. The title of a table always appears *above* the table whereas the title for a figure appears *below* it (see Figure 7.2).
- *Numbering*: There are two ways to number tables and figures. The first method is to simply label them in numerical order – for example, Table 1, Table 2, Table 3. The second way is to label the table/figure with the number of the chapter first and then the numerical order of the table or figure. If the tables appear in the third chapter, for example, they would be labelled Table 3.1, Table 3.2, Table 3.3.
- *Placement*: Figures and tables should be inserted into the report as soon as possible after they are first mentioned, taking spacing and presentation into consideration. Large tables or figures should be placed on a page of their own, but those smaller than half a page should appear in the text. When referring to specific findings in the report, note the figure by number, for example 'In Figure 4.3, it is apparent that the number of female competitors has steadily increased over the past forty years', or 'The number of female competitors has steadily increased over the past forty years (see Figure 4.3)'.

Table 3.1 Number of female athletes competing in the Summer Olympic Games, 1972-2012.

DATE	NUMBER	PERCENTAGE
1972	1095	14.8
1976	1260	20.7
1980	1115	21.5

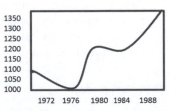

Figure 4.3 Number of female athletes competing in Olympics Games from 1972-2012.

Figure 7.2 Sample table and figure for a research report

- *List of tables/list of figures*: If tables and/or figures are included in the report, you should add a list of tables and/or a list of figures after the table of contents. These should not be conflated into one list, even if you only have a small number of each. List the tables/figures by number, title and page number in the order that they appear. There are functions in most word processing packages to create lists of tables and figures automatically.
- *References*: If you are using a table or figure from another source, then you will need to reference it appropriately. The reference is located underneath the table/figure, and also indicates if it is an exact copy or a modified version.

SUMMARY

1   Reports are designed to communicate information rather than an argument. The use of specific sections, each with its own subheading, enables a reader to find specific details without having to read the entire report.
2   At university, reports may be used to write up the results of laboratory or practical classes, to record field notes during observational studies and to develop various styles of business plans.
3   Reports typically include recommendations that outline appropriate future steps, based on the information presented.
4   Although there are slight differences according to discipline, reports tend to be formatted similarly, using visual displays of data, such as tables, graphs and figures.

EXERCISES

1   Find a report online from a government department, a sports federation or a not-for-profit organization. Review the structure, paying close attention to the executive summary and how detailed it is, the subheadings and the recommendations.
2   Examine the presentation of data in the report, noting how large amounts of information are succinctly displayed in tables, graphs and figures. In particular, notice how data that are visually organized are not described in detail in the text.
3   Explore the relationship between the data, conclusions and recommendations to understand how the latter derive from the former.
4   Take a report you have previously written and consider how you might restructure it according to the format presented here.

REFLECTION

Think about how writing styles differ between essays and reports. Of the three different styles of reports presented here, which are you most likely to encounter in your studies? How confident are you that you can translate findings into recommendations?

FURTHER READING

Borowick, J. (2000) *How to write a lab report.* Upper Saddle River NJ: Prentice Hall.
Emerson, L. and Hampton, J. (2005) *Writing guidelines for science and applied science students.* Melbourne: Thomson/Dunmore.

8

ACADEMIC WRITING

Incorporating evidence and avoiding plagiarism

OVERVIEW

This chapter outlines:
- the importance of supporting evidence and demonstrates how to incorporate evidence into an argument;
- various referencing systems and explains how to accurately cite research sources;
- the concept of plagiarism and offers techniques to avoid inadvertent copying.

INTRODUCTION

The validity of a research paper rests entirely on using convincing evidence to support an argument. Without indicating the source of information, the reader cannot help but be sceptical about the reliability of the evidence and is unlikely to trust or accept any conclusions drawn from it. The process of collecting academic research was outlined in Chapter 4; this chapter focuses on incorporating evidence into an assignment and explaining how to reference, cite, or acknowledge sources of research properly. Importantly, this chapter examines the serious issue of plagiarism and outlines techniques to avoid inadvertently cheating.

INCORPORATING EVIDENCE

In order to understand how to incorporate evidence, it is necessary to revisit the process of building paragraphs. As noted in Chapter 6, each paragraph is designed to communicate a single main point and to link this idea to the research topic. A paragraph also needs to support that point by providing sufficient detail and evidence so that the reader can accept the argument. The Paragraph Formula confirms this structure, noting that each paragraph requires: a) a topic sentence; b) further detail; c) evidence; and d) a summary and link to the next paragraph.

Taking a paragraph of the sample essay from Chapter 6, we can see that the topic sentence makes a claim about why children drop out of sport:

> One of the main reasons that teenagers drop out of organized sport is body image.

Although this is an unambiguous statement, a reader is nevertheless going ask: a) how body image plays a role in sports participation; and b) how you know that it is a *significant* reason why children drop out of sport. You will need to pre-empt their questions by providing a more detailed explanation as well as reference to the research that confirms your assertion. The next sentence in the sample essay expands on the topic sentence to provide some additional detail:

> One of the main reasons that teenagers drop out of organized sport is body image. Girls, in particular, are often concerned that physical activity detracts from what they perceive to be 'feminine'.

You have now made your claim and explained it in some more detail, and have reached the point where the reader can no longer go on trust; they need to see some hard evidence. In other words, you need to demonstrate the basis upon which you are making this assertion, so it is time to support your position by providing some specific evidence and acknowledging the source of that evidence.

Evidence is absolutely critical in a research paper. Without evidence, the reader has no idea whether or not to trust your argument as evidence confirms that the paper is not simply your own opinion or made up out of thin air. Furthermore, there is, quite frankly, no point doing extensive research for your paper if you do not show this work to the reader. As with the court room analogy from Chapter 6, bear in mind that the more evidence you can provide, the stronger your argument is likely to be. Refer to research findings, conclusions from studies, examples or case studies that explicate the point or other specific details that confirm your assertion has merit. It is not possible to incorporate such evidence into your paper without acknowledging where this information comes from, but unlike a courtroom, you cannot bring the actual witnesses and pieces of evidence in to your tutor to support your argument. You need to use other strategies to demonstrate the source of your ideas.

The following sample paragraph demonstrates how specific evidence lends weight to the assertion made in the topic sentence, and how acknowledging the source of these ideas substantiates the evidence so that the reader can be assured your claims are founded:

> One of the main reasons that teenagers drop out of organized sport is body image. Girls, in particular, are often concerned that physical activity detracts from what they perceive to be 'feminine'. Several studies suggest that girls are less inclined to

participate in activities that may make them look too masculine (Whitehead and Biddle 2008; Guillet *et al.* 2000). Whitehead and Biddle (2008) argue that most inactive teenage girls are concerned that being physically active will negatively affect their appearance, as playing sport involves exertion that can cause them to perspire. This is often viewed as masculine within their social groups, and teenagers will typically avoid situations that position them outside the social norms of the group. Changes during puberty can provoke further self-conscious behaviour, heightened in situations where a girl's body is more exposed or she is required to wear tight-fitting uniforms during physical education or matches (Allender *et al.*, 2006; Whitehead and Biddle, 2008).

TIP

If you refer to 'several studies' or 'many studies' in your paper, then you need to include reference to more than one study to confirm that you have seen this point made in several locations, otherwise your suggestion that 'many' or 'several' studies make this point is unsubstantiated.

A direct quote can be a useful way of adding support:

One of the main reasons that teenagers drop out of organized sport is body image. Girls, in particular, are often concerned that physical activity detracts from what they perceive to be 'feminine'. Several studies suggest that girls are less inclined to participate in activities that may make them look too masculine (Whitehead and Biddle, 2008; Guillet *et al.*, 2000). As Whitehead and Biddle (2008: 246) note, many girls do not 'embrace the idea of being active and "ruining" their appearances'. They further argue that most inactive teenage girls are concerned that being physically active will negatively affect their appearance, as playing sport involves exertion that can cause them to perspire (Whitehead and Biddle, 2008).

You should add as much evidence as you feel is necessary to validate your assertion and to demonstrate that the idea has been thoroughly researched. The latter point is the reason that each main point needs support from several sources – namely, to provide depth and strength of research to your argument.

After you have added evidence and acknowledged the source of the evidence, the next step is to summarize the main point and link it to the next topic sentence:

One of the main reasons that teenagers drop out of organized sport is body image. Girls, in particular, are often concerned that physical activity detracts from what they perceive to be 'feminine'. Several studies suggest that girls are less inclined to participate in activities that may make them look too masculine (Whitehead and Biddle, 2008; Guillet *et al.*, 2000). Whitehead and Biddle (2008) argue that most inactive teenage girls are concerned that being physically active will negatively affect their appearance, as playing sport involves exertion that can cause them to perspire. This is often viewed as masculine within their social groups, and teenagers will typically avoid situations that position them outside the social norms of the group. Changes during puberty can provoke further self-conscious behaviour, heightened in situations where a girl's body is more exposed or she is required to wear tight-fitting uniforms during physical education or matches (Allender *et al.*, 2006; Whitehead and Biddle, 2008). Although body image concerns are significant, it is also important to recognize that for many teenagers, the main obstacle to participating in sport is simply a matter of time.

Children in their mid-teens often have a series of demands that compete for their attention and time.

It may be more appropriate to break a main point into two paragraphs (or more in longer papers). This is a useful technique if there are two or more aspects to the point or if the evidence is too detailed to include in one paragraph. If you decide to split a main point into two paragraphs, you will need a topic sentence for each one and you will still need to link each paragraph to the next:

One of the main reasons that teenagers drop out of organized sport is body image. Girls, in particular, are often concerned that physical activity detracts from what they perceive to be 'feminine'. Several studies suggest that girls are less inclined to participate in activities that may make them look too masculine (Whitehead and Biddle, 2008; Guillet *et al.*, 2000). Whitehead and Biddle (2008) argue that most inactive teenage girls are concerned that being physically active will negatively affect their appearance, as playing sport involves exertion that can cause them to perspire. This is often viewed as masculine within their social groups, and teenagers will typically avoid situations that position them outside the social norms of the group. Changes during puberty can provoke further self-conscious behaviour, heightened in situations where a girl's body is more exposed or she is required to wear tight-fitting uniforms during physical education or matches (Allender *et al.*, 2006; Whitehead and Biddle, 2008). While girls have specific body image concerns, boys are not immune to this issue.

Teenage boys also find sport a challenging experience as a result of concerns about their physical appearance. Those who have not yet gone through puberty may be concerned about revealing their boyish bodies in front of girls or those with more mature masculine physiques. Ricciardelli *et al.* (2006) identify that improved social status and popularity are motivations to play sport, whereas Davison (2000) acknowledges that not excelling in physical education exposes boys to questions about their sexuality or even physical assault. Although body image concerns are significant, it is also important to recognize that for many teenagers, the main obstacle to participating in sport is simply a matter of time.

DIRECT QUOTES

Direct quotes can be used to introduce evidence into a paper. A direct quote is an extract or exact copy of words, phrases or sentences from a research source.

They are always presented in 'inverted commas', which acknowledges that the words contained therein are taken entirely from another source and are not the words of the author. You will see direct quotes in newspapers, novels, reports and all kinds of written documents, and in every instance the author is either reporting direct speech or the actual words from another source.

While direct quotes can be useful, if overused or not incorporated effectively, they can detract from your paper. Direct quotes are a heavy imposition on your argument, so you need to use them expertly and judiciously. As a student using research sources, perhaps for the first time, it will feel as though everyone else has already said everything much better than you could ever write it. You may use a lot of direct quotes because you are not confident that you can communicate these ideas as effectively. If, however, you remember that the basic purpose of a written assignment is for you to present your argument based on the evidence that you have found, then it is clear that someone else's words, written for a different purpose and published some time before your assignment, are not necessarily the most useful way to communicate the main points that address your research topic. Your professor wants to see how you can synthesize an argument by drawing together relevant research, establishing the main points and key ideas, and presenting them in a logical order to the reader. For this reason, quotes are actually not the best way to present your research. They are the view of one source only, and you should always try to use several sources to support each point to strengthen your argument. It is much better and more impressive to use your own words to express your main points, even though you still need to acknowledge the source of those ideas. Significantly, direct quotes are rarely used in scientific writing, though they are more common in sports history, sociology of sport and other social scientific disciplines.

Direct quotes should be used only for 'earth-shattering' comments, clever turns of phrases or when you need to invoke the authority of an expert, and in all cases they need to be used sparingly. A paper peppered with a series of direct quotes looks less like a carefully produced argument and more like a jigsaw of comments patched together. When considering including a direct quote in your paper, consider whether the quote is so insightful that it absolutely must be included, or whether it is a fairly standard line that would just as easily be communicated in your own words. If used carefully, quotes add power and emphasis to a point; however, used poorly, they do little more than disrupt your argument.

It is also important to understand what direct quotes cannot achieve within the context of a paper. Most notably, direct quotes cannot argue for you. They only ever support what you have already stated, so it is not possible, for example, to begin a paragraph or even an entire paper with a direct quote. If you have not yet argued anything, there is nothing for the quote to support. Not only does it look out of place but if you do not begin a paragraph with a strong assertion, then the point of the paragraph is not established. You need to present your topic sentence, and no one else's words are able to link your main point to your research topic. Similarly, quotes do not typically belong in an introduction or conclusion, as these are guiding your reader to and from your paper. This cannot be achieved by quoting someone who has no knowledge of your argument.

When copying down notes that might be used later as direct quotes, record the specific page number on which they appear, in addition to all the pertinent bibliographical details of the source. Write down the phrase or passage *exactly* as it appears in the original using the same blue/red system discussed in Chapter 3. Even if the quote has a spelling or grammatical error, you must copy it as it appears. Do not fix any errors, do not leave any words out, and do not omit parts that are not relevant to you. After copying down a quote, remember to record your 'moment of genius' by writing down *why* you think this quote is useful or important. Try to avoid writing down lengthy quotes; if you need to record a longer passage in order to remember the context, underline a shorter phrase that might serve as a quote.

INTRODUCING QUOTES

Left to their own devices, quotes add very little to a paper. They cannot stand on their own because they have been plucked from a different context and inserted into the middle of your argument. As such, they need to be skilfully added to your paper so that they work for you and are not disruptive. The most effective way to integrate direct quotes is to weave them into your sentences, which is known as *introducing* the quote. There are several ways to introduce quotes effectively into your paper, and in all cases, the quote needs to link directly to the point you have made:

- Mention the author(s) by name in the text:

    As Whitehead and Biddle (2008: 246) note, many girls do not 'embrace the idea of being active and "ruining" their appearances'.

- Use only short phrases to substitute for your words rather than an entire sentence:

    Many girls are not keen on physical activity as it may lead to them '"ruining" their appearances' (Whitehead and Biddle, 2008: 246).

- Use clever terms or ideas, but not entire passages:

    Many girls are not keen on physical activity as it may lead to them 'ruining' their hair and make-up (Whitehead and Biddle, 2008: 246).

POOR USE OF QUOTES

Take a look at the following example of a poor use of quotes:

One of the main reasons that teenagers drop out of organized sport is body image. 'These girls would not embrace the idea of being active and "ruining" their appearances' (Whitehead and Biddle, 2008: 246). 'Involvement and perseverance of girls in sport will remain problematic as long as some activities are connoted as being stereotypically masculine, particularly for girls for whom conformity with stereotypic images of femininity is all-important' (Guillet *et al.*, 2000: 420–21). 'They did not want to get sweaty during physical activity' (Whitehead and Biddle, 2008: 246). Although body image concerns are significant, it is also important to recognize that for many teenagers, the main obstacle to participating in sport is simply a matter of time.

You will notice how the quotes seem awkward and do not flow as part of an argument. They do not support anything, and they tell the reader nothing about *why* these comments are relevant to the topic sentence. In fact, the author of the paper is almost entirely absent, so it is not clear what their argument is. In essence, direct quotes are useless unless *you* make sense of them for the reader by linking this form of evidence to your argument.

EFFECTIVE USE OF QUOTES

Compare the previous passage to this one:

One of the main reasons that teenagers drop out of organized sport is body image. Girls, in particular, are often concerned that physical activity detracts from what they perceive to be 'feminine'. Several studies suggest that girls are less inclined to participate in activities that may make them look too masculine (Whitehead and Biddle, 2008; Guillet *et al.*, 2000). Whitehead and Biddle (2008: 246) suggest that many girls do not 'embrace the idea of being active and "ruining" their appearances'. In particular, girls were concerned with being too 'sweaty' and 'disgusting' after sport, as this is often viewed as masculine within their social groups and teenagers will typically avoid situations that position them outside the social norms of the group (Whitehead and Biddle 2008: 246). Changes during puberty can provoke further self-conscious behaviour, heightened in situations where a girl's body is more exposed or she is required to wear tight-fitting uniforms during physical education or matches (Allender *et al.*, 2006; Whitehead and Biddle, 2008). Although body image concerns are significant, it is also important to recognize that for many teenagers, the main obstacle to participating in sport is simply a matter of time.

The number and length of direct quotes have been reduced and better integrated into the paragraph so that it now flows seamlessly. This is an example of how you can make quotes work *for* you rather than *against* you.

TIP

Never run quotes back to back. You are not providing any argument when you are using quotes, so the more quotes you include, the more 'you' disappear from your paper. For this reason, many professors do not include direct quotes as part of the word count.

REFERENCING

It is always perplexing to professors that students either seem terrified about referencing or groan at the thought of the horrible imposition they are forced to endure. In fact, referencing is a positive process that is nothing more than simply acknowledging the source of the information you use in your papers. It is not complicated or difficult, and definitely nothing to be concerned about. It is an essential part of the research and writing process, and it is easy to include references as you go along.

WHY DO I NEED TO REFERENCE?

It is critically important that you reference your argument, because all research is based on evidence. Without acknowledging the specific evidence you used to generate your argument, the reader can only assume that you have done no research or might suspect that you have used poor sources. In short, including references is the only way to demonstrate the depth, breadth and quality of your research. Frankly, there is little point going to the effort of conducting research if you are going to hide the sources from the reader.

Referencing clearly demonstrates to the reader how much work you have done, how many sources you have consulted and how effectively you have integrated these sources into your argument. Here are other reasons why it is important:

- provides sufficient detail so the reader can consult the source themselves;
- gives your work legitimacy;
- protects you from allegations of simply 'making it up';
- protects you from allegations of plagiarism;
- shows your ability to research widely and thoroughly;
- demonstrates your ability to synthesize information from a variety of sources into an argument.

WHAT NEEDS TO BE REFERENCED?

Part of the anxiety about referencing comes from not being sure what needs to be referenced. Essentially, all material that comes from a source needs to be referenced. This does not include 'common knowledge', which varies between subject areas. For example, in sports history, we may not reference the fact that the modern Olympics began in 1896, as this is common knowledge within sports history, though we might reference the fact that the first President of the International Olympic Committee was Demetrius Vikelas. If you are not sure what is 'common knowledge', simply include a reference. It is better to have too many than too few.

There are specific occasions when a reference is absolutely necessary:

- when you quote directly from someone else's work;
- when you mention an author by name;

> ## TIP
>
> A good rule of thumb is 'If I didn't know it before I started this assignment, then it needs to be referenced'.

- when you refer to 'many' or 'several' studies (in which case you will need at least two or three references to support your contention that this idea is widespread);
- when you refer to a particular theory, argument or viewpoint;
- when you have used specific information, such as statistics, names, dates, places or case studies;
- when you have used something as background reading and it has influenced your thinking towards your piece of work;
- when you can actually pinpoint the source of particular information that appears in your assignment.

A good way to test whether or not you need a reference is to ask yourself 'How do I know this?' as you go through your paper. If you can recall the source, then you will probably need to reference it.

HOW DO I REFERENCE?

There are many different types of referencing systems, and there is no consistency across – or even within – the various sports studies disciplines. Thankfully, all of them collect the same bibliographic details, the main difference being simply a matter of formatting and presentation. The type of referencing system you will use in your assignments depends on your discipline, your institution or department and/or your lecturer's preference. Referencing systems can roughly be divided into main types:

- *Author/date references*: The author's name, year and page number (only for direct quotes) appears in the actual text of your paper.
- *Endnotes/footnotes*: The reference is denoted by a small superscript numeral that corresponds to the relevant source either at the bottom of the page (footnote) or at the end of the article, chapter or book (endnote).

The most common referencing systems in sports studies are contained in Table 8.1.

AUTHOR/DATE REFERENCES

Author/date references appear in parentheses in the text and are supported by a comprehensive reference list at the end of the paper. These in-text references

Table 8.1 Common referencing systems in sports studies

Referencing system	Type of reference	Sports studies disciplines
APA (American Psychological Association)	author/date	Sports psychology, sociology of sport, applied social sciences
Harvard	author/date	Sports management
Chicago/Turabian	end/footnote	Sports history, philosophy of sport
Vancouver	end/footnote	Sports/exercise science

or citations should be brief and unobtrusive, and provide just enough information to enable the reader to locate the full bibliographic details in the reference list at the end of the paper. This usually means including the author's surname and the year of publication. In-text references for direct quotes will include the specific page number(s) where the quote can be found.

In the following passage, note the author/date references:

> One of the main reasons that teenagers drop out of organized sport is body image. Girls, in particular, are often concerned that physical activity detracts from what they perceive to be feminine. Several studies suggest that girls are less inclined to participate in activities that may make them look too masculine (Whitehead and Biddle, 2008; Guillet *et al.*, 2000). Whitehead and Biddle (2008: 246) note that many girls do not 'embrace the idea of being active and "ruining" their appearances'.

The first reference includes two sources separated by a semicolon. The second reference includes only a year and a page number within the parentheses because the authors' names are already mentioned in the essay, and it would be redundant to repeat them when the reader can easily see who the authors are. Page numbers must be included in the in-text reference for direct quotes so that the reader can find the quote in the original source without having to read the entire paper.

As mentioned above, author/date references are just a gesture to the reference, so they should be subtle and not dominate the text. For this reason, it is *never* appropriate to include the title of the source or the full bibliographic details within the parentheses, and it is usually unnecessary to mention the name of a book or article in the text. The reader is more than capable of looking up the reference for themselves, and too much detail is distracting. See how clumsy and awkward the following passage would be if the entire reference was included in the text:

> One of the main reasons that teenagers drop out of organized sport is body image. Girls, in particular, are often concerned that physical activity detracts from what they perceive to be feminine. Several studies suggest that girls are less inclined to

participate in activities that may make them look too masculine (Whitehead, S. and Biddle, S. (2008) Adolescent girls' perceptions of physical activity: a focus group study. *European Physical Education Review*, 14: 243–62; Guillet, E., Sarrazin, P. and Fontayne, P. (2000) 'If it contradicts my gender role, I'll stop': introducing survival analysis to study the effects of gender typing on the time of withdrawal from sport practice: a 3-year study. *European Review of Applied Psychology*, 50(4): 417–21). Whitehead and Biddle (Whitehead, S. and Biddle, S. (2008). Adolescent girls' perceptions of physical activity: a focus group study. *European Physical Education Review*, 14: 243–62) note that many girls do not 'embrace the idea of being active and "ruining" their appearances'.

PLACEMENT OF IN-TEXT REFERENCES

References should be placed in the text at the nearest point to the information as is practical, usually at the next natural pause in the sentence, such as before a comma, semicolon or full stop/period. References are also enclosed in parentheses and placed inside punctuation marks:

> Several studies suggest that girls are less inclined to participate in activities that may make them look too masculine (Whitehead and Biddle, 2008; Guillet *et al.*, 2000).

References appear within punctuation marks:

> Many girls do not 'embrace the idea of being active and "ruining" their appearances' (Whitehead and Biddle 2008: 246). The authors further argue that most inactive teenage girls are concerned that being physically active will negatively affect their appearance, as playing sport involves exertion that can cause them to perspire (Whitehead and Biddle 2008).

References are further shortened if the authors' names are included in the text of the paper:

> Whitehead and Biddle (2008: 246) note that many girls do not 'embrace the idea of being active and "ruining" their appearances'.

> Whitehead and Biddle (2008) argue that most inactive teenage girls are concerned that being physically active will negatively affect their appearance, as playing sport involves exertion that can cause them to perspire.

ENDNOTES/FOOTNOTES

Endnotes or footnotes are even less obtrusive than author/date references and allow for more information to be included than just bibliographic details. Rather than including the author's name, year of publication and perhaps the page number, end/footnotes are referenced by the insertion of a small, superscript numeral that corresponds to a reference located either at the bottom of the page (footnotes) or at the end of the paper (endnotes). In some numeric

TIP

A useful way to familiarize yourself with referencing is to take some research articles and examine how they reference. What referencing system do they use? Where do they place the reference? What information do they support with a reference? How often are references included? How are the references formatted?

referencing systems, such as Chicago/Turabian, the numbers appear in the text in ascending order, with each numeral referring to a new entry in the foot/endnotes; in others, such as Vancouver, the numbers refer to a specific source in the reference list and may appear out of sequence or be repeated in the text. The placement/location of end/footnote numbers is similar to in-text references as outlined above, though they sit outside punctuation marks.

Here is the sample paragraph replacing author/date references with end/footnotes using the *Chicago Manual of Style* referencing system:

One of the main reasons that teenagers drop out of organized sport is body image. Girls, in particular, are often concerned that physical activity detracts from what they perceive to be feminine. Several studies suggest that girls are less inclined to participate in activities that may make them look too masculine.[1] As Whitehead and Biddle note, many girls do not "embrace the idea of being active and 'ruining' their appearances."[2] They further argue that most inactive teenage girls are concerned that being physically active will negatively affect their appearance, as playing sport involves exertion that can cause them to perspire.[3] This is often viewed as masculine within their social groups, and teenagers will typically avoid situations that position them outside the social norms of the group.[4] Changes during puberty can provoke further self-conscious behaviour, heightened in situations where a girl's body is more exposed or she is required to wear tight-fitting uniforms during physical education or matches.[5]

ENDNOTES

1   Sarah Whitehead and Stuart Biddle, "Adolescent girls' perceptions of physical activity: A focus group study," *European Physical Education Review*, 14 (2008): 246; Emma Guillet, Philippe Sarrazin and Paul Fontayne (2000) "'If it contradicts my gender role, I'll stop': Introducing survival analysis to study the effects of gender typing on the time of withdrawal from sport practice: A 3-year study," *European Review of Applied Psychology*, 50, no. 4 (2000): 420–21.

2   Whitehead and Biddle, "Adolescent girls' perceptions of physical activity," 246.

3   Ibid.

4   While the influence of social groups is beyond the scope of this study, it is worth mentioning that peer pressure is a powerful influence on attrition from sport, particularly for teenage girls.

5   Steven Allender, Gill Cowburn and Charlie Foster, "Understanding participation in sport and physical activity among children and adults: a review of qualitative studies," *Health Education Research*, 21, no. 6 (2006): 826; Whitehead and Biddle, "Adolescent girls' perceptions of physical activity," 249.

In this system, the end/footnotes can also be used to provide additional information that would have disrupted the argument but is nevertheless important for the reader to know, as per the fourth note.

Here is the same passage using the Vancouver system. Note how the references are numbered according to their first mention in the text:

One of the main reasons that teenagers drop out of organized sport is body image. Girls, in particular, are often concerned that physical activity detracts from what they perceive to be feminine. Several studies suggest that girls are less inclined to participate in activities that may make them look too masculine.[1, 2] As Whitehead and Biddle[1] (p 246) note, many girls do not 'embrace the idea of being active and "ruining" their appearances'. They further argue that most inactive teenage girls are concerned that being physically active will negatively affect their appearance, as playing sport involves exertion that can cause them to perspire.[1] This is often viewed as masculine within their social groups, and teenagers will typically avoid situations that position them outside the social norms of the group. Changes during puberty can provoke further self-conscious behaviour, heightened in situations where a girl's body is more exposed or she is required to wear tight-fitting uniforms during physical education or matches.[1, 3]

REFERENCE LIST

1   Whitehead S, Biddle S. Adolescent girls' perceptions of physical activity: a focus group study. *European Physical Education Review* 2008;14(2):243–62.
2   Guillet, E, Sarrazin, P, Fontayne P. 'If it contradicts my gender role, I'll stop': introducing survival analysis to study the effects of gender typing on the time of withdrawal from sport practice: a 3-year study. *European Review of Applied Psychology* 2000;50(4):417–21.
3   Allender, S, Cowburn, G, Foster C. Understanding participation in sport and physical activity among children and adults: a review of qualitative studies. *Health Education Research* 2006;21(6):826–35.

REFERENCE LIST

A reference list is provided at the end of a paper to allow readers to see the full bibliographic details of every cited source. Occasionally, you may be asked to provide a bibliography, which is a full list of every source you have consulted when preparing the paper, even if it is not cited in the final submission. Either way, this list enables the reader to locate the original source. Please note that a reference list or bibliography alone is *not* enough to suggest that your paper is based on research. You need to link the sources to specific ideas in your assignment using author/date references or end/footnotes to properly acknowledge which points derive from each source.

Both reference lists and bibliographies are presented in alphabetical order by the surname of the first author, with the exception of the Vancouver system where references are listed in the order they are first cited. They always appear at the end of the paper and should begin on a new page. The format of the reference list or bibliography depends on the specific referencing system you are using, but essentially the same bibliographic information will be required for all and is outlined below. While you might memorize the format for one or two systems that you use regularly, it is just as easy to refer to a referencing guide or handout, or one of the many online systems or programmes that help you prepare your notes.

FORMATTING THE REFERENCE LIST

There are many institutional and regional variations in all referencing systems, so it is advised that you check your university's referencing guidelines for specific formatting requirements. In general, the kind of bibliographic details you need to record for inclusion in the reference list are detailed below:

Academic book
- author(s)
- year of publication
- *name of the book* – always in italics and any subheading as well
- city of publication
- publisher.

Chapter in an edited book
- author(s) of the chapter
- year of publication
- 'title of the chapter'
- names of the editor(s)
- *name of the book* – always in italics and any subheading as well
- page numbers of chapter
- city of publication
- publisher.

Journal article
- author
- year of publication
- 'title of article'
- *name of journal* – always in italics
- volume number
- issue number
- pages.

PENALTIES FOR INCORRECT/ABSENT REFERENCING

There are two main consequences for not providing adequate references in your research papers: a poorer (or even a failing) grade and/or academic penalties. A poor grade is based on the fact that your research essay does not contain any actual research to support the claims made in your argument. A reference list appended to the end of a paper is not enough to confirm your paper is supported by evidence as there is no indication how the sources relate to the information in your paper. Academic penalties may be applied if your professor sees that you have copied material directly from other sources without appropriate acknowledgement. This is known as plagiarism and is considered a form of cheating.

CASE STUDY

Joel is in a study group with three others from his class. They had been discussing their assignment and reviewing each other's work when Joel noticed that one of the other students, Ryan, had neglected to include references in his paper. Joel pointed out the omission, and Ryan replied that because he had not used any quotes, he did not need to include references in the text, only a reference list, and that he did not want the professor to think that he had just rehashed everyone else's ideas.

→ How should Joel respond to Ryan's explanation?

→ Explain how Ryan has misunderstood both the purpose of referencing and the purpose of writing a research paper.

Another member of the study group, Erin, is a little unsure about how to format her paper, so Joel offers to email her his paper so that she can see the layout, and she gratefully accepts. Several weeks later, Joel is called to a meeting with the Dean to explain why he has submitted the same assignment as another student in the class, and he realizes then that Erin must have just downloaded his paper and handed it in.

→ How would you feel if you were put in this position?

→ In what way are Erin's and Ryan's actions similar?

PLAGIARISM

Plagiarism is a serious form of cheating where a person tries to pretend that they are the author or originator of material that is presented in their assignments. In other words, it is the use of material that is taken directly, without appropriate attribution, from another source, such as published materials, the internet, a previously submitted assignment or another student.

It includes 'lifting' ideas, text, results, tables or any other material without referencing its origin.

Plagiarism is academic theft and intellectual fraud, and for these reasons it is considered to be serious misconduct. It can result in severe academic penalties and disciplinary action, including formal exclusion from your institution. It can also have a lasting impact on your reputation and affect your employability. In recent years, several high-profile politicians, college presidents and others have been forced to resign their office when it has been publicly revealed that they had plagiarized in their university studies. All colleges and universities will have a formal plagiarism policy, and you should read this at your earliest convenience to ensure you are fully aware of how plagiarism is defined and the penalties that are applied in your institution.

Plagiarism: any time you take someone else's work and pretend it is your own, either *deliberately* or *by accident*.

Plagiarism includes:

- copying written text word for word from a hardcopy or online source;
- cutting and pasting passages from another source into your paper;
- changing just a few words or rearranging sentences to make it seem a bit different from the original;
- copying from another student;
- using the same essay in different courses; also known as 'double dipping'.

It is important to note that plagiarism is the *act* not the *intention*, which means that you do not have to *intend* to steal the work: *accidentally* plagiarizing is *as punishable* as deliberately stealing. It is similar to the World Anti-Doping Agency's policy of strict liability. If an illegal substance is found in your body, you are liable for punishment, even if it was an accident and you did not intend to cheat. There is no valid excuse for plagiarism. Claiming not to understand is *not* a viable justification for plagiarism.

AVOIDING ACCIDENTAL PLAGIARISM

Inadvertent plagiarism is entirely avoidable, and begins by developing good note-taking techniques, as outlined in Chapter 3. Sloppy or lazy note taking, such as writing out lengthy passages, forgetting to record bibliographic details and not summarizing ideas in your own words can cause you to accidentally transfer copied material from your notes into your assignment. When you are working on different research projects or leave a period of time between research and writing, it is easy to forget which notes are from the source and which were your own comments. Using the blue/red note-taking system helps keep your research well organized so you always know what is copied material and what can be used freely in your paper. Furthermore, always summarize main points in your own words, rather than copying out or cutting and pasting passage after passage. If you must record a quote, make sure it is brief, and explain the context in your own words.

STUDENT VIEWPOINT

I was really nervous about accidentally plagiarizing when I went to college because I heard that you can fail the class or be kicked out altogether, so I was really pleased to learn that it is very easy to prevent. You just need to take care when you take notes and make sure you clearly identify which is original source material and what are your own words.—Sophie.

SUMMARY

1   Research assignments must be based on strong evidence that is incorporated into the text with reference to the sources.
2   Far from being difficult or an imposition, referencing enables students to demonstrate the breadth, depth and quality of research they have conducted on the topic, by acknowledging the research sources upon which the argument is based.
3   Different disciplines within sports studies employ different referencing systems, though most are categorized as author/date or foot/endnote systems. Refer to your institution or department's referencing policies for details on appropriate systems and specific formatting requirements.
4   Plagiarism is the unacknowledged use of other people's ideas or data. At its most extreme, material is copied and pasted straight into a student assignment without any indication that it is a direct quote. Plagiarism is recognized as the act, not the intention, and even inadvertent plagiarism attracts penalties.

EXERCISES

1   Look at one or two research sources and examine how evidence is incorporated into the paper. Where are the references placed? Are you more convinced by a point that has many references to support it or only one or two?
2   Look for your university or department's guidelines on referencing. Which system do they ask you to use? Do they provide specific examples for different kinds of sources or do you need to find your own handbook to learn how to format references properly?

3   Write two paragraphs, utilizing the Paragraph Formula and incorporating references to support your argument. Create a reference list to place at the end of the page.

4   Complete an online plagiarism quiz or tutorial to learn more about the mechanics of good referencing. Your university learning skills or library may have links to several options.

REFLECTION

Think about the purpose of using evidence in your assignment as well as the relationship between good-quality sources and your argument. Reflect on the purpose of referencing and how accurate referencing can actually help your argument. Consider what is meant by plagiarism and why it represents a breach of academic integrity. Think about what it would mean to you if your work was published in a book under someone else's name without acknowledgement. How would you feel? Would you want to be recognized for the hard work you have put in?

FURTHER READING

American Psychological Association (2009) *Concise rules of APA style*, 6th edn. Washington DC: American Psychological Association.

Neville, C. (2007) *The complete guide to referencing and avoiding plagiarism.* Maidenhead: Open University Press.

Patrias, K. and Wendling, D. (2007) *Citing medicine: The NLM style guide for authors, editors, and publishers*, 2nd edn. Bethesda MD: National Library of Medicine. Available at: www.ncbi.nlm.nih.gov/books/NBK7256/?redirect-on-error=__HOME__ &depth=2.

University of Chicago Press (2010) *The Chicago manual of style.* Chicago IL: University of Chicago Press.

9

ACADEMIC WRITING

Digital forms and reflective practices

OVERVIEW

This chapter outlines:
*   reflective writing and how it contributes to learning;
*   several online writing formats, such as wikis and blogs, that may be used at college;
*   the pitfalls of social media and the thoughtful development of online persona.

INTRODUCTION

Although the book has so far focused on structuring traditional research assignments, there are many other assessment forms used to evaluate your learning at college. In an increasingly online world, there are new and innovative ways of interacting with material and demonstrating your engagement with ideas, texts, yourself and each other. Most of you will already have vast experience of interacting online, and the growth of fantasy sports, official and fan websites, sports-related blogs and discussion forums means there is a plethora of sporting content at our fingertips. Some professors might ask you to blog on a particular issue or develop podcasts or videos to upload to YouTube or other content-sharing websites, or you could be asked to contribute to discussion boards or work collaboratively in virtual meetings. You might be asked to reflect on topical issues in sport or on your learning practices and experiences as you prepare for employment. This chapter begins with a discussion of reflective writing and then outlines some of the more common digital or online assessment strategies.

REFLECTIVE WRITING

We think reflectively all the time, analysing our actions and making decisions about how we might behave in the future. Indeed, on the field of play these skills are invaluable as we strategize based on effective plays, regroup when something goes awry and think critically about our next steps. Similarly, in the locker room the coach will review and discuss our performances, encouraging us to reflect on where we can improve personally or as a team. At college, students are increasingly encouraged to be more conscious of their reflective practices and to use these as part of their learning. Indeed, many contemporary teaching and learning strategies discourage students from simply rote learning facts to be regurgitated later in an exam, and prefer you to demonstrate how you respond to ideas raised in class, to the literature or to topical events that relate to course content. Writing reflectively means more than simply describing or summarizing what you have seen or experienced. It asks you to think carefully about not just the 'what' but the 'why' and the 'how' and to critically analyse these in relation to what you already know or have learned.

There are many ways that reflection can be incorporated into your course. It might be used to think about how to apply concepts to your own 'real world' examples, or to step back from an issue to consider it from another angle. Reflections can help you make sense of new information, real-life situations, texts that you read and even sports events you watch on television. These moments provide opportunities to think critically about what we are seeing, reading or hearing and to assimilate these prompts into a broader intellectual context. For example, the literature suggests that a good coach should have technical ability and excellent interpersonal skills, but in your coaching internship you noticed that your mentor was gruff, quick-tempered and almost rude to her athletes and everyone around her. Nevertheless, she still earned the respect of her players and was admired by her colleagues and peers. Your reflection might consider the reasons why this coach succeeded despite having difficult interpersonal skills and what you might learn from her.

Reflection encourages you to explore the relationship between theory and practice – for example, in a work placement or an internship. In these situations you would summarize your experience or a specific scenario and then explain what your future actions might be and how they might be changed or affected as a result. This makes it a particularly important skill for practitioners such as physical educators, athletic trainers and coaches – and any other profession in which you are responsible for the well-being of others. Being able to reflect critically on your actions in a given situation in order to determine better or more efficient courses of action for the future enhances your praxis as a professional within the sports industry. It is only when we reflect on a situation that we can appreciate our mistakes and achievements to derive lessons from them. Experience alone only engages our learning at a surface level.

In interview situations, potential employers often ask you to outline specific examples where you may have solved a problem or overcome an obstacle, or where you have demonstrated good leadership or taken an initiative. If you are skilled in the process of reflection, addressing these sorts of questions will be second nature, particularly if you already have experience within, for example, the context of an internship portfolio or reflective journal.

Like most forms of writing, reflective writing is a genre that has generic conventions that will be discussed below; however, it is important to stress that reflective writing is a highly individual process. Your comments and insights will be unique to you and will change as a result of your personal circumstances and knowledge base. On different occasions the same situation can inspire entirely different reactions and reflections from a single individual, let alone across a larger group, as each person draws upon different backgrounds and previous experiences to analyse the moment.

TIP

Just because reflective writing is *personal* does not mean that it is *informal*. You should endeavour to write formally, even though the content is your personal response rather than a researched argument.

HOW TO REFLECT

Students often find reflective writing challenging, particularly if they are used to producing research papers or learning 'the right answer'. It takes practice to be able to communicate your feelings effectively, and it is not always easy to link theory to the 'real world'. There are a number of models to guide us, and the Gibbs' (1988) Reflective Cycle depicted in Figure 9.1 is a popular schematic that outlines the various steps involved in a reflection. Depending on how much you are expected to write, you may not need to consider each one in great detail, but it does lead you through the process of reflective writing.

Description

Begin by briefly summarizing the event, experience or issue. It is important for the reader to understand what happened and the context in which it happened. It is easy to spend too much time describing the incident rather than reflecting on it, so try to be succinct.

Feelings

Record how you felt about the incident or moment. What was your initial reaction? Were you confused? Elated? Doubtful? At the time, were you pleased with your behaviour or how you handled the situation? How do you feel about it now? What may have changed your thoughts on the event? Step outside yourself and really try to identify your feelings.

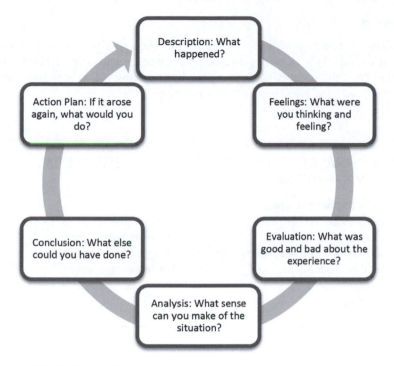

Figure 9.1 The Reflective Cycle

Source: Gibbs 1988

KEY PHRASES YOU MIGHT USE WHEN *DESCRIBING* AN EVENT, EXPERIENCE OR INCIDENT

Last week . . .

After the lecture . . .

During our induction . . .

Before my first client arrived . . .

As I arrived at the office . . .

First . . . second . . .

Initially . . .

Then . . .

Next . . .

Finally . . .

KEY PHRASES YOU MIGHT USE WHEN OUTLINING YOUR *FEELINGS*

I was happy with . . .

I was impressed by . . .

I really enjoyed . . .

I loved . . .

My favourite part was . . .

It was just what I expected.

I didn't enjoy . . .

I wasn't pleased with . . .

I didn't like . . .

I hate . . .

It wasn't what I expected/imagined.

I was very unhappy with . . .

Evaluation

The next step is to provide your appraisal of the experience; how you would rate it overall. What positive and negative aspects were there? How does it compare to similar experiences you have had? Taking everything into consideration, how would you assess the experience?

KEY PHRASES YOU MIGHT USE WHEN *EVALUATING* YOUR EXPERIENCE

It was a terrific experience.	I feel that . . .
It was/was not very good.	I believe that . . .
It was fine.	The main reason was . . .
I was/was not (reasonably/very) satisfied.	I suggest this was owing to . . .
I was disappointed . . .	The main issue was . . .
It was quite poor.	This could have been a result of . . .
I would say that . . .	

Analysis

This is your opportunity to link your experience with some literature in the area. How does the experience concur with your expectations based on the theory you have learned? Look outside the event and draw together other ideas about what it might mean to you.

KEY PHRASES YOU MIGHT USE WHEN *ANALYSING* THE EVENT

Several authors argue that . . .	I agree with A, who argues that . . .
XYZ claims that . . .	I do not agree with X's suggestion that . . .
A, B and C suggest that . . .	

Conclusion

Summarize your experience by outlining what you have learned. Consider how the event has affected you, and identify how you might respond to a similar situation in the future. Will you do the same thing? Will you change your behaviour/actions?

KEY PHRASES YOU MIGHT USE WHEN
SUMMARIZING YOUR EXPERIENCE

Overall . . .   I could/should have . . .
Altogether . . .   The main thing I learned was . . .
On reflection . . .   I also learned that . . .
It might have been better to . . .

Action plan

The final part of any reflection is to think about the concrete steps you need
to take in order to avoid the same sort of situation arising again or to improve
further on the learning experience you have just had. You may identify
additional training that you need or further study on a particular topic. You
may want to seek further practical experiences to strengthen your skill set.

KEY PHRASES YOU MIGHT USE WHEN OUTLINING
YOUR *ACTION PLAN*

The next step for me is to . . .   The first thing I need to do is . . .
I would like to now . . .   It would be better to . . .
I will try to . . .   I won't . . .
I've decided to . . .   It is best for me to . . .
I plan to . . .   I this happens again, I will . . .

TIP

Learning journals record learning *over time*, so if you are required to submit your
journal for assessment, it cannot be written the night before it is due.

CASE STUDY

Nicole made the following entry in her reflective journal as part of her prac teaching in physical education:

2.10.2012

Tennis

Today, I was responsible for teaching tennis to the Year 9 class (mostly 14 year olds). I began by having them sit down in a group on the court while I described what we were going to do for the class. I showed them how to hold a racket properly and then showed them the basic principles of a serve, forehand and backhand. It probably took only about 15 minutes, but the class was getting pretty restless and I had to stop several times to reprimand some students who started rolling balls around the court. The class teacher had to intervene once as well. Then we broke into small groups, and each student got a racket. They were supposed to first learn how to hold the racket correctly and then stand in a line, side on to the net, placing the feet in the right position and rotating the body, leading with the hips. A couple of the boys wanted to start swinging the racket and hitting balls, but for the most part the students listened to what I was describing. I then showed them how to draw the racket back and swing through in rhythm with the footwork and body movement. By the end of the class, most of the students were performing the forehand quite nicely, and we ended with just five minutes of hitting some balls, which got a little chaotic. For the next lesson, I will focus on the backhand, and if there is time, maybe the serve.

→ To what degree does this entry follow Gibbs' Reflective Cycle?

→ Is it evident from the entry what Nicole has learned from her experience or the changes she might make for her next class?

→ Which parts of Nicole's entry would benefit from more analysis and reflection?

Is the lecturer really interested in my opinion?

After emphasizing how inappropriate personal opinions are in the context of academic assessment, it is only natural for students to be a little sceptical about whether their opinions really are wanted in reflective journals. The short answer is 'Yes'. Your professors would not ask you to reflect on an issue if they were not interested in your thoughts, analysis or interpretation. The slightly longer answer, however, is that your opinions need to be informed

2.10.2012

Tennis

I taught my first tennis class today to a Year 9 class consisting of mostly 14 year olds. It was moderately successful, but there were some challenges, particularly in the area of behaviour management, which I will reflect on in this entry. I wanted to start the class with an overview of the skills that we were going to learn, and so I talked the class through the exercises and showed them what to do. Some of the students became quite restless at this point and were not paying attention and were messing around with the equipment. In hindsight, I probably spent too much time talking and not enough time letting them try the activities for themselves. I should have kept in mind that this is a private school in a relatively affluent area, so it is highly likely that some if not most have already played tennis, and some may even have had professional coaching. It would have been better to identify those students who could already play tennis and use them as peer educators. They could demonstrate holding the racket and the forehand swing to smaller groups of less skilled students. Even then, I would need to keep them actively engaged because poor classroom behaviour can result from boredom. I was embarrassed when the class teacher had to step in and resolve the situation, but I note that several recent studies identify that student teachers (Johansen *et al.* 2011), and student physical education teachers in particular (Lavay *et al.* 2012), have insufficient training in behaviour management, so this will be an area that I will need to educate myself on. For the next class, I will revise how I structure the activities and try to incorporate students who are already well skilled into the class.

and demonstrate intellectual engagement. The passage above demonstrates how Nicole, from the above case study, reflected more concertedly on her experience.

LEARNING JOURNALS AND E-PORTFOLIOS

A learning journal is a collection of reflections, ideas, notes, observations and other components that together create a record of your learning in a particular field over time. Learning journals are valuable during professional or clinical placements and when completing internships as they allow you to document your experiences, your evaluation of those learning opportunities and the way that these moments have informed or modified your later actions. They can also be used to record learning in any class you might be taking, and encourage you not just to record lecture notes but to think about what they mean, how the ideas link to one another and how you have improved your understanding of a topic as the class goes on. Learning diaries are also a place to identify what you know and what you need to know, noting down topics or areas that might need further or additional study.

Learning journals are a chance to be honest with yourself. What have you learned? What is the significance of this learning? What are you struggling with? Why do you think you are struggling? How might you overcome the obstacles in your path? Perhaps you are encountering statistics in college, and your previous performance in mathematics has not been particularly noteworthy. A learning journal will track your progress, indicate areas of improvement and reveal weaknesses that still need to be worked on. In addition, you can list the skills that you have learned and think about ways to maintain or improve these. Document examples of how and when you have successfully employed these skills and also examples where you needed to improve.

Even if you are not expected to submit your learning journal, it can be a valuable experience to keep a record of what you have done over the course of a semester. It will help you to make connections between different classes and to see patterns that might not have been otherwise evident. You can record your own thoughts and feelings about your learning experiences and the ways in which your preconceptions are being challenged, as well as highlight how the knowledge and skills you are gaining might be employed in the work place. A learning journal can be as simple as a word processing document or as elaborate as an online e-portfolio, but whichever form you choose, the key is to make regular entries.

Keeping a learning journal may be required as part of a work placement, and if it is online, then you should establish whether your thoughts are entirely private or whether they are open to the rest of your class or even to the general public. It may be that your supervisor or coordinator dips in and out of your online learning journal to see how you are getting on. You may even be asked to comment on your peers' entries, just as they might comment on yours. In instances where your reflections are visible to others, it is important to remember that this is not a personal diary. It is not an opportunity to vent about your employer, professor or classmates but rather a way of making lucid observations about your learning experience.

ONLINE WRITING

A QUICK WORD ON SOCIAL MEDIA . . .

Before moving forward, it is important to say a quick word about social media, in terms of both private use and also its increasing incorporation into higher and further education. The advent of Web 2.0 technologies revolutionized the way that we communicate with one another. No longer restricted to reading static content on web pages, we are now able to comment on web pages, join discussion forums to post our thoughts, create and publish our own blogs for the world to see, curate our own galleries of images, curiosities or other items of interest and work collaboratively on projects or to build repositories of knowledge. In short, Web 2.0 allows us to connect electronically with people from around the world quickly and easily, and in ways that were inconceivable only a few years ago.

The development of social media tools, such as Facebook and Twitter, has inspired millions of people around the globe to set up pages and to publish their opinions on any issue imaginable, with little regard to where that content ends up or how it is managed. While social media tools have varying degrees of privacy, it is important to understand that not only are you committing your thoughts or photos to the public sphere but you are also delivering them to a corporation who may not have the same regard for your privacy in the future as they appear to now. Your information, thoughts and ideas are stored on private servers around the world, and deleting your content from the internet is very difficult, if not completely impossible. For this reason, you need to be judicious about your online interactions.

A number of high-profile athletes have been caught out, and punished, for inappropriate online comments. Australian swimmer Stephanie Rice lost a lucrative sponsorship deal for making homophobic slurs on Twitter; she had previously been reprimanded for uploading inappropriate images on to her Facebook page; in 2012 Greek triple jumper Voula Papachristou became the first athlete banned from an Olympic Games because of a racist tweet; soccer star Joey Barton was released from his contract with Newcastle United after a public bust-up with the club on Twitter; and scores of student athletes have been suspended for online comments that were thought to violate their respective college's code of conduct.

For those of you working towards a career as a professional athlete or in the sports industry more broadly, it is not too soon to learn how to protect yourself by using social media tools to enhance rather than damage your reputation, particularly as employers and intern supervisors will check out your online persona. Here are a few useful guidelines for online interaction:

- Treat every online interaction as if it is written on a postcard to your grandmother. If you are happy for her to read it, then it is unlikely to be embarrassing in the future.
- Review your privacy settings on a regular basis.
- Do not post when upset, angry or inebriated. Write your gut reaction on a piece of paper and leave it for twenty-four hours. You can always rip up a piece of paper, but you cannot always rescind an online post.
- Think of social media tools as an extension of your 'brand image' and only use them to build, not destroy, that image.

BLOGS

As online interaction becomes further entrenched in many college courses, you may be asked to blog about particular issues. 'Blog' is a contraction of 'web log' and is essentially an online diary. There are a number of excellent sports-related blogs online, such as Edge of Sports (www.edgeofsports.com), One Sport Voice (www.nicolemlavoi.com) and The Science of Running (www.science ofrunning.com), and the way that these reflect on various aspects of sport are useful examples of how blogs can be used in class.

Like a learning journal, a blog provides the opportunity to discuss a particular issue, drawing upon your own opinions and experiences as well as those raised in class or in the literature. Blogs can be used to encourage students to think about topical issues before they are discussed in class, to link theory to real-life examples and to review relevant books or articles. Blogs can also be used to speculate about what a forthcoming field trip or lab might be like, and a follow-up blog might compare your expectations with the reality. As such, there is really no end to the number of ways that blogs might be used in your course.

Although they are designed to communicate your opinion, please note that in the context of higher education, blogs should be *informed* opinions. They are less formal than a research essay, but research should still inform your posts. The basic structure of an introduction, body and conclusion remain, but the discussion and interaction may be less formal. If you are asked to write a blog, spend some time looking at different sports-related blogs online. There are some excellent examples that delve into considered and informed analysis of sport rather than engaging with sport on a superficial level.

Regardless of the topic to be discussed, it is always important to understand the parameters of any blogging assignment. Will you be expected to comment on other students' blogs and will they be expected to comment on yours? Will your blog be private, visible to just your class or entirely public? The answers to these questions might change the kind of information you post. Indeed, a public blog will remain available on servers for a long time, so you should be particularly careful about what and how you post.

WIKIS

One of the most exciting aspects to Web 2.0 technology is the ability to work collaboratively with people all around the world to produce a single piece of work. The best example is, of course, Wikipedia: tens of thousands of people have helped build the single largest online repository of knowledge. Wikis are simply online documents that anyone can edit, and can be set up for open access – as Wikipedia is – or restricted to just a class or small group. They might be publicly accessible or limited to a few viewers only.

Wikis are increasingly used at university to develop resources for your class. You might be asked to contribute to a set of class notes to accompany a lecture, create a glossary of terms or share relevant examples to explicate some key themes of your course. A wiki might be used to collect useful study materials or research that can be shared among your peers. Regardless of how a wiki is used, the key feature is collaboration, and wikis succeed or fail on the input from members.

One of the best uses of wikis is for study groups or a group work project. By having online access to the group, the number of face-to-face meetings can be reduced as each member of the team can contribute to an online brainstorming session, post resources that might be useful for the whole group, upload their contributions and work together to edit a single project document. This reduces the temptation to divide the assignment into sections where each person works on their section independently and one person is left to cut and paste the project together.

Wiki etiquette or Wikiquette

As with all online interactions, there is a specific etiquette when it comes to wikis. Here are a few of the most important considerations when contributing to a collaborative online document:

- Make positive edits that improve the document.
- Do not vandalize other students' contributions.
- Correct errors of fact as well as formatting or presentational errors.
- Do not use the Wiki to make personal attacks.
- Do not take edits to your contribution personally but rather as an opportunity to learn.

If you would like more detail on how to interact in wikis, check the Wikiquette page on Wikipedia. While it specifically focuses on manners within the Wikipedia community, many of the basic principles, such as treating others as you would like to be treated, apply to university-based wikis.

STUDENT VIEWPOINT

I really love working online. It means I'm not tied down to my computer and can just use my phone to check the discussion boards. If we've had a pretty intense discussion in class, it's nice to be able to keep that going rather than having to shut everything down because the hour is up. I guess my best suggestion for online learning is to stay on top of things. It's really easy to think that you can write a blog piece off the top of your head, but it actually takes some thought to come up with an interesting, but educated, take on a topic.—Joshua.

DISCUSSION BOARDS

In many institutions, there is an increasing use of online spaces as a way to encourage student interaction and discussion. This is particularly the case when it comes to e-learning and online courses, where most, if not all, class interaction will be virtual. Discussion boards can also facilitate interaction with your peers for on-campus modules, and might be used to work through ideas collaboratively, to pose questions about topics or issues you do not understand and to share relevant resources. Your lecturer might prompt you with specific topics or you might post questions that you would like addressed. It is an effective way to extend peer discussion beyond the classroom, and most can be easily accessed from your smartphone, laptop or tablet, enabling you to engage at your convenience.

There are several ways that discussion boards can be utilized as part of your class, and each mode requires a different level of input and formality. A discussion board may be set up entirely for the students' use, as a place to chat about course content or other issues. These boards are not normally moderated, or even monitored, and are not typically part of the assessment. Alternatively, your lecturer may post a 'question of the week' or several topics to inspire discussion. These might be related to the material being delivered in lectures or other items of interest. In this case, the board may be monitored, and your lecturer could probe further with follow-up questions. In this scenario you may be encouraged, or even expected, to participate. Finally, you may be required to participate in a discussion board, and your professor will outline how many original contributions you need to make, how many responses to other students' contributions are expected and what level of analysis you should demonstrate in your posts. In all cases, especially when your online interactions are graded, it is important that you understand the criteria against which you will be assessed.

Tips for successful posting

Regardless how discussion boards are employed in your modules, it is up to you to make the most of them. Follow the tips below to communicate effectively in this online environment:

- Read posts carefully so that you understand the perspective or question being presented. Do not shoot off a response in haste. Take time to think about how you can contribute meaningfully to the discussion. Before you press 'send', read the original post and your response again.
- Be polite and courteous and respect other opinions. The golden rule is as important online as in the real world: treat others as you would like to be treated. Offensive language and behaviour is unacceptable. If you are not sure about what you have written, think about whether you would say the same thing to the recipient's face.
- Use simple, grammatically correct language, but please note that tone is not easily translated into written form. You might think you are being sarcastic or ironic, but you might be 'read' as rude and disrespectful.
- Avoid the use of abbreviations, emoticons, slang, txtspk or other informal ways of writing. It is a good idea to get into the habit of writing properly whenever you are in a professional context, such as college. This is particularly important if you are being assessed for your online contributions.
- Keep posts concise and to the point. Nobody likes to read rambling musings, but equally, a single sentence or just a few words are unlikely to convey much useful content. This is not to say you cannot write a lengthy reply if the topic requires some careful thought, but always read your contribution before submitting to ensure it is all relevant to the discussion.
- Help facilitate discussion by asking new questions or inviting comments on your response. If there is a closing time/date for posts, remember that

'discussion' cannot occur in the final minutes. You need to make regular contributions and keep up to date on what others have posted.

- Link to other sources or add an attachment, rather than repeating information that might be interesting but not specific to the topic.
- If you are replying to a specific post, stay on topic. If you have a new idea or want to pose an unrelated question, start a new thread.
- Use clear subject lines so your peers know what the post is about. Obscure descriptions irritate other participants.
- Use evidence where possible to support your statements. This is an intellectual exercise, so do not resort to anecdotal evidence. Opinions should be informed.
- Do not post while under the influence of alcohol or other drugs. You might be checking in on your smartphone at midnight, but leave posting until you are lucid.

Finally, given the transient nature of discussion boards, it is important to keep copies of your comments and posts so that you have a full record of statements that you have made. This gives you some additional resources to use when studying for exams. It might also be useful to keep copies of relevant posts that your peers have made, particularly if these suggest resources for further study. Keeping copies is as simple as taking a screen shot and storing the image electronically. You could crop the image to save just your comment and either save these individually or add them all to a single word processing document. If you are using a note-taking programme, the screenshots could be added to the relevant topic to create a complete record of the issue under consideration.

EXAMPLES OF DISCUSSION BOARD POSTS

You are responsible for coaching a group of athletes, and as part of your nutritional strategy, you ask each one to keep a food diary for a week so that you can assess their nutritional intake. One of the athletes is evasive about submitting her diary and claims to have forgotten it every time you ask her for it. You suspect she might be suffering from an eating disorder. How might you raise your concerns with the athlete and/or her family?

Poor response: 'I'd call a meeting with her parents to let them know she's anorexic and that she has to start eating food. Everyone knows that you need to eat properly to be a good athlete. An exercising body needs fuel!!'

Good response: 'Eating disorders are a very sensitive issue and a situation like this must be handled with delicacy, care and respect. First of all, it is important to determine whether or not your suspicions are justified. In my opinion, not being willing to hand over a food diary alone is not necessarily evidence of an eating disorder. Plenty of athletes might be reticent if they have a poor overall diet. They don't want the coach to know that they are eating rubbish in case he/she uses it as a reason to drop them from the team! But if there is other evidence (e.g. sudden, rapid or dramatic weight loss), then the research would suggest the most appropriate way would be to be sensitive, empathic and non-judgemental when discussing their eating habits. Use "I" statements, rather than "you" statements, e.g. "I've noticed you've lost a lot of weight lately" or "I've noticed you always seem to skip breakfast and lunch". Be prepared for a hostile response. People with eating disorders have developed good systems at keeping their behaviours secret, and are not always receptive to people "interfering". A coach would be responsible for expressing their concerns to the athlete's parents/ guardians and recommending medical assistance. However, it's also important for coaches to be aware of their limitations when they are stepping outside the area of their expertise and not to hesitate to call in expert assistance where needed.'

ASSESSING ONLINE CONTRIBUTIONS

If your contributions to wikis and discussion boards are assessed, then your professor is likely to have a criteria-based marking sheet or rubric so that you understand clearly what is expected of you. You might be assessed on:

- the number of useful original contributions and responses you make;
- the quality of your posts in terms of content, analysis and synthesis;
- your role in sustaining the discussion or contributing to the content;
- the mechanics of your posts, including a professional presentation, good use of language and no emoticons, hyperbole or excessive punctuation (!!!!!).

SUMMARY

1 A number of non-traditional writing formats are used in higher education, including reflective journals that allow students to consider the impact of course content on their personal and professional development. Reflections can also be used to identify strengths and weaknesses in various subject areas, and to integrate experience with theory.

2 Web 2.0 technologies have revolutionized e-learning by enabling students to interact and collaborate with one another through blogs, wikis, social media and online work spaces. Although the mode of communication may be less formal, the content should still be informed and based on evidence.

3 There are particular procedures and etiquette that apply in online forums and collaborative digital spaces, including wikis and discussion boards. Students should be aware of both their lecturer's expectations and the conventions for online communication.

EXERCISES

1 Write a reflective piece of around 500 words on a recent sports-related experience using the Gibbs' (1988) Reflective Cycle as a guide.
2 Start a reflective journal to think about your learning at university. Try to write entries at least weekly, and reflect upon lecture content, its practical application in labs, your response to the ideas and areas that you might like to follow up for more information.
3 Set up a blog to communicate some of your thoughts about the classes you are taking. Invite other members of the class to read and comment on your entries.
4 Register as a contributor to Wikipedia and edit some pages based on research you have done. Engage in the 'talk' behind the scenes to discuss your contributions.

REFLECTION

Reflect on your experiences (or expectations) of reflection. What contribution do you think it will make to your learning? How might you integrate it into a weekly study session? Is a reflection something you might be able to do within a study group or is it only a personal activity? Think about how you might utilize social media as a tool to enhance your learning. Would a closed Facebook group be useful as an online space to discuss ideas and share problems with your study group or would it become too social?

FURTHER READING

Moon, A.J. (2005) *Reflection in learning and professional development*. Abingdon: Routledge Falmer.

Watkins, R. and Corry, M. (2011) *E-learning companion: a student's guide to online success*. Boston MA: Wadsworth.

10

COLLABORATIVE LEARNING

Working as a team

OVERVIEW

This chapter outlines:
- the value of working collaboratively in groups;
- strategies for working together effectively;
- how to identify constructive and disruptive behaviours within teams;
- troubleshooting techniques to keep the group on track.

INTRODUCTION

It would not be out of place to expect that group work within sports studies courses would be readily embraced by students who, for the most part, have an interest, if not a future career planned, in sport, where teamwork is fundamentally required for success. Athletes, coaches, medical staff, trainers and other support personnel all work together with the gold medal, world championship, league cup or other ultimate achievement in mind. Though the stakes may not be so high in the classroom, the ability to work as part of a team is a critical skill to learn and one desired by employers.

Yet nothing inspires as much fear, trepidation or outright hatred as group work, particularly when the outcome is a collaboratively produced assignment. Dedicated students may resent having to carry 'freeloaders', whereas weaker students may be intimidated when asked to work with more accomplished peers. Extroverted students may feel that introverted students are making no audible contribution, while shy students might feel their voice is lost among more dominant classmates. In almost all cases, students resent having their grades influenced by others. Nevertheless, group work remains a standard assessment practice in many university curricula, so this chapter is written with a view to helping you navigate both traditional and innovative group work formats. The chapter begins by reviewing the benefits of collaborative learning, and then explains how to establish and maintain groups, assign specific roles, and set goals, milestones and agenda, before discussing strategies for when it all goes wrong.

WHY WORK IN GROUPS?

Within higher education, group work is a valuable way to learn and practise the collaborative processes that you will experience within the workplace regardless of the field you go into. By collaborating with your peers, you learn how to work towards a common goal, improve your communication and negotiation strategies, develop your interpersonal skills and produce a much stronger piece of work. Group work allows you to identify your own strengths and weaknesses within a team environment, and encourages the development of personal skills such as time management, the ability to prioritize tasks and meet deadlines. It also allows you to understand your accountability to a team, which will be applicable to other assessments as well as industry. Finally, collaboration means that you can be part of much more complex tasks than you would be if you worked independently, and lets students bring a wealth of diverse perspectives, opinions, knowledge and experience to enhance the overall learning outcomes.

In many respects, the *process* of working collaboratively is as important as, if not more important than, the final product, and keeping that in mind will ensure a more positive group work experience. Your attitude towards group projects will have a significant impact on your overall experience, so be open to the idea of working together and you will reap the rewards of collaborative learning.

DIFFERENT TYPES OF GROUP WORK

Although we typically think of a group project when it comes to group work, there are a number of ways that you might be asked to work together at college. Some of these will have written papers or oral presentations as part of the assessment process, but in other instances group work might be used informally to encourage discussion, debate and the sharing of ideas. It is a powerful way to ensure you understand course content, can articulate your understanding and can argue a particular position, so you may be asked to participate in some or all of the following during your time at university:

- *Informal groups*: During a lecture, seminar or tutorial you may be asked to divide into small ad hoc groups to discuss a particular point raised in the class. The time allocated for these discussions is usually only a few minutes, so you need to focus on the task at hand.

- *Group projects*: The final outcome of a group project might be to produce a report where each member has made a contribution to the research and the writing of the final paper. Group reports are often accompanied by a presentation of the report during which some or all of the group members have to speak and answer questions.
- *Presentations*: You may have only to do a group presentation rather than produce a final written paper. It is more likely that every member of the group has to speak and answer questions if there is no report to accompany the presentation.
- *Debates*: Groups might be formed to debate a particular position. An informal debate might take place within a class, whereas you might be given a few days or weeks to prepare for a more formal debate.
- *Guided discussions*: In a class, tutorial or seminar, you may be asked to work in small groups, either ad hoc or within the same group throughout the semester, to discuss course content, relevant readings, other material or to work through specific questions. Although you work in small groups, you may be required to write up the results of the discussion individually.
- *Online discussion groups*: The various types of online collaborations, such as blogs, wikis or discussion boards may be used to facilitate interaction outside the classroom. See Chapter 9 for more detail.
- *Study groups*: These are normally informal groups of students who meet to discuss course content, supplementary readings, assessment (including individual assessments) and other related material to help each other to learn and succeed. The structures in this kind of group might be more flexible than for project groups.

Despite the range of group tasks, this chapter focuses on group projects, though many of the principles and techniques will be applicable for any formal or informal collaboration.

SELECTING GROUPS

Deciding who should be included in a group is a strategic decision. In some instances, the decision is out of your hands and you are allocated to groups by the lecturer, whereas in others students will be encouraged to form their own groups. Lecturers may build groups based on the students' skill sets or different personalities. They might want to ensure that there is at least one academically strong student in each group; they might choose to break up students who always work together to give them the experience of working with others; or they might want to ensure that a range of different experiences and perspectives are represented in each group. Every way of forming groups has advantages and disadvantages, but regardless of how your group is created, knowing how to respond will make the group work process more effective.

Students tend to prefer choosing their own groups; however, this can be fraught. Many will gravitate towards their friends, which makes it difficult for students who do not know anyone else in the class. If a few students are absent that day, then they might be overlooked during the group selection process. A fundamental trap that many fall into when creating their own teams is not adequately considering the skills and experiences that each individual brings with them. It might be easier initially to work with people you know and like, but it can also be much harder to pull friends into line if they are not contributing or if their work is sub-standard. Not dealing with issues as they arise can breed resentment and, in some cases, even lead to the end of the friendship. When forming your own group, think about the skills you need and what each member might be able to contribute. Do you have a natural leader or someone who will be able to set the agenda? Do you have someone with good written skills? Is there a member who excels in research and can help with finding good sources? Will one of the members be able to monitor the group's activities and keep everyone on track? Familiarize yourself with the various roles within groups and be certain that you utilize your members effectively.

CONSOLIDATING GROUPS

GETTING TO KNOW EACH OTHER

Creating a team out of a group of individuals does not happen automatically and requires effort to ensure that the group develops a sense of cohesion. If you are working on a larger project, you will need regular meetings, so it is important to spend time during the first session learning a bit about each other, particularly if you have been assigned to groups and do not know each other well.

At the first meeting, swap contact details, look at your schedules and determine meeting times that will work for everyone. Face-to-face meetings might suit, or you might prefer to have meetings primarily in a virtual meeting space. Establish how often you will meet. Weekly? More/less often? Once you have worked through the organizational logistics, the next step is to establish clear expectations for the group and to confirm that you all understand the assessment task. Think about the overall group and project goals and agree on some larger milestones to ensure that you have a realistic picture of what can be achieved in the timeframe.

The final task in your first session will be to allocate roles to each group member based on their individual strengths. Determine what each member's prior experience in group work has been and ask each member to specify the contributions that they can make to the project. Individual members should identify their strengths and weaknesses, using an online survey tool if they are not sure where their talents lie. Allow each person to nominate two or three roles that they would be most suited to, and establish what each role will require. In some classes, the professor might allocate specific roles to individual students, so make sure you are familiar with each one and how they work together to create an effective team.

ROLES WITHIN GROUPS

Whereas groups should aspire to a sense of cohesion, it is also important to recognize that it is a coming together of individuals who each have their own talents and skills, experiences and knowledge. Like sports teams, everyone's contribution is responsible for achieving the final result. Each member of the team needs to be utilized in the most effective way and should occupy the position that best suits their skills. Some students will have natural leadership tendencies; others will prefer to focus on monitoring milestones; and others still are happy to do whatever grunt work is necessary but are more reticent about setting the agenda. Utilizing each student's strengths creates an overall stronger group, whereas shoehorning people into roles that they do not feel comfortable with may breed resentment, disinterest and outright dissent. A quarterback is not going to be successful – or even happy – playing linebacker.

Roles do not have to be fixed throughout the entire project and may fluctuate as the group develops or as a result of a deliberate team decision. Each position can be rotated to ensure everyone has an opportunity to lead, timekeep or try out another role that interests them or will extend their skill set. For example, you may agree from the start that the leadership position rotates each week, or you may decide that all roles will be reviewed at the halfway point. There could also just be a natural shift where one member's role changes as they take on different responsibilities. Although flexibility can be built into the process as one of the ground rules, too much flexibility can be destabilizing.

Roles can be divided into three main categories: *task* roles, *maintenance* roles and *disruptive* roles. Task roles are those that help progress the project, including activities such as developing ideas, researching and writing. It would be expected that all members of the group have some responsibility for a task role. Maintenance roles are those that contribute to the smooth running of the group and may include activities such as timekeeping, recording, encouraging and compromising. Disruptive or 'self-centred' roles are those behaviours that detract from the conduct of the project or the cohesion of the group by focusing on individual rather than group needs. These include members who make personal attacks, dominate the conversation, miss meetings on a regular basis, whisper and giggle during meetings or are overly critical without offering alternatives.

Table 10.1 summarizes a number of key roles that are needed for successful group work. There are a number of online tools that can help you determine the kind of team member you are and which of these roles would suit you best.

DESCRIPTION OF GROUP ROLES

The coach: the leader

The coach is responsible for the overall running of the team and for ensuring that the work needed to complete the assessment is effectively organized and delegated to the group members. To this end, the coach sets the agenda and chairs meetings. They are also responsible for: establishing and maintaining a

Table 10.1 Overview of group roles, responsibilities and personality traits

Role	Also known as . . .	Key responsibilities	Individual suitability
Coach	Leader	Responsible for the overall running of the team. They set the agenda, chair the meetings, ensure the strategy is worked out, and keep the group focused on the groups' goals and the final outcome.	Suits someone with an outgoing personality and natural leadership tendencies.
Captain	Summarizer/ Clarifier	Responsible for both clarifying the team strategy for the entire group as well as summarizing the group's discussion and decisions. This role also mediates between the leader and the rest of the team, providing support by explaining the leader's decisions and elaborating on the team's ideas and suggestions.	Suits someone who is more detail oriented and who can both expand upon and summarize quickly.
Vice-Captain/ Deputy	Encourager/ Compromiser	Responsible for encouraging the team as motivation or enthusiasm starts to wane. Ensures the team remains harmonious by mediating between conflicting members and ensuring the group's goals remain at the forefront.	Suits someone with an empathic personality who can identify and resolve conflicts, provide encouragement and support.
Playmaker	Ideas person	Responsible for coming up with key ideas to move the project forward. Seeks solutions to challenges.	Suits someone who is creative and energetic. Needs to be able to problem-solve.
Senior player	Evaluator	Responsible for keeping the group from making rash decisions. Asks questions, seeks alternative perspectives and encourages the team to think through decisions carefully before committing to a course of action.	Suits someone who can think critically 'outside the box', offer alternative suggestions and inspire debate.
Scorer/ Timekeeper	Recorder/ Timekeeper	Responsible for keeping members focused on the group's goals. Monitors timelines, reminds members of due dates as well as recording minutes of meetings, decisions and action plans.	Suits someone who is well organized and pays attention to detail. Needs to be a good communicator.

positive atmosphere by making sure everyone is included and is on board with the task; ensuring everyone has a chance to speak; and encouraging discussion. The coach needs to identify individual skills and employ these to the team's advantage and delegate tasks to those who are best suited to executing them. As team members report back to the coach, he or she needs to keep an overview of the project. The coach should be careful not to dominate or drive their opinion through, although, at times, the leader does need to make the final decision. Finally, the coach is responsible for ensuring that the group has the resources it needs to complete the task.

A coach might say:

- I think what the task is really asking us to do is . . .
- Matthew and Lola said they always get great feedback about their researching skills, so I think they should take the lead in gathering the resources we will need.
- Let's brainstorm the key ideas for the project and then select the direction we want to take.
- Everyone's had a chance to speak, except for James. James, what do you think about the structure of the presentation?

The captain: the summarizer/clarifier

The captain's role is twofold: they act as a conduit of information from the top down and from the bottom up. The captain represents and explains in more detail the coach's strategy to the team, but is also responsible for elaborating on team members' ideas and ensuring that the coach understands their suggestions. They also link ideas together. The captain seeks to establish clarity among the team and steps in when the discussion starts to lose focus or is becoming confused.

A captain might say:

- What I think Anna is really saying is . . .
- Ruth, that's a great point. Can you elaborate a little more on it?
- That's a really useful suggestion that relates back to what Robert was saying earlier.
- I think we're talking at cross-purposes here. Let's just establish what we've agreed so far before moving the discussion forward.

The deputy/vice-captain: the encourager/compromiser

The deputy tries to maintain an overall positive atmosphere by encouraging the team as a whole as well as individuals. As the project progresses, the initial enthusiasm might wane and group members may start to lose interest, at which point the deputy will try to motivate the team. They will listen to each team member's ideas, and where there is conflict over a course of action, suggest compromises that satisfy all parties. The deputy needs to be diplomatic and intuitive to try to defuse conflict while ensuring everyone's contribution is valued.

The deputy might say:

- I think that you both have a valid point. Perhaps the way forward might be to . . .
- Come on, guys, we're nearly finished. Let's just work on getting the final draft finished.
- We're really making some good progress at this meeting. But maybe we need a short break to regroup.
- That idea certainly has merit, Peter, but let's explore Mia's suggestion first.

The playmaker: the ideas person

The playmaker likes to jump in and get the task started, sometimes even before the basic formalities have been completed. They maintain momentum by suggesting ideas, approaches and sources of information as well as solutions to challenges and conflicts. They are creative thinkers who like to brainstorm the big picture and come up with many different suggestions, not all of which will necessarily be useful. A playmaker does not usually take offence when ideas are discarded and is happy to leave the final decision to others on the team who might spend more time developing their initial suggestions.

A playmaker might say:

- What about this idea? Or this one?
- Here are three ways we could approach this topic.
- Quick! Someone write down these suggestions.
- That doesn't work? OK, then, what about . . . ?

Senior player: the evaluator

The senior players on any team are the voice of experience and reason. They have seen it all and know the pitfalls. Whereas the rookies might be eager to rush into quick decisions, the senior player tries to slow down the pace of the discussion until they are convinced that a decision has been carefully considered. These are the analysts of the team and are able to examine different ideas and perspectives before drawing their conclusions about the most viable steps to take. They are not afraid of suggesting alternative courses of action based on their experience or knowledge.

A senior player on the team might say:

- Let's not rush into a decision.
- I think we could think about this in another way.
- Does anyone else have a suggestion about how to proceed?
- We tried that in the past and it didn't work. How about we try. . .?

The scorer/timekeeper: the recorder/timekeeper

This is an important organizational role that keeps the whole team in check. The scorer/timekeeper is responsible for recording and circulating the minutes of meetings, keeping meetings on schedule, drawing up and circulating action plans, monitoring team goals and milestones, sending reminders to individual team members when due dates are approaching, and ensuring the overall smooth administration of the team.

The scorer/timekeeper might say:

- We only have ten minutes before the end of the meeting, so we need to start making a decision.
- Helen, your report is due at the next meeting. Can you circulate it to the team by Friday?
- A reminder that the actions from the last meeting will need to be completed by Monday in time for Tuesday's meeting.
- At the last meeting, we didn't finish all the key agenda items. We'll need to start with those today.

CASE STUDY

Ellen is a member of a group with her three best friends. They all share an apartment together, so figured that it would be easiest to work with each other when it came to group work. They decided not to allocate specific roles because it is only the four of them, they are completely open and honest with one another, and they see each other all the time, so they felt that assuming rigid roles was excessive for their situation. The project begins very well, and instead of organized group meetings, they just catch up with each other at home.

→ What advantages and/or challenges are associated with this group's approach to working together?

After a few weeks, Ellen starts to notice that two of the girls tend to socialize a lot in the evening when the other two are working on the project. She wants to check in with them to see how much they have completed, but each time she tries to raise the issue, the girls roll their eyes and tell her they are working on it and to stop being so bossy. She knows she is not the leader, but she feels as though someone has to take charge.

→ What would you suggest Ellen does at this point?

→ Do you think group roles can be allocated once a project is underway?

ESTABLISHING GROUND RULES

Working together in groups is most effective when there is a degree of structure in place, and establishing ground rules confirms the expectations that the group has for its operation. Without an agreed structure, each member is more likely to do their own thing and there is no accountability for poor performance. Ground rules are a record of the values by which your team will operate, offering guidance on how you will communicate, meeting format and frequency, the kinds of behaviours that are appropriate or acceptable, and the overall expectations you each have for working together. In fact, you can include anything that your team feels is important to clarify from the outset. A good set of ground rules will help avoid conflict by developing a positive atmosphere and an open and honest dialogue about each member's expectations.

Spend some time discussing what each member expects from the group, what they feel contributes to a stronger team and the behaviours they consider unacceptable. Start off with some general themes, using your prior experiences with group work as inspiration, but as you discuss these in more detail, try to become more specific. Vague rules are open to more interpretation, and this is one area where everyone should be on the same page. Build in penalties for breaking the rules. This might be as simple as having to buy everyone a coffee if you arrive late or working on some of the less exciting parts of the project.

Some of the ground rules might be based upon the following themes:

* treating each other with respect at all times;
* attending meetings prepared and on time;
* engaging in, not derailing, discussions and meetings;
* being inclusive;
* responding to emails in a timely manner;
* offering *constructive* criticism and, where possible, suggestions to improve;
* taking personal responsibility for your contribution;
* regarding group deadlines as non-negotiable.

Regardless of the rules your group decides upon, writing them down and having each member sign their name ensures everyone is aware of the basic expectations for the team.

RUNNING EFFECTIVE MEETINGS

Students today are spoiled for choice when it comes to communication. With smartphones, laptops and tablets, there is little excuse for not staying in touch with your teammates, even when on the go. Online or virtual meeting spaces are becoming more popular, particularly for students who have conflicting schedules or extra-curricular responsibilities such as part-time employment, coaching or sports practice to work around. There are a number of free online sites that allow you to set up a group, create, store and edit documents, schedule and hold meetings, establish to-do lists and communicate with one another.

Many of these sites also work on mobile or cellular devices, which means you can check in with the group and upload your contributions even if you are not tethered to your desktop.

Although these technologies create additional opportunities to interact, face-to-face meetings should never be completely abandoned. Tone, intonation, facial expressions and body language can be lacking in virtual spaces, so it is easy to take offence or misunderstand intent. Try to schedule regular face-to-face meetings, particularly for brainstorming sessions or other times when you need to discuss some of the big picture or conceptual ideas that underpin the project. Virtual meetings are useful for updates or reports or keeping others informed of your progress.

Conducting an effective meeting

Regardless of the type of meeting you hold, there are ways to ensure they run smoothly and lead to useful outcomes. It is usually only when you attend a poorly managed meeting that you realize how effective well-organized meetings can be. Like the group overall, meetings need to have some structure and formality to ensure that the right decisions are being taken and action items are created. Running a meeting efficiently requires good preparation, execution and follow-up, including setting a clear and achievable agenda, keeping to the schedule, being inclusive, recording key decisions, allocating actions to individual team members, circulating these to the group in a timely manner and following up prior to the next meeting. The following outlines in more detail some of the key components of the meeting process:

Agenda

The coach organizes the agenda and chairs the meeting. In conjunction with the scorer/timekeeper, they will determine what needs to be included on the agenda and how much time should be allocated to each item. The agenda should be circulated to the group in advance so that everyone is informed about the purpose of the meeting and whether or not they will be expected to report on their progress. In the workplace, you would receive an agenda usually around a week ahead of the meeting, but in the context of a university project, a day or two is probably sufficient.

A typical agenda would include the following items:

- time/date of the meeting;
- apologies;
- outstanding issues from the last meeting;
- discussion points;
- reports;
- other business;
- evaluation;
- date for next meeting(s).

Timekeeping

The scorer/timekeeper is responsible for keeping the meeting on track and ensuring that a discussion of any one point does not go on so long that the rest of the agenda cannot be covered. Build in a few minutes for everyone to settle into the meeting and catch up with each other.

Minutes

The scorer/timekeeper should keep an accurate record of the meeting, noting down in particular important discussion points, the main decisions and actions. The minutes should be circulated to the rest of the group promptly so that everyone knows what has been decided and what they are expected to do before the next meeting. If you are using an online meeting space, then the minutes can be posted so that everyone has easy access to them. The minutes reflect the agenda and include more detail (see Figure 10.1).

Actions

Sometimes the actions listed in the minutes can be overlooked, so it is a good idea to compile a separate list of actions and circulate it to all members. Include a 'finish by' date that is linked into your schedule of meetings. See Figure 10.2 for an example.

Evaluation

Leave time for a quick evaluation of the meeting and the group's performance so far. If you have peer assessment of performance built into your assessment, then noting down how valuable each member's contribution has been and recording any poor behaviours will help you when coming to a final decision about your teammates' performance on the task. An evaluation can be a simple table as per Figure 10.3.

If any member rates any aspect below the level expected, have a quick discussion about what can be done to improve for the next meeting. This might mean reassigning a role or reminding individual members to show a greater commitment.

STARTING THE PROJECT

Once the logistics have been settled, it is time to start the project. Start by asking each member to outline what they think the main objectives of the assessment are and come to a consensus about the project's central focus. Make sure you have a clear understanding of the requirements and what the final outcome should be. If you are not sure at this point, then you should seek clarification from your professor. It is better to ask for assistance in the developmental stage than after you have already committed to a flawed approach.

The next step is to develop ideas about the content of the project, and there are several methods you can use to get the discussion started. Brainstorming is a popular method to inspire creative thinking and works by encouraging

DATE/TIME MEETING STARTED
- THE NAMES OF THOSE PRESENT
- APOLOGIES FROM MEMBERS WHO COULD NOT ATTEND
- ANY ITEMS ARISING FROM THE PREVIOUS MEETING
  - POINT 1
    - RAISED BY
    - DECISION
  - POINT 2
    - RAISED BY
    - DECISION
- DISCUSSION 1
  - DECISION
  - ACTION
- DISCUSSION 2
  - DECISION
  - ACTION
- REPORT 1
  - PRESENTED BY
  - ACTIONS
- REPORT 2
  - PRESENTED BY
  - ACTIONS
- EVALUATION
- NEXT MEETINGS
- TIME MEETING CLOSED:

Figure 10.1 Format of minutes of team meetings

ACTION	PERSON RESPONSIBLE	FINISH BY
ROOM BOOKINGS @ #80P.N.	CONOR	5 OCTOBER
SEATING QUOTES	FIONA	10 OCTOBER
CONFIRM CATERING	CRAIG	5 OCTOBER
QUOTE FOR DRINKS	CRAIG	8 OCTOBER
FOLLOW UP WITH TV STATION	SARAH	10 OCTOBER
QUOTE FOR HIRE OF PHOTOGRAPHER/ VIDEOGRAPHER OR EQUIPMENT	JOHN	8 OCTOBER

Figure 10.2 Sample list of actions following team meeting

	EXCEEDED THE LEVEL EXPECTED	AT THE LEVEL EXPECTED	BELOW THE LEVEL EXPECTED
TEAM ORGANISATION		X	
AGENDA		X	
TIME-KEEPING		X	
CRAIG	X		
JOHN		X	
FIONA	X		
CONOR	X		
SARAH			X

Figure 10.3 Example of a meeting/peer assessment

everyone to make suggestions and to build upon each others' ideas. While some suggest that there should be no criticism during the initial ideas stage so that the group's imagination is not curtailed, the most effective brainstorming sessions are actually those where rough ideas are debated, added to, subtracted from, analysed and critiqued by the group to gradually polish them into workable solutions.

An effective alternative to brainstorming is to allow group members to develop ideas by themselves before sharing and discussing their suggestions. This can be included as part of a meeting, where the team is given time and space to individually note down relevant ideas, important issues or potential challenges. When the group re-forms, ideas are presented in turn and each one is written on the board for consideration. Team members can evaluate ideas collectively or individually by casting a secret ballot in favour of their preferred options. The votes are used to determine the group's general position, which may provoke further discussion to refine the ideas or approach. With the initial focus on logistics and team roles, there is often insufficient time during the first meeting for the team to generate ideas, so this could be set as the first 'homework' task, with members bringing their suggestions to the second meeting for discussion.

GOAL SETTING AND ASSIGNING TASKS

Athletes are very used to setting goals to guide their training and focus on important competitions. Short-, medium- and long-term goals keep them focused and motivated, but achieving small objectives along the way also reminds an athlete that they are on track to their final target. It is no different when working in groups on a college assignment. Setting goals in this context keeps the team focused on the tasks necessary to achieve the final outcome and establishes milestones from the outset to keep the project moving forward.

As a group, you will determine short-, medium- and long-term goals. Break the project down into smaller, measurable tasks that can be prioritized and assimilated into an overall time management plan. In some cases, the level of priority will be clear – research will need to come before writing, for example; in others, however, you may need to negotiate the relative importance of each component. Goals need to be specific and measurable, but flexible enough to take into consideration unforeseen events or unexpected circumstances. Determine the start and end point for each task. Perhaps your group wants short-term objectives met on a weekly basis, whereas other groups might expect tasks to be completed by the next meeting. An online 'to do' list not only tracks individual tasks but also keeps everyone apprised of the team's progress, and seeing items checked off can bolster flagging enthusiasm.

As useful as short-term goals can be, you must always keep the big picture in mind. A project Gantt chart graphically displays all tasks in relation to one another along a timeline, and should be reviewed weekly to ensure the entire project is progressing as planned. Establish some larger milestones, perhaps at the halfway point and a week before the submission date, to allow the group to review the overall project rather than only focusing on compartmentalized achievements. The scorer/timekeeper is responsible for monitoring the short-, medium- and long-term goals and for sending out reminders when due dates are approaching.

Tasks should be allocated to specific members; otherwise they may either slip between the cracks, as everyone assumes someone else is taking care of them, or the workload is doubled, as several members take the initiative to work on the same item. Consider using sub-teams of two people to work together on tasks. Not only does this retain the benefits of collaboration but there is also a back-up in the case of unforeseen difficulties. Allowing team members or sub-teams to nominate their preferred assignments ensures that they will take ownership of their contribution. Even though members will be responsible for different components of the project, it is important to remember that everyone is ultimately accountable for the entire project. This tends to be the time when the group disperses, with everyone working by themselves with the expectation that someone will simply bring the sections together in a final draft. Although some aspects can be worked on individually, the main analysis or conceptual work needs to be done as a team, so you need to ensure that you set aside time to discuss the results of your initial work rather than assume that all the pieces will somehow just fit together.

WORKING AS A TEAM

Part of the reason for assigning group projects is to develop your ability to work collaboratively, a skill much sought after by employers. Working together involves good interpersonal skills, strong communication skills as well as the ability to listen and compromise. In a group environment, it is unlikely that every member will agree with each other all the time, and learning how to create a positive environment where conflict is well managed is one of the skills you should hone through this process.

Good communication is critical for successful teamwork; conversely, the most common problems arise as a result of poor communication. Disagreements can and will occur in any team, but the manner in which the disagreement is conveyed will be the difference between a solution and a fight. Communication at its most basic requires a speaker and a listener, and each one plays an important part in the process. Effective communicators have mastered the following skills:

- *Active listening*: It is frustrating when you have carefully explained a point and the other person just replies without regard to what you said. Did they even listen? Do they know what you said? Or are they just ignoring your contribution? Active listening takes more effort than simply hearing sounds or thinking about what you are going to say; active listening means you take in what the other person has said, you respond by repeating back the salient points or summarizing their ideas. Once they feel as though their point has been heard, they will be more receptive to receiving your critique, alternative or opinion.

- *Asking questions*: Good communicators indicate that they have understood your point by following up with a question or two. This demonstrates they have listened to you and processed your ideas before probing a little further to encourage you to add to your idea or clarify a point.

- *Letting teammates speak*: You will have been in the situation where you are trying to explain your perspective and someone else jumps in and tries to finish your sentence for you or change the essence of what you are saying or even just starts talking about their ideas. We all want to have our ideas heard, so extend the same courtesy to your teammates and allow everyone the chance to speak and the opportunity to finish.

- *Being assertive*: Being assertive is not the same as being aggressive. Being assertive simply means ensuring your voice is heard and that you communicate your points rather than simply going along with the rest of the group. It can be easy just to agree with everyone else, but you may have some strong, valid points to raise, so make sure your ideas are noted.

- *Being respectful*: Common courtesy and manners go a long way when working in a group, and the golden rule of doing unto others as you would have them do unto you is never more apt than in this situation. Show respect and you will be respected.

- *Body language*: Try not to turn your back on group members when speaking or avoid looking at them when they have the floor. You might not be intending offence, but they might read your body language differently.
- *Compromise*: You cannot always be right, you cannot always get your own way, and not everything has to be done according to your expectations. You need to know when to stand firm and when to compromise. If you feel strongly about a particular issue, make sure the rest of the team understands your perspective, but recognize that the team has the right to choose another option.

COLLABORATIVE WRITING

One of the mistakes that students make when it comes to writing up a group project is to divide the project into sections for individuals to work on, with perhaps one person left to pull it all together and create a seamless, coherent piece of work at the end. Although it might be the common modus operandi, it is unfortunately not the most successful approach. Unless you have spent a lot of time working out precisely what content is included in which section, you run the risk of repeating material or, worse still, leaving out critical ideas. Furthermore, if everyone is given the same deadline, it will not be possible for any real analysis of the data to occur. A better strategy will be for the group to impose staggered deadlines. The literature review needs to be written first, as this will inform the data collection. The data need to be collected and collated before the analysis can take place. If each group member takes responsibility for one section, they should write up their material with a list of ideas, tips and suggestions for the team member whose own section depends on their initial contribution.

The alternative is to try to write collaboratively, where everyone has a stake in each section of the report. At the very least, you should try to write the introduction, conclusion and recommendations (if applicable) together as these are the sections that require a good overview of the entire piece of work. It is difficult for one person to write these effectively without input from other team members. If you like to work together in person, schedule a writing afternoon, where you bring drafts of what you have already done, suggestions and ideas, and work together as a group to improve each section. If you prefer to work in a digital environment, online collaborative tools offer excellent opportunities to work on documents collectively. An initial list of inclusions could be developed, with each member contributing to and editing the document. One person can take the lead on each section to give it a final polish, but every member of the group should take an interest in the content and make contributions. Finally, it is critical that every team member goes through the final draft and makes comments and edits. It is a group project after all. You are not usually assessed on your individual contribution, so your responsibility does not end with writing a single section.

ASSESSMENT

A significant reason why students avoid group work if possible is their trepidation that other members of the class may have an impact on their grades. This is not an insignificant concern, and depending on how well the group works together, a high achiever might find they receive a lower grade than they might be used to. There are several ways that professors try to mitigate the impact of group work on final grades, including awarding grades for the process of group work rather than the final product; asking students to complete peer assessment forms; and allowing students to award marks based on contribution as well as final product.

- *Divided grade*: In this scheme, a grade is allocated for the final product – which each team member receives – and for the group process – which is negotiated for each student. The project itself might receive 14/20, which each member of the group receives. A further 10 marks might be available to recognize individual contribution to the project: either the students assign a mark to every other student in the group or the group sits together and negotiates the mark each student receives based on input. The two grades are added together to arrive at the final mark for each student.
- *Differential allocation of marks*: This process combines a professor's grade with a negotiated peer assessment. If the final project is awarded 7/10 and there are five members in the team, then 7 is multiplied by 5 to give a final result of 35. The group essentially has 35 marks to divide up among the five members. The group negotiates the allocation of marks – those who have made the strongest contribution might receive 8 marks each, those who have made a smaller contribution might receive 6 marks each. Regardless of how the marks are divided up, the process is collaborative and negotiated.
- *Team/peer/self-assessment*: In this process, group members privately evaluate the performance of the team as a whole, the other members of the group and sometimes themselves according to specified criteria. The marker takes the peer evaluation into consideration along with the quality of the final product when awarding a final result to individual students.
- *Individual journal*: Like the divided grade, the final product receives a mark that each group member receives. At the same time, students submit for individual grading their reflective journal of their contributions and progress through the project. The two marks are added together for a final result.

If your lecturer does not offer any of these, perhaps ask whether it might be possible to put in a system for differentiating grades, but do not be surprised if they suggest that group projects in the 'real world' do not usually recognize individual contribution or reward team members differentially.

WORKING IN VIRTUAL GROUPS

If you are studying via distance education, you might be expected to work in groups with people you have not yet met and may never meet in person. Although many of the above suggestions apply, such as establishing ground rules, organizing a meeting schedule and recognizing roles, there are also some additional considerations you need to have when working in online or virtual groups.

Good communication is critical for successful virtual interactions. Being available for one-on-one chats and group meetings or to respond to queries is fundamental for successful online group work. This means staying in regular contact and checking in at least daily to discussion boards or virtual meeting spaces to see if there are any new queries, ideas or documents for you to consider. Make good use of your smartphone or tablet, and check discussion boards when you have a few free minutes here and there.

Online conversations can move quickly, particularly when people are 'chatting' to each other one-on-one, so make sure you schedule regular virtual meetings to make group decisions and to inform everyone of the ideas and suggestions that have emerged from individual conversations. It is important that actual decisions are made only during group meetings; otherwise team members will increasingly act independently and there will be little oversight. Having a set time each week that the group communicates together online provides structure to the group's operations and also allows members to touch base, which is particularly important when working in cyber-groups. Online conference calls may work well for these group sessions.

It is important to note that online forums are notoriously difficult spaces in which to communicate effectively. A misplaced comma, an omitted word or a brief reply can lead to team members feeling attacked, and without the benefit of facial expressions or body language, a joke or sarcastic comment is more likely to be misinterpreted. Though not deliberate, these seemingly trivial incidents can destabilize the team as group members may feel more defensive and escalate a perceived conflict. Recognizing the limitations of online com-munication means you can employ strategies to keep interactions clear and professional.

First, you should ensure that your group knows that you are engaging with them. Reply to comments posted online, ask follow-up questions, respond to chat requests and otherwise make yourself available. You do not, of course, have to be in contact every minute of the day, but you should check in at least daily and make your presence known. The other members will not know that you are giving their ideas careful consideration if you simply read a post and then log off. Acknowledge your peers' ideas online, even if it is just to say that you need some time to think about them.

Second, be aware that written criticism always comes across more harshly, so try to provide meaningful feedback gently. Summarize your teammate's key ideas first before stating your critique or alternative suggestions. This means that they understand their ideas have been taken on board rather than overlooked or ignored and that your response has taken their ideas into consideration. When receiving feedback, try not to take comments personally. While using emoticons is not usually good practice in a professional context, during online communications a strategically placed smile or wink may diffuse some of the tension that accompanies critique. Finally, avoid writing sarcastic retorts or trying to make jokes, particularly at another team member's expense. These rarely translate well in an online environment and could not only be an unintended cause of group tension and discontent but also reflect poorly on your professionalism.

WHEN IT ALL GOES WRONG

Despite best intentions and using the above systems and suggestions, sometimes teams simply do not work. Students are used to working in a competitive environment, and collaboration is not easy for everyone. Furthermore, conflicts can arise between members as individuals try to dictate the direction the project should go, as others abandon their tasks or go AWOL, and as deadlines come and go and progress is not made. Resentment starts to grow and the group implodes. As part of the process of collaboration, you will be expected to try to manage the situation and resolve the conflict rather than turning to your lecturer to sort out the mess for you. Understanding the source of the conflict and resolving the issues you face will work in your favour, even if you still need to seek intervention at a later date.

Most of the disruptions to the group process and atmosphere can be avoided by clarifying ground rules for the group, reminding people about their responsibilities and being willing to compromise. We are never going to work

STUDENT VIEWPOINT

For our first group project in our senior year, we had a bit of a disaster – at least, at the start it was. One of the four group members just didn't turn up to meetings and it was hard to contact her by phone. She was responsible for the first part of the project, and without her research we just couldn't move forward. We weren't really sure what to do, but in the end the team leader managed to get hold of her, and it turned out that her mother had been in hospital and she was trying take care of her as well as her younger brother, as her dad was away for work. So as a group we decided to reallocate the tasks so that she was responsible for the final draft, as she would have more time at the end of the project once her dad was back, and I took on the early research that was needed. It was a win–win situation all around, and I felt pretty good that we were able to help out our team member and also fix the problem ourselves rather than running to the professor to sort it out for us. I thought that as seniors we needed to take more responsibility, and in this case it really paid off.—Charlie.

Table 10.2 Overview of disruptive roles within groups

Role	Description	Key phrases
Aggressor	The aggressor is rude, disrespectful and dismissive of other members' ideas and offers very little in return. They may attack other members' personally or ridicule their contributions.	I think that's a really dumb idea. Then again, dumb person, dumb idea.
Solution	Remind the perpetrator of the ground rules they agreed to and the need to treat everyone with respect. Everyone has the right to speak, make suggestions and offer ideas in a supportive environment. The coach might explain how the comments are disruptive to the group.	
Dominator	The dominator tries to take over the discussion, interrupts team members and feels that their opinion is more important or better than everyone else's. It seems like theirs is the only voice being heard. They may be patronizing, try to usurp the leader and try to take control of the direction of the project.	(interrupts) Well, that might be what you'd do, but I already came up with a better suggestion. Let me explain it again.
Solution	Establish a ground rule whereby everyone gets a turn at speaking and impose time limits on each person if necessary. If the dominator interrupts, the coach should ask them to wait their turn and then make a point of asking others in the group for their input before returning to the dominator for their comments.	
Avoider	The avoider avoids discussing the task or taking on any roles and does not appear to be taking part in the project. They may have a lot of excuses why their work has not been completed.	I was going to start this week, but, well, you know. I'll just start that section next week.
Solution	Try to establish why the student has been avoiding meetings and missing deadlines. Are there time management problems? Do they have outside responsibilities (family/work/sport) that might interfere with their ability to contribute to the group? Do they have a work style that thrives under pressure? Figuring out what the obstacle is will be more productive and lead to a more effective resolution than simply criticizing the student or 'writing them off'.	
Critic	The critic always shoots down everyone else's ideas and has reasons why they will not work or are the wrong way to proceed. They rarely offer alternatives.	Oh, that's a really stupid idea. It'll never work because . . .
Solution	Establish a process whereby constructive criticism must be followed by an alternative or a solution. Critique is an important part of working together, but negative criticism does not inspire creativity. Try to add to an idea or think about how it could be made to work. If someone still criticizes without contributing their own ideas, it is up to the group to point out their lack of contribution.	

	Description	Example
Help-seeker	The help-seeker appears quite helpless and unable to do any of their assigned tasks. They express their insecurities and may be overly self-deprecating. This may be a way of avoiding work or simply playing the victim to garner sympathy from the group.	I've never done this before. I'm so useless. Can someone help me? Maybe it's better if another person does this part.
Solution	You need to encourage self-confidence in the team member. Suggest ways to break down their assignments into smaller, more manageable tasks, and set some additional deadlines.	
Self-confessor	The self-confessor talks only about things that are of interest to them and not necessarily to the group.	We might be doing a marketing plan for the gym, but disability access is a really important issue that we should be considering.
Solution	Reference to the ground rules is also important in this situation, with the coach drawing the discussion back to the task at hand. If this behaviour is repeated, the group may need to actively ignore attempts to derail the meeting, and the coach may need to reiterate the direction the group has decided on.	
Deserter	The deserter withdraws from the process either physically or mentally. They may not attend meetings, or not engage if they do. The desertion might happen from the start or gradually over the course of the project.	There are no typical phrases because they do not attend meetings.
Solution	Try to discuss the team member's non-participation and establish whether there are any underlying issues that are preventing them from engaging more fully in the group.	
Blocker	The blocker refuses to take part or to follow other people's suggestions. They might stall the discussion by trying to raise issues that have already been decided.	I'm not doing that.
Solution	The basis of all group work is collaboration, so the team member should be reminded that no one member is bigger than the assignment.	
Narcissist	The narcissist will try to draw attention to themselves, their ideas and their contributions, by boasting or manipulating others to comment on their strengths. They need the group to reaffirm that they are bright, clever and intelligent. They might refuse to do what they believe are menial or inferior roles and prefer to take on tasks that will keep them in the limelight.	Well, the last time I was in a group project – actually, I was the leader – we worked on something similar so we could adapt that approach for this project if you like, and I'd happy to lead again.
Solution	As with the blocker, the narcissist should be reminded that every contribution to the task is critical and that each member must complete their assigned tasks.	

effectively with every single person we encounter, and personality clashes can and do occur. Conflicts of this nature can be an opportunity to learn to adjust our fixed ideas in order to create a more harmonious working environment. Try to account for different learning and working styles as well as personality types and establish whether your issue is a process or task issue, or simply a difference in approach. While individual personalities can contribute to an awkward working relationship, there are specific roles that are destined to sabotage any team.

DISRUPTIVE ROLES

Just as there are roles that assist in both the running of the group and the conduct of the task, there are also roles that inhibit the group's ability to function. Being aware of these disruptive or self-centred roles means you are more likely to recognize these behaviours and be in a position to counteract them. Table 10.2 describes the main disruptive roles you may encounter as well as suggestions on how to deal with these personalities.

SUMMARY

1   Group work is a valuable way to learn how to work cooperatively, to draw upon the strengths and weaknesses of individual team members and to develop interpersonal and communication skills.
2   The types of group work at college range from informal and ad hoc groups through to lab and project groups and online collaborations and discussions. While the final product may differ, the process of working together is important regardless of the style of interaction.
3   Understanding the key roles within a group means that individual students can accept responsibility for an area that best suits their personality and characteristics. Although most roles contribute to the task or maintenance of the group, there are also disruptive roles that derail otherwise effective teams.
4   It is important to establish a set of ground rules to underpin the group's operation and short- and long-term milestones in order to ensure that everyone is working towards the same deadlines.
5   Working in virtual groups presents a unique set of circumstances, and participants have to be particularly appreciative of the peculiarities and limitations of online discussion and collaboration.

EXERCISES

1   Write down the main benefits and challenges of working in a group rather than on an individual project. How does working in a group at college differ from working together as part of a sports team? Are there any teamwork skills you can transfer from the sports field to the classroom?

2   Consider your strengths and weaknesses when it comes to group work. Write down your personality characteristics that you think would enhance a group project. How do these align to the various roles within groups and which role best suits your strengths? Do you think other group members will see you the same way? Which role would you not want to take on?

3   If you were in charge of forming a group of four members, what skill sets would you need to complement your own?

4   Imagine you are in a group with two people who are contributing and two who are not. As leader, what would you do to bring the group together to ensure all are making a fair contribution?

REFLECTION

Do you enjoy working in groups? If not, write down the reasons you prefer individual projects. Think about the last time you worked in a group. What role(s) did you have? Were you successful in those positions? What might you have changed in order to contribute more to the group? Alternatively, could you have encouraged other members to make stronger contributions? Was the group well structured or too informal? Did you feel the process was as important as the final assignment?

FURTHER READING

Learning Higher (2012) *Group work video resource.* Liverpool: Liverpool Hope University Centre for Excellence in Teaching and Learning. Available at: www.learnhigher.ac.uk/groupwork//index.php.

Levin, P. (2005) *Successful teamwork!* Maidenhead: Open University Press.

11

ORAL PRESENTATIONS

Tips and tricks for effective delivery

OVERVIEW

This chapter outlines:
* how to prepare, structure, rehearse and deliver oral presentations;
* how to design effective visual presentations;
* ways of engaging the audience and responding to their questions;
* strategies to overcome public speaking anxiety;
* tips on working with technology.

INTRODUCTION

One of the most dreaded university assessments is the oral presentation. The thought of standing in front of your peers and professors to deliver a polished performance is enough to send many students into a tailspin. Indeed, public speaking is so generally feared that it is regarded as a fate worse than death. At the same time, we have all sat through interminably boring presentations where the speaker meticulously reads every word on a screen densely packed with text and graphics or listened to an athlete mumble through a post-match interview. The ability to speak confidently in front of your colleagues is a desirable skill to have and one that is easily practised during your studies. This chapter outlines strategies for creating and delivering presentations while using effective visual aids and keeping your nerves under control.

PURPOSE OF A PRESENTATION

Presentations come in many forms. You might be asked to stand up and deliver an impromptu speech without any preparation; your project group might have to present your report findings to the class; you might have to participate in a debate; and for graduate students, you might be required to defend your dissertation to an expert panel or present at conferences. Equally, in most work places, you will at some point be called upon to speak to a group of people. A coach might have to face a press conference; an athlete might be interviewed or asked to address their fans; a trainer might need to talk to a group of athletes; a sports scientist will be required to present to a learned audience; a sports marketer will pitch their goods and services to potential clients.

Although the specific objectives may differ, the overall purpose of presentations is to communicate to an audience. Communication at its simplest means conveying ideas, thoughts, concepts, messages or information from one person to another. In such a model, there is one person who sends the message (the sender) and another who receives it (the receiver). Successful communication occurs when the receiver understands the message transmitted by the sender as the sender intends the message to be understood. Although this seems a straightforward process, the message is not always understood correctly. A message is often filtered through a medium (television, phone, third party) at which point it can be interrupted by 'noise'. Noise might be actual noise that makes it hard to hear the message or simply differences of interpretation based on prior knowledge, cultural differences or an inability to understand the words used. This means that the receiver does not understand the message in the way that the sender intended. With this basic model of communication in mind, it is important to think about how and why you are communicating information to ensure your audience understands clearly what you want them to know. Regardless of whether you are trying to simply inform your listeners, persuade them to agree with your perspective or to buy whatever you are selling, the presentation is an opportunity to make a personal appeal to the group and to explicate your perspective or standpoint. A successful presentation is one where your audience walks away with the message you wanted to communicate.

When planning a presentation, understanding its purpose is the first step towards success. As part of your college classes, you are likely to be asked to prepare either informative or persuasive presentations, and the style of each of these is further dependent on your discipline. A persuasive argument in a sports science presentation will be quite different from one presented as part of a sports philosophy module.

An *informative* presentation asks you to present factual information on a particular topic. If you are presenting on the use of fast skin swimsuits in swimming, an informative presentation might list the various types of swimsuits that are available in swimming, specific examples of each type of swimsuit, perhaps a timeline of when the suits were accepted into and banned from swimming, and an overview of the changes to swimming and the number of world records that resulted from these new innovations. Your presentation might have a number of lists or graphics to display the information, and the accuracy of your presentation would depend entirely on the accuracy of your facts.

A *persuasive* presentation, on the other hand, presents a particular perspective with the intention of altering the audience's opinion or standpoint on a particular issue. This means that you need to do more than offer information, and will need to contextualize the 'facts' into a meaningful argument that will make the audience think about a topic in a new way. A persuasive presentation on the merit of fast skin swimwear might take a particular stance, such as arguing that there is no rationale for banning the high-tech suits. Rather than presenting information about the types or impact of these swimming costumes, this presentation would explain why banning fast skin suits makes little sense, use case studies to demonstrate flaws in the basic philosophical foundation for prohibition and draw upon scholars who argue a similar standpoint.

PREPARATION AND PLANNING

PLANNING

As with most academic assessments, the initial planning stage is critical; however, unlike other assessments where you have time to review and revise your final product, you have only one opportunity to present. It is thus no surprise that the more time you put into research, organization, structure and practice before the presentation, the more likely you will deliver a high-quality end product. Yet it is not only the presentation itself that will be more effective; knowing that you are well prepared increases your confidence and concomitantly reduces your nerves. There are a number of planning checklists online, but here are some of the key areas that need consideration when putting your presentation together:

- *Purpose and objectives*: First and foremost, you need to establish the purpose of the presentation. Should it be an informative or a persuasive talk? The topic should give you some guidance, but if you are not sure, confirm with your lecturer. Second, you need to be aware of your objectives. What do you want to convey to the audience? How should the audience feel about the topic once you have finished? Answering these questions will help you develop your presentation.
- *Audience*: You need to determine who the audience is. In most college presentations, your professor and peers will be the only members of the audience, so you can safely assume that they will have a similar level of base knowledge. In some courses, however, and particularly at the graduate level, you might be working on a 'real world' problem, which means the client may also be in attendance. In this case, you should find out more about their specific needs and tailor your presentation to match. Make sure you include sufficient context so they understand your recommendations or conclusions.
- *Logistics*: You need to confirm all logistical issues, such as how long the presentation should be, whether there is a required format or template you

should use, the location of the presentation and the availability of equipment. If you are presenting the results of a group project, you should check whether every member is required to speak for an equal amount of time, or whether you are permitted to select the best speakers. In the latter case, you should try to include the rest of the team when taking questions from the audience. Check out the location of the presentation to see the layout of the room and the available equipment. Can you change the seating to better suit your presentation? What kind of lighting will you need? If there is no audiovisual equipment, you may need to book it in advance.

- *Topic*: Make sure you understand the topic clearly. In the case of a debate, you will need to conduct research to find arguments to support your position as well as to debunk opposing ideas. If you are presenting the results of a project, then you will need to pare down your lengthy report to create an effective and meaningful presentation.
- *Key ideas*: A presentation is limited in the amount of information you can communicate, so you need to think about the key ideas you want your audience to take away, and build your presentation around them. A useful rule of thumb is to identify three main points, because audiences typically struggle to remember more. If you are presenting the findings of a report, then you could, for example, focus on the main recommendations rather than every last detail.
- *Supporting materials*: Once you have established your key points, it is important to think about the kind of additional materials that will support your assertions. Can you use visual images, graphs or other data? Do you need to foreground the literature you have examined to add strength to your argument? Are there any audiovisual materials, such as videos, that will add interest to the presentation? Can detailed information be provided in a handout for the audience to read later? Remember that these should only support your presentation, not become the main focus.
- *Create a storyboard*: Go 'old school' and use squares of paper to create a storyboard. Write the key points you wish to cover on each one and move ideas and points around so that they are presented in the most effective way possible. A presentation gives you a lot of flexibility, so if you are presenting the results of a report, your presentation does not need to follow the structure of the report. You could begin with the recommendations and then explain how you reached them; or you could start with a series of inspiring ideas or questions before outlining the key ideas. Be creative in how you present material, but always make sure the structure flows logically from point to point and builds from simple to more complex ideas.
- *Contingencies*: Plan for the things that can go wrong. Bring an extra set of your notes in case you drop yours during the presentation and decide what you will do if the technology fails. Many of the problems you might encounter will be averted by good planning, but there are always unexpected hiccoughs that can disrupt your presentation.

STRUCTURE

Presentations follow the same structure as essays or reports. Begin with an introduction, present the main ideas in the body and then wrap up the presentation in the conclusion:

- *Introduction*: Use the basic Introduction Formula to create an effective introduction to your presentation. Begin with a broad overview of the topic, explain the purpose of the presentation, the main points you will cover and then preview the main sections of the presentation. The audience will then know what to expect, which will keep them more engaged throughout. You can foreshadow the outcome you expect the audience to take away – a new idea or technique; a revised opinion about an issue; information for them to think about – to help the audience link the material you are presenting to the expected outcome.
- *Body*: Divide the presentation into the three or so main ideas you want to present, and order them so that one point logically flows to the next. It is difficult for audiences to retain information delivered verbally, so create a structure whereby each point builds on the one that precedes it. Each key point should be dealt with in turn as if it is a mini essay: outline the main idea, explain in some more detail, review the main point before linking it to the next idea. If you are expected to change speakers during the presentation, allocating one speaker to each main point keeps the transition between speakers reasonably smooth.
- *Conclusion*: Restate the main points that you have presented and then link these back to the overall topic under consideration. This gives the audience the confidence that you understand the topic and have successfully engaged with it. Finish with a strong statement about what the key points mean – the 'take-away' message for the audience – or identify areas for future consideration.

Be quite ruthless when putting a presentation together. You will have a lot of information that will need to be condensed into a small number of points, so you should focus on outlining key ideas rather than trying to explain every issue in depth. Avoid getting bogged down in tedious detail. The audience will not remember it and it just obscures your actual point. If there are important details that you feel the audience must know, consider giving them a handout to examine later.

ENGAGING THE AUDIENCE

The most effective presentations are those where audience members feel personally addressed and leave inspired, and yet many speakers neglect the specific needs and interests of those listening to their presentations. When a speaker does not make them feel included in the presentation, the audience may start to drift off, to plan their weekend or to think about everything on their 'to do' lists. There is little that is more disheartening to a speaker than to see an audience member so bored with what you have to say that they fall asleep while you are speaking. Given that in a work situation, capturing the audience's imagination may be the difference between making a sale and going home empty-handed, it is critical that speakers learn how to engage their audience.

One of the easiest ways to keep your audience focused on your presentation is to foreground the structure. Outlining the talk in your introduction sets the scene for the presentation, but as you go through, make good use of signposts and transitions to establish explicit links between ideas so that your audience understands how the ideas all fit together. Your listeners are being expected to remember a lot of information, so signalling the argument keeps them on track. For example, you might begin with 'I'm going to start by outlining the four main reasons countries have boycotted the Olympic Games. The first reason is . . .' and then you could wrap up with 'So those were the four key reasons that countries have boycotted the Olympic Games. The next aspect I will discuss is the effect that boycotts have on the host nation'. Though it sounds repetitive to someone already familiar with the content, it is actually a highly effective technique to keep the audience on track.

As noted above, you need to understand who your audience is, their general experience of the topic and what your outcome for them will be. But besides ensuring the content is relevant to the audience's interests and pitched at an appropriate level, there are a number of practical ways to keep the audience focused on your message. For example, you can invite them to participate for a few moments: ask them to write down their ideas or turn to their neighbour to discuss a point of interest or come up with their own examples. You might even pose a rhetorical question for them to consider. Rhetorical questions engage the audience by articulating reservations that the audience members might share: 'So why did we insist on a ninety-second rest period between sets?' or 'What would be the right approach to avoiding injury in this cohort?' If time is short, you can engage listeners by directing them to think about a particular issue, to imagine a relevant scenario that they have experienced, or to think about how your ideas could apply to them. Each of these creates the illusion of a dialogue between you and your audience. Depending on how much time you have, encouraging the audience to participate, and thereby create their own meaning from your presentation, keeps the audience focused on you and your ideas.

Body language is also an important part of engaging with the audience. Simply keeping good eye contact with many people in the room will make the entire audience feel as though they have been personally spoken to. If the group is large or spread across the room, move your head and look at someone in each area. Try not to linger too long on any one person, but gradually scan your room to keep everyone involved. If you are nervous about making eye contact, try looking at the forehead or between the eyes. It has the same effect as making direct eye contact. Use expansive arm gestures to draw the listeners to you, or direct an open palm towards individuals to suggest you are speaking to them directly. Your facial expressions can also keep the audience connected to the material by expressing what they might be feeling. Inspire confidence through good posture. A straight back looks poised and self-assured, whereas a stooped or bowed head looks insecure.

A final technique for engaging the audience is to use inclusive language throughout your presentation. The types of phrases you might use include 'what we can learn from this is . . .' and 'if we look at this graph, we can see . . .'. By referring to 'we' rather than to 'I', the audience is taken on a journey of discovery with you.

PRACTICE

Like all skills, public speaking improves with practice, practice and more practice. Just as a professional tennis player cannot 'wing it' on the court, very few people are able to stand up and deliver a polished speech the first time they are invited to present. Like top-level athletes, the one characteristic that confident speakers have in common is adequate preparation. There really is no substitute for practice when it comes to oral presentations, and there are several areas that need specific attention during your preparation.

The first step is to familiarize yourself thoroughly with the content of your presentation. Read through your written speech aloud several times and think carefully about what you are saying. Do you understand each of the points you are making and could you explain them without reference to your speech? When you feel completely comfortable with the content, condense your speech down to key terms and phrases (cues) on some palm cards and practise speaking to the various points. Use these practice sessions to refine your speech to ensure the content is logical and structured so that the audience can follow easily.

Once you feel confident that you know *what* to say, practise *how* you will say it. Listen carefully to how you speak. Do you speak at a good pace or do you need to work on slowing down? Are you projecting enough for the size of the room and audience? Are you pronouncing words properly? Record yourself speaking to hear the tone, pitch and speed of your voice.

The third step is to practise speaking in front of an audience. Gather together some willing friends or family, and run through your presentation. By now, you should be confident with the content, so you can concentrate on the delivery, taking eye contact, arm/hand gestures and other body language into consideration. An audience provides direct feedback to you about your performance and indirect feedback in terms of how they respond during your presentation, as well as valuable experience speaking in front of a group. If you cannot organize an audience, deliver your presentation in front of a mirror until you feel you have a natural stance and comfortable body movements.

Finally, practise your presentation while working the technology and equipment you will use on the day, ideally in the actual location in which you will present. See how your voice carries in the space, bearing in mind that the more bodies there are in the room, the harder it is for sound to travel. How much time does it take to change slides and can it be easily accommodated within the set time limit? If there are a number of speakers, how much time is lost by transitioning between them? Can you move seamlessly between your speech and the technology without interrupting the flow of the presentation? If you find you cannot change slides or start videos, ask someone to assist you. Provide them with an overview of the speech that indicates when they should change slides or turn on other equipment, or work out a subtle signal that you can give them. Practise working together to deliver the presentation; do not assume that it will all work out on the day.

TIP

Do not try to memorize your speech. You are more likely to forget key parts, and even if you get through it, the presentation will sound rehearsed and unnatural. There are no bonus points for word-perfect presentations, so focus on understanding and communicating your points.

PERSONAL PRESENTATION

Although there is usually no strict dress code at university, and students in sports courses are notorious for wearing tracksuits and trainers, for a formal presentation you should dress for the occasion. Not only will you feel more professional if you are dressed smartly but you will appear to the audience to be more authoritative and knowledgeable about the topic, which means they will be more accepting of your message. Think about whether you are more likely to trust a politician dressed in jeans and a scruffy T-shirt or one who is wearing a suit. If a doctor enters your operating theatre with ripped trousers and a stained shirt, will you be convinced of his ability to operate hygienically? A team who arrives in the formal team uniform looks like a slick, well-oiled machine compared to one that turns up in whatever they feel like wearing. Your outfit inspires confidence, so dress well when presenting.

DELIVERY

We have all endured presentations where the speaker's monotone voice is more sleep-inducing than stimulating, and yet it takes only a few small steps to deliver strong, effective and compelling presentations that will keep your audience engaged and leave them inspired. The most effective presentations occur when the presenter is simply speaking to the audience to create what feels like a one-on-one dialogue rather than standing motionless, eyes cast down, reading from a prepared script. While writing out the entire speech word for word means you are sure to include all the relevant material you need, it is rare that you would actually read out pages and pages of text during your presentation.

Remember that *you* are the centre of the presentation; there would be no point gathering people to listen to you speak if you are simply reading printed material. You could save everyone time and effort and just email them the document to read at their leisure.

Delivering a presentation means speaking to the main points that you want the audience to understand by providing enough evidence and detail to convince them of your position. The more you practise, the more you will remember to emphasize the central points and examples, even if the specific way that you communicate them differs each time you rehearse. A presentation should connect to the audience and does not need to be as perfect as a written submission. As such, a successful presentation is one where the key message has been understood by the listeners, not one where you have successfully read through a lot of detailed information.

Some students feel quite vulnerable without a detailed script or any kind of notes in front of them. In this instance, palm cards are a good compromise. Reduce your speech to key words or phrases that serve as prompts, in much the same way that you use 'cues' in your Cornell notes to remind you of lecture content. Allocate a palm card for each part of the presentation: one for the introduction, one for each main point and one for the conclusion. You could have some lengthier bullet points on the back of each card to help if you really get stuck, but you will likely find that just the process of summarizing notes and creating palm cards, as well as practising the presentation, will be enough to cement the key points in your mind. Always number your palm cards or notes. It only takes a moment of carelessness to send them all flying. Indeed, a well-prepared presenter will have a second set ready to go in case the palm cards are dropped.

Here are some additional tips that will help your delivery:

- Use appropriate language during your presentation. Avoid unnecessary jargon, slang ('it's not over until the final whistle', 'it's a game of two halves') and any words that are difficult to say, but do explain unfamiliar terms. Be as professional and as polished as possible. Although you are just speaking to a group, it is not chatty or informal.
- Speak a lot slower than you feel is normal. You know what the presentation is about, but your audience does not. It takes time to hear, understand and assimilate information that is delivered orally, so allow the audience time to grasp your key messages.
- Do not be afraid to use your voice, intonation and gestures to emphasize particular points. Practise these so that they come across as natural rather than awkward or forced. Equally, do not be afraid of silence. A dramatic pause or a brief moment to leave a point lingering in the air for the audience to ponder also adds to a presentation and emphasizes important points.
- If it is necessary to put a block of text on the screen, do not read every word. Stay quiet while the audience reads through it, and then, if necessary, highlight one or two key phrases.

- Avoid having anything noisy on or about your person, including coins or keys in your pocket, bracelets or other jewellery. These can be distracting for an audience, and you want them focused on what you are saying, not listening to the jingling keys in your trousers.
- Turn off your own cell phone.

ANSWERING QUESTIONS

At the end of a presentation, the audience and/or professor are typically offered the opportunity to pose questions to the speaker(s), who in turn have the chance to explain their points in more detail. Nevertheless, asking questions is not merely a way to test your understanding of the material you have just presented; it allows the audience to ensure that they have understood your key points. Strong, confident responses will inspire the audience and reaffirm that you are knowledgeable and that your content is trustworthy; however, fudging answers or avoiding the question makes you look ill-prepared and uninformed about the topic.

While you may have been able to deliver a confident speech, answering unknown questions 'off the cuff' can be quite anxiety-inducing. There are, however, some techniques to ensure you respond well:

- Before the presentation, compile a list of questions that might arise and think about how you would respond to them. You might even consider 'planting' a question with a friend, so that the first question you are asked is something you expect, just to ease you into the question-and-answer session.
- Listen carefully to the question and let the speaker finish. Jumping in and trying to answer before they finish is not only impolite but risks missing the actual question the audience member is posing.
- If you are not sure what you are being asked, politely request for the question to be repeated. This gives you a little more time to structure a response that will best address the query.
- Repeat or paraphrase the question back to the speaker. This ensures that you understand what is being asked, allows the entire room to hear the question and also buys you a few moments to think about your response.
- If the question is quite lengthy, note down the key points so that you can address all of them. You can respond to each issue in a different order from how they were asked, so deal with the more straightforward points first and work up to the difficult issues.
- Be brief in your response. Address the question clearly and comprehensively, but avoid introducing new areas or other ideas and do not start another lengthy speech.
- Do not be afraid to indicate that you are not sure, as an audience will know when you are just speaking for the sake of speaking. You do not need to say 'I don't know', but rather simply indicate that this touches on an area that you have not yet looked into but that it would be a worthwhile point

to examine in future. If you are representing a team and are not sure of the answer, ask for a moment to confer with your group or nominate another member of the group to address the question.

- Take a moment or two to think about how to respond. The audience does not expect you to make quick comments to complicated or thought-provoking questions and will respect you for giving due consideration to your answer.
- Do not make a judgement about the question being posed ('that's an excellent question') because the audience members who are not commended may feel a little offended that their question was not worthy of an accolade.
- Avoid responding to just the person asking the question. It is more than likely that others in the audience had the same query, so once you start speaking, address the room. When you have finished, look briefly at the person who raised the question to see if they are satisfied with your response and to see if they have a follow-up question.
- If an audience member just wants to make a comment rather than ask a question, do not feel compelled to respond. Thank them for their comment and move to the next question.
- Wrap up the presentation with a few lines thanking the audience for their participation and summarizing one or two points that emerged from the questions. This leaves you as the last speaker and gives the audience some additional ideas to take away.

The question-and-answer session really does have the power to enhance or severely compromise your presentation, so make sure you are prepared for questions and have practised a few obvious examples.

VISUAL AIDS

We live in a highly visual culture and are used to being stimulated by a number of senses at once, so incorporating images, short phrases, graphics, sounds, music, videos and even artefacts or other objects has the potential to enhance the overall presentation. The audience is more likely to connect your ideas to visual depictions, and the thoughtful use of overview and review slides will allow them to follow the logic of your argument. Despite the value of visual aids, there are many who wait for the demise of PowerPoint and other multimedia presentation software, as these applications are typically overused and the resultant presentations are often designed with little creativity or insight into how audiences experience them.

A fundamental principle when designing a slide show is that your visual aids should enhance your presentation, offering something in addition to what you are saying rather than repeating your words or distracting the audience. Remember that the speaker is the main focus, not a series of slides, so think about whether the presentation makes sense without you speaking. If an audience can read the slides and understand the presentation in its entirety, then you have not designed an effective visual aid. Visual aids should provide an added dimension to your words, but not replace you. You are the key part of the presentation; do not elide your significance by cluttering up slides with so much text and detail that your audience simply reads them rather than listening to you. They cannot do both.

WHEN TO USE VISUAL AIDS

When it comes to knowing what to include in a slide slow, a good rule of thumb is to depict information visually. For example, images can pack quite a powerful punch. If you are discussing the treatment of compound fractures sustained on the football field, showing pictures of the injuries will elicit a more visceral response in the audience than simply describing how a bone was poking through the skin. A graph or table, on the other hand, concisely presents a large amount of data so that you need focus only on the relevant results. Visual representations reinforce the old adage that 'a picture is worth a thousand words', so use them to save time or create compelling memories of the presentation.

It is always useful to have a title slide where you include the title, the name of the speaker(s), the class code, and name and the date of the presentation. The title page might be branded with your school or group's logo, and it is usually visible as the audience are taking their places. Some of the structural elements of a talk are also best highlighted in a slide. Rather than trying to describe the 'roadmap' of the presentation, a simple outline of the main points in the order that they will be presented lets the audience see what you are going to discuss and allows them to make some initial connections between the various components of the talk. If you are using any terms or jargon that may be unfamiliar to some members of the audience, a slide to define the term when you first use it saves you having to stop and explain a concept for a small handful of people.

DESIGN

Effective slide presentations should embrace principles of good design. There are many online tutorials that help you design effective visual materials, but here are some basic ideas to get you started:

- *Do not be afraid of white space*: Keep slides clear of clutter and use space to create a calm, professional look.
- *Simple, consistent backgrounds*: Use a plain colour that is not distracting to the audience and use it consistently through the entire presentation. White is the most effective background. Do not use images, pictures or other distractions as backgrounds.
- *Remember the 'eight second rule'*: You have under ten seconds to hold the audience's attention, so do not fill the slide with so much information that it cannot be viewed and understood in around eight seconds.

- *One main point per slide*: Bearing in mind that most people cannot retain too much information in their short-term memory, try to keep the number of main ideas on a slide to an absolute minimum. If you include one main idea, then you can speak to the point rather than having the audience read the text.
- *Images rather than text*: Use images to support your points rather than writing lengthy descriptions for the audience to read, but avoid peppering your presentation with clip art or graphics that are simply there to make your presentation pretty. If it is not directly relevant to what you are saying and you do not refer to the image, then remove it.
- *Graphics*: Only include a graphic if it is referred to in the presentation, and keep it as simple as possible. The audience should understand at first glance what they are seeing. Use concise data, and do not include information that is irrelevant to your presentation or that is not referred to in your speech. If you are using graphs or tables, be consistent throughout the slides and use the same format all the way through.
- *Use brief text*: If you absolutely cannot live without putting words on your slides, keep the number of words to a minimum. There should be no more than six words per line and no more than six lines on any one slide. More than that is just clutter and means your audience is reading, not listening.
- *Clear, readable text*: Any text you include should be clear, readable and a size that can be seen all over the room. Do not use fancy fonts; stick with plain, sans serif fonts such as Helvetica, at least 36 points in size. You can use a contrasting font for the headings, but avoid using more than two fonts in a presentation.
- *Avoid animations*: Although most presentation software will have a plethora of animations, transitions and sounds, these are distracting. It is far more professional to use a simple fade than to have text or images flying in from angles, spinning around and glowing in the dark,. If you absolutely must include quirky transitions or animations, make them consistent. It is never necessary to use laser shots, smashing glass or other gimmicky sounds to emphasize your bullet points in college or other formal presentations.
- *Proofread*: Carefully proofread your slides for spelling and grammatical errors. Mistakes are bad enough in your own written assignment; they are literally magnified for all to see when displayed on a screen.

TECHNICAL ASPECTS

Although technology is an important aspect of most presentations these days, it should fade into the background rather than being the main attraction. And yet when things go wrong, the technology is suddenly propelled to the forefront of the talk while the speaker scurries around trying to fix the problem. Indeed, if technology can fail, it is most likely to fail in the middle of your presentation. It has happened to world leaders, heads of industry and almost every student who has ever presented at college. Laptops crash, software stalls,

CASE STUDY

Take a look at Jason's brief slide presentation on the golf grip:

→ What are the positive features of this presentation?

→ How might you change this presentation to make it a more effective support to an oral presentation?

internet connectivity is lost and files are corrupted. Nothing is more disruptive to a presentation and disconcerting for an audience than to see the speaker grind to a halt as they try to fix the problem.

To avoid wasting time on error messages and crashed computers, it is best to have a contingency plan in place. If you have already thought about everything that can go wrong, you will have an immediate solution up your sleeve, so that your presentation can continue with little disruption. Here are some tips to avoid a technology failure interrupting your presentation:

- Test all the equipment before your presentation. You may have practised with the same technology the day before, but still make sure that everything is in working order before you start.
- If you are using your own laptop, make sure email, scan updates or other notifications are turned off.
- Always bring at least two copies of the presentation with you, ideally on different media (data stick/flash drive, SD card, email), or have access to a copy online. A corrupted file is a nuisance, but your entire presentation should never be dependent on one copy of the slide show. Remember the rule of thumb that digital files exist only if they exist in at least three different places, so back up along the way and make sure you keep copies elsewhere.
- If you are using a web-based presentation, make sure you also have an offline copy in case the internet connection is weak.
- Bring handouts of the slides for the audience to look at in case the technology fails irreparably. Have someone on hand to distribute the handouts if needed.
- Practise how you will handle a technology failure. Do you have a spare laptop? If technology support is not available, bring someone along who can work on the problem while you continue presenting.
- Apologize for the delay, but remain calm and composed. The audience will feel confident if you exude confidence, but if you start to crumble, the audience will start to feel anxious for you.
- Use a little humour to set the audience at ease as your contingency plan is activated.
- If the problem cannot be resolved quickly, move on. You have practised your presentation without slides, and given the audience is there to see *you* talk, losing the slide show should really be a minor irritation rather than the end of your presentation.

MANAGING ANXIETY

One of the hardest parts of public speaking is overcoming nerves. For some people, these are just a slight feeling of butterflies, whereas for others it can be absolutely crippling. However severely it affects you, the symptoms are quite common: sweaty palms, quick breathing, dry mouth, increased heart rate, a feeling of nausea and even aching fingertips. And yet rather than being designed

STUDENT VIEWPOINT

I absolutely HATE public speaking. I get so nervous I want to be sick. I have found that being well prepared cuts down the nerves somewhat, and combined with some relaxation techniques I learned at yoga, I can just about get through it. I still think it's important to learn, so I don't avoid classes with presentations because I will only get better the more often I do them.—Grace.

to debilitate, 'nerves' are a physiological response to unfamiliar or uncomfortable situations that allow the body to respond to perceived danger with 'flight or fight'. As adrenalin is released, your senses are heightened and your body prepares either to take on the risk or to run away, which are precisely the choices you have when preparing to speak in front of a group. As it is a physiological response, it will not be possible to get rid of nerves all together, but it is certainly possible to manage them and to use the sensation to your advantage rather than your detriment. Many experienced presenters actually look for this nervous feeling as the hormonal response helps them deliver a more engaging presentation. And if they are not feeling nervous at all, they will actually rip up their notes in order to generate the level of anxiety they require to perform well.

Here are some tips to help you manage your nerves:

- *What are you afraid of?* Write down the three main concerns you have about speaking in public. Students are usually concerned about forgetting what to say or looking stupid in front of their peers. But delve into each of these a little further. If you are well prepared, with palm cards to prompt you, is it really likely that you will forget what to say? Similarly, will you look stupid if you have prepared and practised your speech? Knowing what you are afraid of and working through those fears can help you manage your nerves.
- *Perspective*: Closely related to identifying what you are afraid of is thinking about what is the worst that can happen. The world will not end, you will not be marched off campus by security, and your family and friends will not abandon you if you falter in your delivery. It is one small part of a much larger university experience. Bear in mind that lecturers are experienced in assessing presentations, and they are more than able to discern when a student who is obviously well prepared has been let down by nerves in the final delivery.
- *Visualize*: Many athletes use this technique to great effect. Visualize yourself in front of the group feeling calm and relaxed. Think about what it feels like to stand there and proudly deliver a confident presentation. See yourself expertly answering questions and remember how it feels to be in control. And just before you step in front of the audience, recall how it feels to be successful from your visualizations.

- *Preparation*: For the average student, the level of nerves is often directly proportional to the level of preparedness, so that the more prepared you are, the more confident you will feel. Practising your presentation builds your confidence, but remember that not every presentation will be perfect. As long as your key message is communicated, it really does not matter if you forget one or two small details. Being familiar with the technology and confident that it works and that you know how to operate it will also alleviate nerves.
- *Breathe*: Breathing exercises can help alleviate some of the effects of anxiety. Breathe in slowly through your nose. Focus on the sensation of air deeply filling up your lungs. Hold the air in for a moment before slowly breathing out through your mouth. Visualize the nervous tension being released as the air leaves your body. Repeat this process a few times to slow down your heart rate and ensure enough oxygen is circulating through your body.
- *Drink*: Settle your dry mouth by drinking water before you speak. Have a drink close at hand during your presentation to refresh if needed.
- *Friendly faces*: Look for one or two friends in the audience to focus on as you get started, but remember that through the presentation you need to scan the room to make everyone feel included. Do not make the mistake of speaking only to one or two people throughout the presentation.
- *Use your nerves*: Remember that adrenalin invokes the 'fight *or* flight' mechanism, and you can choose which one prevails. Rather than fleeing from the situation, use your anxiety to fight, or in other words, to make a powerful, exciting and enthusiastic presentation. Replace your negative thoughts with positive affirmations: you are prepared and you will do an amazing job.
- *'Fake it till you make it'*: Even if you feel crippled with nerves, no one in the audience needs to know that. Do not broadcast your nerves; it will only make the audience feel nervous on your behalf, and every stumble or pause will make them worry you are having a breakdown. Smile as you begin; make a point of speaking slowly, and basically act as though you are calm and confident. If your hands are shaking – which they sometimes will, even if you are not feeling nervous yourself – obscure them by foregoing the use of a laser pointer or large pages of notes that will just magnify the shaking. Instead, use broad arm gestures to point out key material and palm cards that can be hidden in your hands.

SUMMARY

1 Even though public speaking is often rated as a 'fate worse than death', it is nevertheless an important skill to develop as it is highly prized by employers.

2 Planning, structure and practice are critical to delivering strong oral presentations. Rehearse speeches in the venue where they will be held using the equipment available on the day.

3   Mitigate technology failures by having contingency plans, handouts and other materials to ensure the presentation continues without a hitch.
4   Keep visual aids uncluttered and focus on presenting images and graphics that support your presentation. Do not overwhelm the audience with a lot of text, because if they are reading, they are not listening.
5   Manage anxiety by being thoroughly prepared and rehearsed, visualizing a successful outcome and using breathing and other calming strategies. However, some adrenalin is needed for an engaging performance.

EXERCISES

1   Take a research paper you have written and convert it into an oral presentation, bearing in mind that you need to focus on delivering a small number of key points so that you do not overwhelm the audience with detail.
2   Video yourself as you deliver the speech so that you can watch it back and assess how confident you appear, how you engage with the audience, your body language and how your voice sounds. This technique reveals the areas that need improvement.
3   Create a brief visual presentation, incorporating the principles of good design. Try different presentation modes, such as slides and online presenters, to find the one you are most comfortable with.
4   Practise speaking without notes by giving 'minute speeches' on any topic of interest. Once you have a topic, just start speaking authoritatively for a minute. You can do this either in your study group as a way of practising or alone if you prefer.

REFLECTION

Think back to a presentation you have done. Were you confident or wracked with nerves? What could have improved it? Do you think you were as well prepared as you might have been? What strategies from the chapter will you use to improve your presentation style? How might you better engage with the audience? If you are shy, what techniques can you use to overcome your dislike of being in front of a group?

FURTHER READING

Chivers, B. and Schoolbred, M. (2007) *A student's guide to presentations: making your presentation count.* London: Sage.
Duarte, N. (2008) *Slide:ology: the art and science of creating great presentations.* Sebastopol CA: O'Reilly Media.
McCarthy, P. and Hatcher, C. (2002) *Presentation skills: the essential guide for students.* London: Sage.

12

EXPERIENTIAL LEARNING

Putting theory into practice

OVERVIEW

This chapter outlines:

- the purpose and value of experiential learning;
- how to prepare for labs, pracs, internships and work placements;
- strategies to make the most of 'real world' experiences;
- how to effectively communicate the skills learned to employers and other professionals.

INTRODUCTION

It is not uncommon for employers to expect students to have gained some practical experience in their field during their time at college. Hands-on experience might be acquired by working during the summer, volunteering at local or varsity sports clubs, or completing coaching courses or internships. Many academic programmes will build in labs, pracs or work placements to allow you to apply what you have learned in the classroom to the 'real world'. You might attend labs in exercise physiology, biomechanics and motor learning where you conduct experiments and record outcomes, or you might engage in activity classes yourself where you learn a range of sports. There might also be 'hands-on' learning opportunities in athletic training where you practise your strapping skills, or in physical education where you learn to teach each other a new skill. Furthermore, various classes might take case studies and actual examples and have you work through these to seek solutions – for example, developing a sports tourism experience in your local region or running a charity football tournament for children. For most students, the opportunity to test out their skills in a real setting is quite exciting compared with learning dry theoretical concepts. Nevertheless, it is important to appreciate how the two interact and reinforce one other. This chapter outlines the rationale for including practical components in academic and extra-curricular programmes and offers strategies for making the most of the theory–practice link as well as tips on how to incorporate these experiences into your curriculum vitae or résumé.

PURPOSE OF EXPERIENTIAL LEARNING

Although the acquisition of knowledge is an important outcome of your university degree, being able to apply this knowledge through the exercise of specific skills is an equally significant part of your education. The purpose of practical experience is, however, much more than simple application; it reinforces the material explained in lectures and seminars by allowing students to experience the described skills for themselves while being guided by a tutor, supervisor or mentor. For subject areas where you learn specific actions, such as physical education, strength and conditioning, and event management, learning the theory is critical, but often not as powerful as actually experiencing the activity for yourself. You may know the concepts underpinning teaching or coaching, but that is not the same as standing in front of a group of students or athletes and teaching them a new skill. Understanding the mechanics of a deadlift is enhanced by lifting weight off a floor and appreciating the interplay of forces on the body and the way muscle groups respond to the exercise. For this reason, in many subject areas you are exposed to experiential situations to learn how to implement theoretical ideas and determine their efficacy in real life.

The laboratory setting also offers opportunities for students to experience the nature and spirit of enquiry by conducting experiments or testing human subjects. Participating in labs introduces the rigours of scientific experimentation, exposes you to research methods, and teaches you to record results and critically analyse those outcomes against a thoughtful discussion of the method and contextual literature. To succeed in labs, and as an exercise scientist thereafter, students learn to be methodical and systematic in their organization and execution, to troubleshoot and problem solve, and to reflect on their role as a researcher within the scientific process. In some labs, you may be given little direct instruction and so must work cooperatively to design and carry out the experiment, test or intervention. Regardless of how experiential learning is built into your degree, the key point is that theory and practice are not either/or: pracs, labs and internships are designed to work in concert with your lecture content to enhance your learning outcomes.

PREPARING FOR PRACTICAL EXPERIENCES

Preparing for practical experiences is no different from preparing for other assessments. You need to understand their purpose, how they align with the curriculum and the expected learning outcomes. You should consider how the lab or placement supports or extends what you have learned in class, and what links you are expected to draw between the two. Regardless of the type of activity, preparation is a necessary part of making the most of your learning experience.

LABS/PRACTICALS

Preparing for labs/practicals typically requires you to read up on the experiment or exercise ahead of time so you understand the protocol and the outcomes. You should familiarize yourself with the equipment, the procedure and the expected results. You will need to have a good grasp of the theoretical perspectives and principles of the experiment, test or intervention so that you will be able to troubleshoot areas that could go wrong. With adequate preparation you will be able to take meaningful notes that incorporate relevant literature to create a more comprehensive lab report.

INTERNSHIPS/WORK PLACEMENTS

There are many steps involved in securing an internship or placement, but if it is structured into your course, it is likely that you will receive assistance in finding a suitable position. If it is not included, there will be careers specialists on campus who will help you access internships and placements, and, of course, there are also online providers who link students to organizations seeking interns. There are many on-campus or online guides to securing internships, and the following is just a brief overview of the areas that you will need to consider when trying to obtain a work placement:

- *Identify your aims and objectives*: To make the most of a work placement, you should think about the kinds of experiences that will contribute positively towards your development as a professional. Write a list of your aims and objectives for the placement, focusing on the type of work you are interested in, the style of organization that best fits your needs (corporate, public, not-for-profit) and the range of skills that you need to learn or enhance. Identifying outcomes for the practical experience ahead of time means that you will be better prepared to recognize placements that are appropriate for your needs.
- *Research the company*: After you have identified potential placements, you should research the organization. What are their main products and/or services? Who are their major clients? What sort of business do they engage in? You are going to find a better 'fit' for your interests, skills and learning outcomes if you invest some time in understanding the options available to you. If you are allocated a placement as part of your course, you should do the same kind of research so you can align your expectations with reality, to make the most of the opportunity.

- *CV/résumé*: Before seeking a work placement, you will need to develop your résumé or curriculum vitae. This document outlines in brief your educational background and your previous work experience, and highlights any awards and honours. The Careers Centre on your campus will run workshops on how to prepare CVs/résumés, and there are many online sites that review the various formats for specific industries. It is important not to exaggerate or lie on your CV/résumé and to detail only those positions and achievements that are relevant to the position for which you are applying.
- *Interview*: Most host organizations will want to interview prospective interns to ensure they will be a good 'fit' for their clients, business and staff. Interviews are also a good time for you to determine whether the organization will be able to meet your needs. Your Careers Centre will run workshops to develop interview skills, and no matter how confident you are, it is worth taking one to learn the intricacies of the interview process. Again, there are online sources that offer tips and techniques for successful interviews. Regardless of the industry, dress appropriately, be polite, err on the side of formality, and ensure that you know and understand the organization as well as what your role will be. During the interview, engage with the questions, using actual examples rather than hypotheticals.

DURING PRACTICAL EXPERIENCES

There are certain behaviours that are expected when you engage in practical experiences, and outlined below are some key areas to be aware of when participating in labs and practicals or working as an intern.

LABS/PRACTICALS

As labs and practicals will involve equipment and procedures with which you may not be familiar, it is important to conduct yourself responsibly and – in the case of client groups or volunteers – professionally at all times. This is not the place to be casual or flippant, as there is always potential for injury to yourself and others. In the first lab/practical you will be introduced to the policies and procedures to which you must adhere. First and foremost, make sure you are familiar with all health and safety regulations. Each lab will have specific guidelines, so read these before you start. You should also locate safety equipment and first aid kits, and know the emergency procedures if there is an incident. Listen carefully to instruction and do not touch anything until invited. Be forthcoming about any personal issue/characteristic/injury that may compromise or prevent your safe and full participation. Before starting out, the specific objectives and requirements for any laboratory or practical will be explained, but you should also be well prepared, having attended the relevant lecture and read through any notes or materials that might have been provided in advance. Know your limits, and if at any point you do not understand what to do, ask for guidance.

INTERNSHIPS/WORK PLACEMENTS

You should treat all internships as training for future employment by applying a good work ethic, professional behaviour, enthusiasm and initiative. You should familiarize yourself with the policies and procedures of the organization, and most hosts will introduce you to these in an orientation or induction session. It is your responsibility to respect the regulations of the work place, particularly in relation to attendance, starting and finishing times. You should dress appropriately for the placement, and deport yourself in a professional manner at all times. Avoid making personal calls or sending text messages, and keep your phone on silent where possible. Be conscious that you are representing the organization and will be perceived by clients as an employee, so you need to behave in a manner that is consistent with the expectations of your host. Finally, ensure you maintain confidentiality at all times and conduct yourself ethically.

Making the most of an internship/work placement

Successfully completing an internship is more than simply clocking up the requisite hours, and there are a number of ways that you can make the most of your placement:

- *Have a sense of direction*: Have clear learning outcomes in mind as well as some specific strategies to achieve these. Discuss your objectives with your supervisor(s) so that they can structure your work to help meet your goals. Use your internship as a chance to learn about your future career options.
- *Develop a good relationship with your supervisor*: Have regular meetings with your supervisor to discuss your progress, accomplishments and areas for improvement. Ask questions about your work, the organization and the industry. Remember to be an active listener and learn as much as you can during these meetings.
- *Find a mentor*: A mentor is someone who guides you and provides advice on your development. They can serve as a sounding board for you to discuss ideas, ask questions and figure out your place within the industry. Your supervisor might be your mentor, but it could also be another person within the organization.
- *Have no fear*: It is natural at the beginning of your internship to feel like you are in over your head. Because these are new experiences, you may be afraid to make a mistake. Realize, however, that even if you do make a mistake, the consequences are not likely to be catastrophic, and you will have had a learning opportunity. Remember that an error becomes a mistake only when you refuse to correct it.
- *Be consistent, responsible, flexible and dependable*: Make sure that those you work with see you as someone they can depend on to get the job done and done well. You should work hard, complete set tasks on time and limit

the time you spend socializing so that you are considered an asset, not a liability. You may not end up learning and doing the things you expected, so be flexible in accepting tasks and learning what you can from every opportunity.

- *Be enthusiastic*: The most successful placements are those where students are enthusiastic and eager to engage in any and every activity, and where they seek out challenges and show initiative. Complete all work assignments – even the dull ones – with the same level of enthusiasm and professionalism. If you show a willingness to be involved and the capability to execute work tasks effectively, you may be offered opportunities to work on more interesting projects as the placement progresses. A poor attitude can ruin an internship from the outset. Avoid complaining, being rude and disrespectful to co-workers, criticizing the tasks you are given and appearing inflexible.
- *Take initiative*: Employers love employees who dive into tackling tough problems and who think 'outside the box' to find solutions. Just make sure you work with your supervisor(s) so you do not overstep your authority. There is a fine line between taking initiative and being perceived as a 'know-it-all', and for interns especially, it is best to err on the side of caution.
- *Ask questions*: Bear in mind that an internship is a learning experience. While the employer expects a certain level of work, you are not expected to know everything. Always seek advice and ask questions, and be open-minded about new ideas and procedures; remember that you do not know everything and that your professors did not teach you everything.
- *Network*: You may be rotated around different departments and supervisors, but if you are not, do not let that prevent you from tackling new tasks, meeting people outside your area and attending company social events. Talk to colleagues about their roles and what they did to get to that position. The more you are exposed to new ideas and people, the more you will learn.
- *Leave with tangible accomplishments*: Try to leave your placement with tangible outcomes for your CV/résumé. Maybe you attended training workshops, gained a qualification, developed a brochure, computerized an inventory system, organized a sales conference, met with clients, initiated a training protocol or tracked industry trends. Keep a copy of any reports, articles and presentations you worked on and create a portfolio of achievements.

UNDERSTANDING YOUR EXPERIENCE

Part of the purpose of experiential learning is to encourage you to understand the relationship between what is learned in lectures and textbooks, and the practical application of those ideas and theories. Too often, theory and practice are considered independent activities, and when the two are housed in separate modules, their relationship is not always apparent. Part of the value of

STUDENT VIEWPOINT

I wish I had paid more attention to the advice of the internship coordinator about getting value out of my internship. I went in with the attitude that I was just clocking up hours to get through it all, especially because it was unpaid and it didn't seem fair that I had to work for no money. The work itself had seemed kind of menial so I just thought I wasn't learning much. It wasn't until the end of the placement that I realized they were waiting for me to show some motivation and interest in the job before giving me more complex projects to work on. The worst thing is that there was an actual job at the end of it and they were going to hold it for me until I'd finished my college degree. I can't believe I made such a mess of things, simply because I thought the internship was just something to get course credit, rather than an opportunity for employment in the exact industry I want to work in.—Alison.

experiential learning is bridging the gap by considering the interplay between theory and practice, and by recognizing that our behaviour as professionals, also known as praxis, draws upon both what we have learned, what we know and what we have experienced. Understanding how each component contributes to our praxis is a critical part of a broader analytical and reflective process that helps us engage with experiential learning.

Understanding how theory and practical application might be used to reinforce one another is often left up to the student to decipher, as it is thought that the relationship between the two will be 'obvious'. Students are expected either to deduce the relationship by beginning with the theory and applying it to the practical situation or to induce a theoretical position from an experience. Either way, trying to make sense of the relationships requires a concerted effort, particularly when little guidance is offered. Begin with a personal reflection on your experiences, identifying the knowledge base you drew upon and any theoretical positions that underpinned your actions, before considering the relative value of each component to your professional praxis.

ASSESSMENT

Practical experiences that are part of a university degree may have specific assessment requirements. For labs and pracs, you may have to write a report detailing your activities, results and interpretation of those results. Lab and field reports have been discussed in more detail in Chapter 7. For internships, you may have to produce ongoing submissions and/or a final report outlining the experience or keep a journal to record your main tasks as well as a personal reflection about what you have learned.

Learning journals and personal reflection

Even if it is not mandatory for assessment, it is highly recommended that you keep a reflective journal to record your experiences and your thoughts on their relevance and value to both your personal growth and professional development. You can list and describe specific activities you have undertaken, explain how you handled tasks, identify key behaviours and then reflect on your performance. It is particularly useful to record challenging situations and the steps you took to resolve them, or to note specific achievements. Translate these experiences and your actions into specific skills that you have developed or improved during the practical experience. Always keep evidence that supports your learning, such as copies of work product, emails congratulating you on an achievement or anything else that attests to how you are developing as an industry professional.

COMMUNICATING YOUR EXPERIENCE

One of the hardest parts of completing practical experiences is understanding how to communicate the skills you have learned to others, especially potential employers. Although the day-to-day internship might feel a little repetitive with a lot of 'busy' work, these activities are all contributing to your development as a professional. Welcoming clients at reception is part of customer service and brand management; entering client details into a spreadsheet is database management; answering phones is learning communication skills, problem solving and customer service. Similarly, executing an experiment demonstrates organization, time management and problem solving skills, and teaching a group of athletes a new skill enhances leadership and communication skills. Learning how to best present your skill set is not about exaggerating 'menial' activities but about recognizing that the skills you develop during even the most rudimentary of tasks can be applied to many other work situations as your career progresses.

To explain what you have learned through your internship, labs or practicals, start by revisiting your learning journal and listing your various activities. Group similar activities together, and look for common skills that you might have learned or improved. Allocate them to one of the following broad headings:

- leadership/management skills;
- organizational/project management skills;
- problem solving/analytical skills;
- teamwork/working independently;
- communication/interpersonal skills;
- flexibility/versatility;
- IT/technical skills;
- research skills;
- professional behaviour.

Table 12.1 is an example of how you can explain the skills you have learned through various practical activities.

Regardless of the kind of placement you had, one of the critical parts of communicating your experiences is providing examples and evidence of your skills and achievements. Evidence can range from descriptions of how you have employed your skills through to physical samples of your work product. For example, if you have noted that you have improved your communication

Table 12.1 Translating experiences into skills

Task	Skills
I had to stop a friend from making an error in the lab by referring to the health and safety drills. This prevented a dangerous incident that could have led to injury	Leadership Problem solving skills
I was able to link the underlying theory from class to what we did in the practical	Analytical skills
I volunteered to be the subject during our lab	Initiative
We had to teach basic aqua aerobics to a group of nursing home residents	Communication Interpersonal skills Professional behaviour
I was responsible for setting up the lab for each experiment	Organizational skills Technical skills
I had to prioritize my tasks each day/across the placement	Organizational skills Time management
I was responsible for summarizing two reports	Communication skills
I arrived and left on time, and stayed longer when required	Professional behaviour
The computer network crashed and my boss needed a document for a meeting, which I was able to retrieve from the hard drive	IT/technical skills Problem solving skills
Halfway through the project I was taken off it for a few days as I was needed to help tailor a sales brochure for a client	Flexibility/versatility IT skills/technical skills
I saw our main project was missing key data, so I spent an afternoon doing some research. My supervisor was pleased as no one else in the team had noticed the gap	Initiative Working independently Research skills
All my projects were delivered on time	Time management Project management
I was responsible for showing two new interns the ropes and was their first point of call for questions about their project	Leadership Team work

skills, explain what you did to improve them. Did you talk to colleagues about how they communicate professionally? Did you observe meetings to see how professionals interact? Did you read reports or other documents to learn how to express yourself more appropriately? Are there any practical examples of you using your new communication skills? Do you have samples of your written work that you can provide a prospective employer with or other evidence of your communication skills? While it may not be necessary to include all this detail in a cover letter or résumé, it is certainly worth understanding what you have learned, knowing how to explain it and being able to demonstrate evidence of your competencies, particularly when it comes to interviews.

CASE STUDY

Liam worked at a professional sports facility during his placement and is applying for a similar full-time position at another venue. As part of his cover letter, he is outlining his previous experience in the industry:

> I worked at a well-known professional sports venue for my internship. I had a number of different jobs to do, both in the office and as part of the facility management team. Part of my placement was working with the marketing and sales team looking at ways of developing packages for corporate sponsors. It was near the end of the season so we were contacting sponsors to see what they wanted for next year and making sure we could deliver. Our ultimate aim was to make sure they kept their corporate box for next season. I also did some work for the PR team, helping out on a charity day and keeping the mascot from running into things. I also just set up chairs and organized the equipment for the speeches. My main role on game day was standing on one of the gates directing everyone to their seats. I had two high school work experience students with me, so I had to make sure they knew what to do at all times. None of the other interns had to 'babysit', so I am not sure why I did. I actually came up with a better way to manage wheelchair access and was allowed to try that out during one game. It worked really well, and one of the managers said they'll use it again. Finally, I set up some forms to help with internal organization. I was surprised that they didn't have a list of the various skills and training that each staff member had, so I made a spreadsheet so that if they were down a few people, they would know which staff members could help out in different areas on game day. Overall, I didn't have a lot of responsibility, but it was fun and I enjoyed my time at the stadium.

→   Rewrite Liam's description of his internship experience to better communicate to a potential employer the skills that he developed during the placement.

SUMMARY

1   Experiential learning opportunities are a valuable part of any sports studies programme as they apply theory and knowledge in a practical or 'real-life' setting.
2   Work placements and internships may lead to future employment opportunities, so it is important to be motivated and enthusiastic and not just 'clock in' each day.
3   Practical experiences require the same level of preparation as other learning opportunities, and may require a higher level of personal responsibility and professional behaviour.
4   Learning journals and personal reflections help you make sense of practical experiences by integrating theory, knowledge and application to inform your professional praxis.
5   It is important to translate the skills developed through labs, practicals and placements into terminology appreciated by employers.

EXERCISES

1   Think about a recent work or volunteer experience. List the main activities you performed and translate these into the key skills you believe this experience developed.
2   Review your performance during a recent work or volunteer experience and nominate areas for improvement. How would you rate yourself as an emerging professional in your specific field?
3   Write a paragraph explaining to a potential employer how the skills you have acquired through work or volunteer experiences are relevant to their workplace.
4   Identify the main skills you think you need in your future career. What practical experiences will help you develop those skills?

REFLECTION

Think about the ways in which theory and practice come together in some of the labs or practicals you have attended. Did you see the relationship? Did you feel that 'doing' the activity gave you a better insight into the theory? How do you think you could incorporate more 'action' into your learning? Alternatively, how can you more effectively incorporate some of the theory you have learned into your current work or volunteer activities? Consider recent work or volunteer experiences in light of this chapter. What worked well for you? What could you improve or change next time to make more of the experience? If you have yet to complete an internship, think about the kind of intern you will be. What tips resonated with you as areas you might need to focus on in order to have a successful placement?

FURTHER READING

Miller, J. and Siedler, T.L. (2010) *A practical guide to sport management internships.* Durham NC: Carolina Academic Press.

Thomlison, B. and Corcoran, K. (2008) *The evidence-based internship: a field manual.* Oxford: University of Oxford Press.

Wong, G.M. (2013) *The comprehensive guide to careers in sports.* Burlington MA: Jones & Bartlett Learning.

13

TESTS, QUIZZES, MID-TERMS AND FINALS

Preparing for and writing exams

OVERVIEW

This chapter outlines:

- the types and purpose of examinations;
- how to prepare effectively for exams by learning rather than cramming;
- time management techniques during exam papers;
- strategies for managing exam anxiety.

INTRODUCTION

Whether formal examinations in large exam halls or pop quizzes in your classroom, exams are a ubiquitous part of higher education. They determine your understanding of course content and your ability to respond to specific interrogation of your knowledge, and they allow you the opportunity to apply your understanding to new examples and case studies. Although exams come in various formats and are administered in slightly different ways depending on your country and institution, it is fair to say that no matter how stringent or casual, exams can be a nerve-wracking experience. Like preparing for an Olympic final, readying yourself for exams takes discipline, dedication and the proper training and practice to make your performance count. Exams also require you to look after your body as well as your brain as you prime yourself for an optimal outcome. This chapter explains the purpose of exams before discussing the types of formal assessments you may be required to sit at college. There is extensive discussion of how to prepare for exams, including reference to logistical issues, study groups, memory techniques and personal care. The chapter then outlines how best to plan your exam strategy, manage your time and deal with exam stress, before concluding with how to appropriately seek feedback on your grades.

WHAT ARE EXAMS?

One of the reasons that exams induce anxiety is a misunderstanding about their intention. Formal assessments are designed to let you show what you have achieved and the knowledge you have acquired over the semester, though students often regard them as little more than a deceptive means to trick you into writing the wrong answer. If you keep in mind that exams are an opportunity rather than a curse, you may be able to approach them with a new attitude. It is likely that each class you are studying will publish some kind of learning outcomes, so from the start of the semester, it is possible to see the kind of knowledge and the application of that knowledge that your lecturer will expect from you. This insight can help guide your studies as it lets you see the main areas of focus. For example, a learning outcome might be something like: 'At the end of the course, students will be able to appreciate the basic concepts and methodologies of long-term athlete development', which tells you that you need to be able to demonstrate your awareness and understanding of these specific coaching methods by the end of the semester. The only way that the teaching faculty have of determining your level of awareness and understanding is to assess you through assignments or exams.

TYPES OF EXAMS

There are many types of examinations that you might write at college. They include:

- *Essay exams*: You will be asked to write several essays, usually selecting a few topics from a longer list. Depending on the course, you might have to write two, three or even more essays, and the length of each one will depend on the detail provided in the topic, the number of questions to answer and the length of time available for the exam. Essays should be structured with an introduction, body and conclusion. Like an essay submitted during the semester, in an exam essay you are presenting an argument, not your own opinions, so it is important to incorporate examples and references to support your position.
- *Short-answer questions*: You will be asked to write short responses to a larger number of questions, and these can range in length from a line or two to a more substantial paragraph. You need to cover all key points but be succinct and use only relevant examples and material. You do not need to structure a response as you would an essay, but you do need to think about the most logical way to respond to the question.
- *Multiple-choice questions*: In this format, you select one answer from a short list of four or five choices. The questions are typically designed so that one or two choices can be discounted, whereas the remaining responses

could be plausible. Multiple-choice exams tend to be used more in subjects where there are specific definitions or concepts to be learned, such as the biophysical sciences, and tend to be more prevalent in introductory modules than advanced classes where you may be expected to apply concepts. Multiple-choice exams can be graded with 'negative marking', where you lose marks for incorrect answers (usually a quarter of a mark or half a mark) to discourage guessing. It is incumbent on you to know the grading system before you start.

- *Open book examinations*: In open book exams, you are allowed to bring in written materials to help you answer the question. You may be permitted to bring in a single page of written notes or you may be allowed to use the course textbook. If you know you have an open book exam, then make sure you understand the restrictions on what you can and cannot bring with you. The exam should not, however, be the first time you open the book; you should be very familiar with the content so that you do not waste time in the exam flipping through pages trying to find relevant material. Detail and accuracy are particularly important in open book exams as you have the relevant information at your fingertips.

- *Practical examinations*: While the format of practical exams in different subjects will vary, they are all generally skill based. In an anatomy exam, you might be asked to identify marked body parts; in a physical education class you might need to teach a skill; in a strength and conditioning practical you might have to demonstrate the correct technique for a squat. To prepare for practical exams, you will need to rehearse the skill, rather than just be able to talk or write about it. Some practical exams may also be conducted in groups rather than individually.

- *Take-home examinations*: Take-home exams are exams that, not surprisingly, you take home to complete. You will be free to use any resources available to you, discuss the material with your study group and spend time thinking about your response before you submit the final paper. There will be a time limit on submission, and you might have a single day, several days or a week or more. Bear in mind that the longer you have, the more depth you will be expected to show in your answers.

- *Oral examinations*: Oral exams are not common in sports studies, but they might be used in conjunction with practical exams, where you might have to explain what you are doing as you are demonstrating the relevant skill. Occasionally, oral exams might be used as an additional assessment if you have not demonstrated sufficient competency through your written or practical work.

PREPARING FOR EXAMS

If you have made it to third-level education, it is safe to say that you have sat an exam at some point in your life. This means that you have also studied for exams before, so you have some experience and knowledge of what it takes to survive an examination period. Before preparing for your college exams, you should take an honest look at your study habits and think about what works and what has hindered your performance in the past. Keep in mind that exams at university are quite different from those at school, so what has worked previously may not work now. Nevertheless, if you know you tend to procrastinate, then you need to make a conscious decision not to put off study until it is too late. There is absolutely no point walking out of an exam thinking 'If only I had studied more' when it is within your power to make that happen.

KNOWING AND REVISING VERSUS LEARNING AND CRAMMING

As soon as you set foot in the classroom on the first day of term, you are starting to prepare for the final examination. Sadly, far too many students think that exam preparation begins the day classes end, rather than recognizing that it is an ongoing process from the start. Ideally, you should reach the revision period already *knowing* the material, so that you simply need to review the main points, draw ideas together and practise writing questions to get your mind and body used to exam conditions. To reach this point, you should follow the note-taking and revision strategies outlined in Chapter 3. After each lecture, revise and edit your notes, annotate them with additional material and think about key questions that arise from the content. Discuss the material with your study group and develop some mind maps or flow charts to help structure the ideas into a logical sequence, so that you are building upon your knowledge week by week. By the time you start revising for the exam, you will already know most of the course content, so you need only revise the course, not learn it all from scratch.

Picture now the student who shuts their notebook at the end of each class and does not spare a thought for the content until revision time. Suddenly, they are faced with ten, twelve or fifteen weeks of course content to *learn*. Their notes are patchy because they have not been edited or annotated, none of the recommended readings have been completed and there have been no discussions with the study group because, well, none was organized. It is little wonder that this student will panic and try to cram ideas to be regurgitated in the exam. They will not demonstrate understanding or comprehension – just the ability to remember some related material. It induces anxiety just writing about it! Slow and steady wins the race, so commit to revising each week and making sure you understand the material each step of the way. Remember that small investments each week lead to a large return at the end.

REVISION

Some universities will have revision weeks built into their semester schedule; in others, the semester may end and exams begin straight away; and in others still, the exams are incorporated into the semester schedule. You will know from the first week when exams are held, even if the precise date and times of individual exams are not yet known. Remember that the study period should be a time to revise, not to learn, as there is just not enough time to learn the content of four, five, six or more different subjects in just one week:

- *Access to labs*: If you have practical exams, you might need access to lab or gym space to practise, so book these in advance.
- *Study groups*: If you have been working in a study group throughout the semester, you will be well placed to draw upon the collective expertise of the group to help you prepare for exams. If you have not been part of a study group, it is not too late to form one. Working together to discuss key issues and test each other's comprehension will help solidify the content in your own mind. Teaching the group an idea or concept helps you to identify whether or not you understand a topic.
- *Reconnaissance*: In some universities, you may have access to previous exam papers, and these are a useful resource when studying. You will be able to see the kinds of questions that have been asked in the past and the level of detail you might need to provide. So do your research on the exam. Speak to students who have taken the module before, ask questions in class about what might be expected from you, and/or enquire whether 'model' responses are available for you to look at. Your professor will provide only as much information as is fair, but it is worth asking the question. Finding out as much as possible about the exam in advance means that there are fewer surprises on the day.
- *Write your own questions*: Use the past exam questions to develop your own practice questions. It really does not matter if these appear on the paper; you are simply practising putting your thoughts on to paper in an organized fashion and drawing upon relevant and original examples. Try writing questions for your study group to answer and then talk through your responses.
- *Practice*: Practising writing responses is a great way to familiarize yourself with exam conditions. Many of us rely so much on computers and typing that we are not used to writing for extended periods of time. Without practice, your hands will begin to ache, your handwriting will slip and you will find it difficult to write down everything you want to. Practising gives you the opportunity to prepare your hands as well as your mind for writing under strict time limits. Use questions from past exam papers or your own examples and set yourself a time limit to construct a response.
- *Concept map*: Develop a mind map, diagram, flow chart or timeline that demonstrates how all the main ideas in one subject fit together. It is sometimes difficult to see the 'big picture' as you go through seemingly unrelated points each week, but an overall chart will highlight links between ideas and themes, and perhaps reveal relationships that were not previously apparent. It will also quickly identify the areas with which you are less comfortable, so that you will be able to focus your attention accordingly.

MEMORY IMPROVEMENT TECHNIQUES

There are some subject areas where, in addition to understanding and applying material, you simply need to remember a lot of data. In anatomy, for example, you need to know the names of every part of every body part, and this is nothing more complicated than sitting down and learning and remembering them. The longer you take to lay down the memories, the more entrenched the information will become, so while there are various techniques for memorizing data, it is always best to begin this process well in advance. There are many techniques to help improve your memory. Two common methods are:

* *Flashcards*: A good way to test your memory of definitions, dates, theories or other basic concepts is to write a prompt on one side of a small card and the definition on the other. These are transportable, so they can be referred to when waiting for the bus or sitting having a coffee. There are also applications that will create flashcards for you to use on your laptop or tablet.
* *Mnemonics*: These are a shorthand way of remembering lists of informa- tion in a particular order by creating a phrase or short sentence with words that substitute for the individual items. You might remember the tarsal bones by the mnemonic 'Tiger Cubs Need MILC', which stands in for the talus, calcaneus, navicular, medial cuneiform, intermediate cuneiform, lateral cuneiform and cuboid bones. You can invent your own or look online to see what other students have come up with. Either way, mnemonics work extremely well and can be quite enduring. This author still remembers the order of the planets based on the mnemonic she learned at the age of ten: 'Many very eerie Martians just sat under nice palms', though, of course, Pluto has since lost its planetary status.

EXAM SCHEDULE

As soon as the exam timetable is released, you can work out your revision schedule. Create a calendar noting down the date, location and time of each exam. If the times are listed as per a twenty-four-hour clock, make sure you understand the correct time, as plenty of students are caught out each year arriving at, for example, 5pm when the exam began at 15:00 (3pm).

By the time the exams start, you should really not be trying to learn more material, so the periods in between exams should be spent practising questions, quizzing each other and going through your lecture notes to check that you are comfortable with the different topics. Trying to cram between exams invariably does not lead to good results.

NUTRITION, EXERCISE AND RELAXATION

As you prepare for exams and during the examination period itself, it is important to take good care of your physical and psychological self. While it is tempting to live on takeout, cold pizza and cups of coffee, this is not nutritious enough to sustain the brain power you need to prepare and execute college exams. Make sure you are eating regularly – several small meals a day will keep your blood sugar stable – and focus on eating protein, low-GI carbs and fresh fruit and vegetables. Avoid too much refined sugar and caffeine. Try to schedule in some exercise every day. It need not be a lengthy workout in the gym; a brisk ten-minute walk every few hours is enough to keep the blood pumping and the oxygen circulating.

Learn some relaxation techniques, yoga or meditation. Allowing your mind and body to relax completely each night before you go to bed will help you sleep more soundly and allow you to feel revitalized and ready for the challenges ahead. Get a good night's rest the night before an exam. Last-minute cramming until the small hours of the morning is unlikely to assist you as much as being rested and refreshed.

STUDENT VIEWPOINT

It seems completely obvious to me now, but having a good night's sleep before an exam makes all the difference. In my first year of college I'd cram and cram all night long, drinking caffeine to stay awake, and then get to the exam feeling tired and sick like I'd been partying all night. And honestly, the cramming didn't make much difference to what I remembered. This year, I tried to learn a little each week so I only had to revise my notes, stayed as relaxed as possible, ate properly and slept well before the exam. My mind was so clear and focused in the exam, it was like I could remember every single point I'd studied.—Ben.

ON THE DAY

WHAT TO TAKE

In most formal examinations, you will be able to take very little into the room with you. It goes without saying that you should take enough writing implements, including several pens and pencils, but there are a few other items that you should have with you, subject to the regulations in your institution:

- calculator – if relevant and permitted;
- student card, if required – always bring some form of ID just in case;
- food and water – while there is little time to eat and drink during an exam, if you are starting to feel tired or the hunger pains hit, it is good to have an energy source with you, such as a banana;
- notes/textbook – if it is an open book exam.

Try to organize these items the day before so that you do not have to rush around packing your bag just before you leave. If you are taking public transport or walking to the exam, think about leaving your bag at home, as you will probably not be able to bring it into the room with you and there may not be somewhere secure to store it.

HOW TO DRESS

It is always wise to dress in layers to account for all kinds of temperatures and physical conditions. Large exam halls can be draughty, particularly in winter, and you may be more attuned to the temperature when sitting still as adrenalin pumps through your body. The more you notice how uncomfortable you feel, the less you will be concentrating on your exam. Bring a sweater or something warm to put on in case you start to feel cold.

GETTING THERE

Look at the schedule again the day before the exam to confirm the location and time (again, keep the twenty-four-hour clock in mind). If the exam is being held in a new location or even off-campus, make sure you know where it is and how to get there. Do not assume you know; go there the week before and check the area so you are absolutely certain you will not get lost.

On the day, allow plenty of time for travel, bearing in mind the likelihood of inclement weather, traffic or other obstacles. If you take public transport, make sure you know the schedule and how long it will take to arrive, and have a contingency plan should you miss your bus or train. Arrive early to give yourself time to use some relaxation techniques to calm down before the paper. You will start to feel the adrenalin pumping if you are running late, and this will take time to abate.

EXAM HALLS

In some institutions, you may take your exams in large examination halls rather than in your classroom. It can be overwhelming walking into what looks like a warehouse with several thousand other students. Arriving early means that you can find your allocated desk and take your seat without panic, and you can assess your surroundings, noting the location of the bathroom and the clock. If you are sitting an exam in your regular classroom, arrive early and sit in the same general area that you normally would. This will give you a sense of familiarity and may help visualize the professor delivering relevant content.

DURING THE EXAM

You have made it to the exam and are sitting quietly waiting for it to begin. This is not the time for recriminations for not studying enough or to panic about what you do or do not know about the topic. Instead, focus on calming yourself. Close your eyes, breathe in and out, and remind yourself that you are as prepared as you can be.

LISTEN TO ALL INSTRUCTIONS

There may be changes to the structure or format of the exam since it was printed, so listen carefully. Read the front of the exam paper and make sure the details are correct. Write your name and/or student number where indicated; you would be surprised how many students forget to do this.

PERUSAL TIME

Some formal exams might allow you a five- or ten-minute period to peruse the exam paper, in addition to the normal exam period. Use this time to read calmly through all of the questions, making sure you understand what each one is asking of you. Look in particular for questions within questions, as inadvertently leaving a sub-section out of your response can be costly. Select the questions you will answer, if there is a choice, and determine the order that you will answer them. For many students, beginning with the easiest question can build confidence, settle nerves and unlock ideas that might be relevant to subsequent questions. For others, however, beginning with the most challenging question is best as it allows them to focus their attention on the harder problem while their mind is still fresh. Decide the best strategy for you. Make sure you are aware of any restrictions on the questions you choose. For example, you might be directed to select one question from Part A and two from Part B. The perusal time is also an opportunity to draft your time management plan, and if you are permitted to take notes, you can start to plan the structure of your responses.

If you do not have perusal time, you should still take five minutes at the start of the paper to carefully and calmly review all your options. Do not be swayed by the students who start writing furiously as soon as the exam starts. They are unlikely to have planned their response.

TIME MANAGEMENT

In most cases, you will know the format of the exam and how much time you have to complete it before you even set foot in the exam hall, which means you will have been able to work out your time management plan in advance. If you are not sure how many questions are on the paper until you see it, do not begin writing until you have determined how many minutes can be spent on each question. Keep your watch in front of you, stick to your schedule and be absolutely brutal. A few minutes extra on one question means not enough time on the next, and this impact snowballs through the paper. Allocating time to each question just requires some quick arithmetic. If you have three essays to write in two hours, then you can spend forty minutes on each one. If you have a combination of short-answer and longer-answer questions, allocate time to each question based on the relative weighting of each. If the paper is worth sixty marks and you have one hour to finish, then each mark receives one minute, so that a short answer worth five marks is allocated five minutes. If you are not finished in that time, you need to stop and move on to the next question. For multiple-choice exams, a good rule of thumb is to answer one question every 30–45 seconds.

HOW TO ANSWER QUESTIONS

One of the most common mistakes that students make in exams is not addressing the question. In haste, they skim read, recognize the topic and then think that they know what is being asked. They then write a response to what they *think* was the question, rather than what is actually on the page. As an examiner, it is heartbreaking to see an intelligent, engaging response that demonstrates that the student clearly has studied hard and is familiar with the material but that does not answer the question, earning them a poorer grade than their level of understanding deserves. Regardless of the type of exam, always begin by reading the question carefully. Do you really understand what it is asking?

Essay questions

When it comes to essay questions, it is imperative you understand the topic; otherwise you risk wasting a lot of time heading down the wrong path. Under-line the task, content and limiting words. Should you compare and contrast, or does the question direct you to analyse a specific issue? Are you asked for your own examples? In this case, do not use ones discussed in class. The professor wants to see how you can apply the ideas to different situations. Are there sub-sections? If so, how many? Number them so that you remember that they need to be addressed. Develop your structure, incorporating the question into your introduction. It may seem a waste of time to rewrite some or all of the topic, but it focuses your attention on the actual question and places the essay on the right track from the outset. Working out the main points of your argument before you begin writing similarly discourages you from scribbling reams of information that may be interesting, but not relevant.

The structure for an essay question in an exam follows the same structure as for a regular essay. Begin with an introduction that outlines the question and indicates the main points you will discuss in your response. Develop one main point for each paragraph. Create a topic sentence (state your point), explain in more detail and then provide an example or reference to the literature or course material to support your point. Move on to the next point. At the end, draw together the points and explain how these address the question that has been posed. Taking a few moments at the beginning of the question to organize your thoughts and sketch out a plan and to identify the main points you will address will ensure you are systematically addressing the actual topic, not what you think is written there.

If you start to run short of time and cannot finish writing the essay, some professors suggest you start writing in bullet points rather than sentences to show the examiner there is more you know about the topic. Unfortunately, this does not really demonstrate how you can apply your knowledge to the specific exam question and often just looks like a random list of terms that the student hopes might be relevant to the question. Instead of bullet points, it is a better strategy to start writing the topic sentences of the paragraphs you will not have time to explain in full. A topic sentence will establish a main point that is linked to the exam question, which demonstrates your ability to apply knowledge. Furthermore, topic sentences will still communicate an argument, even if the detailed explanation is missing, and you will be able to write a meaningful conclusion at the end. Leave some space after each topic sentence and if you still have a few minutes remaining, go back and add in some examples or additional points after each one.

Short answers

These tend to require concise responses, but usually more detail than just one or two words. If you are given space to fill in, use the amount of space provided as a guide for how many lines you should write. Another tip is to look at how many marks are allocated to each question. This should guide you in terms of how many key points you should raise. For example, if a question is worth eight marks and there are eight lines, it may be that there are eight key points you should be able to identify. If a question is worth two marks, it could be two main points or four smaller points that the professor is looking for. If it is not clearly stated, then you will need to use your judgement.

Multiple-choice questions

Use a piece of paper to cover the answers as you read the question. This stops your eye from being distracted even for a microsecond. See if you know the answer before looking at the options. Go through the questions and answer all the ones you find the easiest first, as this may buy you a little more time to think about the more challenging ones.

NERVES

Experiencing anxiety before exams is perfectly normal. You are entering into unknown territory, you might not be sure if you have revised the right material, and you feel as though your mind has gone completely blank. Exams are a necessary part of university life, so learning to manage your nerves is an important step that will enable you to perform to your best intellectual ability. As with presentations, the level of anxiety you experience is often related to your level of preparation. If you have implemented the suggestions in this chapter during the semester, it is unlikely that you will feel so nervous that you cannot function. Nerves become a problem when they are disproportionate to your preparation. If you know you have prepared well, and yet are so terrified that you are having physical responses, then you need to focus on techniques to manage your anxiety. Here are some tips to help you calm your nerves before and during an exam:

- Think of the exam as an opportunity not an imposition. You are being given the chance to demonstrate what you have learned about the topic,

CASE STUDY

Emily is sitting her first exam at college, and the paper is divided into three sections:

PART A (40 marks)
Multiple-choice questions

PART B (40 marks)
Short-answer questions

PART C (60 marks)
Essay questions (must answer 2)

She has allocated an equal forty minutes to each part of the exam, and starts working through the paper in order as she finds it easier to start with multiple-choice questions before moving on to longer answers.

→   What difficulties do you think Emily might encounter using this strategy?

→   How much time would you allocate to each part of the exam? And why?

With thirty minutes to go, Emily realizes she is running out of time and has started only one of the essay questions. She calculates that she will have only ten minutes left to do the final essay. She is feeling incredibly anxious and starts to panic.

→   What would you do in this situation?

→   How might you calm yourself so that you can finish the paper?

→   How might you revise your strategy to ensure you can write something for both essay questions?

so think about the exam as the deliverable at the end of the semester, the point you have been working towards. Turning the experience into a positive rather than a debilitating negative will help adjust your attitude and ameliorate the nerves.

- Avoid caffeine, including coffee and fizzy or high-energy drinks. If you are already feeling jittery, you do not need to add more stimulants to your bloodstream.
- Exercise before the exam. A brisk walk around the campus or exam hall will increase your heart rate and the circulation of oxygen to your brain.
- Breathing exercises also help increase the oxygen to your brain. Close your eyes, take deep, slow, deliberate breaths in and gradually release so that you focus on your breathing rather than on your sense of impending doom.

- Do not panic if you do not know an answer immediately; just move on to something you do know. As you start to work through questions, you will start to relax and the information will come flooding back.
- Keep everything in perspective. It is only an exam. This is one paper in one subject in one semester of one year of your degree. In the context of your entire life, it is a minor event. Try not to blow it too much out of proportion.

If your anxiety rises to and remains at a high level during the period leading up to exams so that you are experiencing panic attacks, insomnia and other debilitating conditions, please seek professional advice from your doctor, student adviser or counsellor. Nerves are a part of the exam process, but extreme anxiety is not and needs to be addressed.

WHAT HAPPENS IF . . . ?

No matter how prepared you are, it is impossible to account for unexpected obstacles. Despite your best efforts, you may be delayed by traffic, you may come down with a severe illness or there could be an bereavement in your family. Every institution will have a policy and procedure to deal with these sorts of situations. It is strongly advised that you read the relevant policy and are aware of the process well before exams so that you know what you are entitled to. It may be that being delayed by peak-hour traffic is regrettable but not grounds for any kind of special consideration, whereas a heavy snowfall that closes most roads is accepted as legitimate.

Your best step is to contact someone in authority as soon as you know you may be delayed or unable to attend. This might be the director of your course, the lecturer responsible for the module, the programme administrator or a student or academic adviser. Do not leave this for a few days or weeks as it is unlikely that they will be able to offer any help or support after the fact.

AFTER THE EXAM

As you leave the exam, try to avoid the post-exam analysis, particularly if you have other papers coming up. It is tempting to rehash your answers with your classmates and worry about the quality of your response compared to theirs, but remember that the paper is over, nothing can be changed and it is time to focus your energies in other areas. Take some time off if your exam schedule allows, even if it is only an hour or two, and allow your brain to close off that chapter and prepare for the next exam. Relaxation in between exams allows you to refresh and restore your body and mind.

SEEKING FEEDBACK

Despite your diligent preparation and revision throughout the semester, it may be that your exam results are not as high as you would have liked. You feel you understood the material and thought that you addressed the questions properly, but for some reason you have not achieved the lofty heights of an A or High Distinction. It is perfectly reasonable in most institutions for you to seek feedback from the examiner. Some colleges will have a formal process where you can view the scripts to remind yourself of what you wrote and see any written comments that might be on the paper before discussing it with the lecturer. On the other hand, it may be a more informal process where you can simply approach your professor for feedback. If the paper is short-answer or multiple-choice, make sure that marks have been added up correctly; if it is an essay question, you may simply receive a grade with no specific allocation of marks to various sections. Read over the detailed grade descriptions that your college provides to understand what each one means in relation to a written paper. This may give you some insight into the grade you were awarded.

Regardless of how you access feedback, keep in mind that you are not going to negotiate a new grade, and most professors are unimpressed with students who are only interested in arguing for a higher mark rather than genuinely wanting to understand how they might improve. When asking for feedback, you are simply asking the professor to explain how you earned the grade and what steps you need to take to improve for next time. If you are familiar with the grade descriptions, you will be able to ask specific questions about why your paper did not meet particular criteria. It is always a good idea to come to the feedback meeting with questions in mind, rather than expecting the professor to explain every last detail of their grading system to justify their mark.

If you remain unhappy with your grade, your institution will have an appeals process. Please note, however, that appeals are generally only accepted in relation to the non-recognition of extenuating circumstances or substantial irregularities in the conduct of assessment. They often do not allow disgruntled students to appeal because they are unhappy with their grade, so before going down that route, make sure you understand the policy. Finally, it might also help to put this experience into some context. You may be upset with a grade, but it is not the only paper you will sit at college and there will be more chances for you to gain higher grades. Even if you disagree with the result, the feedback you receive from your lecturer will have some useful tips for future papers, so regard it as a learning experience where you can.

SUMMARY

1   Examinations are a ubiquitous part of the higher education experience, though there is significant national, regional, institutional and disciplinary variation in terms of the style and delivery of exams.

2   Preparing for examinations should not be left until the end of semester, but should be integrated as part of the weekly study and revision sessions. Arriving at the end of semester already knowing the content of the module means a student need only revise the material and practise writing exam questions rather than having to cram in several months' worth of lecture notes and readings in a few days.

3   Physical and psychological health should not be neglected when revising for exams. Eating properly, exercising and limiting the intake of stimulants improve the mind, making students more receptive to learning and more alert in exams.

4   Normal exam stress can be managed by being prepared, using relaxation techniques and sleeping well the night before. Extreme anxiety may need professional help.

5   Post-exam post-mortems should be avoided. It is over, and no matter how much students check answers against one another, there is nothing to be gained other than contributing to exam stress. Take a small break before moving on to preparing for the next paper.

EXERCISES

1   Build exam preparation into your weekly study timetable. Try a memory improvement technique such as flashcards to help you learn during these sessions.

2   Determine the types of exams that are usual in your programme. There is little point practising essay questions if you are more likely to have multiple-choice or short-answer tests.

3   Practise answering different types of exam questions so that you get used to planning and writing a response within the time allocated for particular types of questions.

4   Find out if your institution offers you access to past exam papers. If so, use these as part of your studies to help you translate study materials into responses that address the exam question.

5   Check out the exam venues in your institution. Do you take exams in your regular classroom or lecture theatre, or are exams administered in central or off-campus exam centres? Familiarize yourself with the location and transport links well in advance.

REFLECTION

Think about the different varieties of exams that you have previously done. Did you have a favourite style? Think about the exams where you felt the most confident or where you were the most successful. Were there any common features, such as level of preparedness? Have you ever felt exam nerves? What strategies did you use to overcome them? Are there other techniques listed in the chapter that will help you manage your anxiety as you approach university exams? What are your biggest concerns about writing university standard exams? What can you do to alleviate these concerns?

FURTHER READING

Hamilton, D. (2003) *Passing exams: a guide for maximum success and minimum stress.* London: Cassell.

Levin, P. (2004) *Sail through exams! Preparing for traditional exams for undergraduates and taught postgraduates.* Basingstoke: Open University Press.

APPENDIX 1

Task words

Task words, or instructional words, are typically used at the beginning of research topics to direct the student to address the topic in a particular way. Understanding what a task word means ensures you are responding appropriately and not omitting any key component. If you are not sure whether your professor's interpretation of a task word is the same as the definitions below, always check to ensure you understand what is expected of you.

Task words	Meaning
account for	Provide reasons; clarify; explain why something happens the way that it does.
analyse	Break the issue into components, discuss each in turn and carefully examine how they interrelate.
argue	Present a case for and against the nominated issue using evidence to support the main points.
assess	Determine the value of something, taking positives and negatives into account. Come to a conclusion on the value, based on the evidence and analysis.
comment on	Provide insight into the main issues, based on research evidence.
compare	Identify and explain similarities and differences between two or more things.
contrast	Identify and explain differences between two or more things.
criticize/critique	Examine an issue from a number of perspectives with a view to making a judgement about its overall merits. Identify criteria upon which the judgement is based and provide evidence or examples of how the criteria are applied.
define	Explain clearly what something means, and ensure the differences from anything similar is apparent. Use a number of approaches to arrive at a comprehensive explanation of the meaning.

Task words	Meaning
describe	Outline specific detail about something or a logical sequence of events or process. Usually does not require analysis or interpretation as much as simply stating what is there or what happened.
discuss	Evaluate an issue from several perspectives, identify main points and present an argument based on evidence, reaching a conclusion one way or the other.
enumerate	Describe an issue by listing the main features one by one, though in an essay format. Do not use bullet points.
evaluate	Weigh up and assess several angles using evidence to come to a final judgement.
examine	An in-depth investigation of a topic or issue.
explain	Outline the features of a topic or issue and describe the reasons they are like that or function in that manner.
illustrate	Use specific examples to describe how something is or how it happens.
interpret	Clarify the meaning of an issue; identify its implications or effects.
justify	Provide reasons and evidence why a particular perspective or argument is appropriate, acceptable or preferable.
outline	Identify and describe the key characteristics of a topic or issue.
prove	Use irrefutable evidence and logical argument to demonstrate that something is true (rarely, if ever, used in the sociocultural study of sport).
relate	Link ideas together by establishing similarities; may identify causal relationships.
review	Consider the key points of an issue and provide a commentary on their merits.
state	Indicate the main features or characteristics without the need for interpretation or analysis.
summarize	Provide a succinct description of a larger issue or topic, noting key features.
to what extent	Consider the degree to which an idea or topic is accurate or how far one item impacts on another.
trace	Describe changes over time, analysing how something developed from one point to another, taking influences and impacts into consideration.

APPENDIX 2

Research summary sheet

Use this research summary sheet to keep a neat, succinct overview of the content of research sources. Include enough information that is relevant to your paper so that when you are piecing your paper together, you need only use this summary – you will not need to go back to the article and wade through pages and pages looking for relevant material.

RESEARCH SUMMARY SHEET TEMPLATE

FULL BIBLIOGRAPHIC DETAILS OF SOURCE

PREPARATION
Two questions I need answered from this source:
1
2

PREVIEW
Thesis statement (as per the article):
Summary of purpose (your own words):
Type of research:

CONTENT

Three key points/findings (in your own words):

1

2

3

Direct quote (in blue):

Reason I wrote the quote down (in red):

FOLLOW-UP RESEARCH

Key words:

1

2

3

Three sources from reference list to read:

1

2

3

EVALUATION

Rating (out of 5):

Value of this paper (your words):

SAMPLE RESEARCH SUMMARY SHEET

FULL BIBLIOGRAPHIC DETAILS OF SOURCE

Whitehead, S. and Biddle, S. (2008) Adolescent girls' perceptions of physical activity: a focus group study. *European Physical Education Review*, 14(2): 243–62.

PREPARATION

Two questions I need answered from this source:

1   What are the top three reasons girls do not participate in sport?
2   What strategies can be put in place to encourage participation?

PREVIEW

Thesis statement (as per the article): The purpose of this study, therefore, was to start to build a comprehensive picture of physical activity as it relates to adolescent girls.

Summary of purpose (your own words): This study looks at teenage girls' attitudes towards physical activity, focusing on a range of reasons why girls do and do not participate in sport. The results come from a series of focus groups.

Type of research: qualitative (because it collects opinions not numbers).

CONTENT

Three key points/findings (in your own words):

1   Girls' perception of femininity/feminine appearance is important in determining attitudes to participation.
2   Girls experience significant changes in priorities in their teenage years: going out, spending time with friends/partners and studying all take away from playing sport.
3   Whether the girls had the support of their parents was critical in whether or not they participated in sport.

Direct quote: p. 246 'Many of the girls were reluctant to be active in case it negatively influenced their feminine images.'

This is a particularly important point. I wasn't aware that body image was such a significant reason why teenage girls might not play sport. This goes together with the others I have identified, such as too much emphasis on winning, poor coaching and studies taking priority. I will need to look up more research to see whether others have also found body image to be a significant issue. If it's a common theme, then I will need to include it. I wonder whether boys are affected by the same issue.

FOLLOW-UP RESEARCH

Key words:

1   participation in sport
2   girls
3   femininity

Three sources from reference list to read:

Biddle, S.J.H. (1999) Adherence to sport and physical activity in children and youth. In S.J. Bull (ed.) *Adherence issues in exercise and sport* (pp. 111–44). Chichester: John Wiley.

Biscomb, K., Matheson, H., Beckerman, N.D., Tungatt, M. and Jarrett, H. (2000) Staying active while still being you: addressing the loss of interest in sport among adolescent girls, *Women in Sport and Physical Activity Journal*, 9(2): 79–97.

Dwyer, J.J.M., Allison, K.R., Goldenberg, E.R., Fein, A.J., Yoshida, K.K. and Boutilier, M.A. (2006) Adolescent girls' perceived barriers to participation in physical activity, *Adolescence*, 41: 75–89.

EVALUATION

Rating (out of 5): *****

Value of this paper (your words): This paper is very useful because it outlines clearly five main reasons why girls stop participating in sport – I was only looking for three. Three of the reasons are common to other studies. However, I haven't come across the remaining two reasons yet. I will need to do more research on these to see if other authors have discussed them. Overall, I will be able to compare the reasons identified in this paper to the reasons determined in the other research papers I have already looked at. It will provide some good evidence for the body of my research essay. The paper did not provide suggestions about how to encourage participation.

APPENDIX 3
Common errors in student writing

This checklist is an invaluable tool when editing your work. Use it to search for specific common errors in your written work, and add your own commonly misspelled words or grammatical mistakes as a reminder to look for these when editing. Once you become familiar with the kinds of errors that appear in student writing, you will no longer have to refer to the list.

COMMON MISUSE OF WORDS

It is not difficult to use the wrong word in the wrong context, and a spell-checker is unlikely to identify the error. Familiarize yourself with these terms, and when proofreading, search for each one and make sure you have used the correct version.

Common errors	Actual meaning	Use in a sentence
there	there – a place, can replace the subject in a sentence	**There** is no milk today. Put the book over **there**. It is neither here nor **there**.
their	their – possessive case of 'they'	**Their** situation will be taken into consideration. What is happening to **their** house?
they're	they're – contraction 'they are' (never use contractions in written work at university)	**They're** not invited to our party. **They're** ordinary people. **They're** going out tonight.
whether	whether – introduces alternatives	I don't know **whether** or not he is reliable.
weather	weather – the thing that is pretty much always gloomy in Ireland	**Whether** he comes depends on the **weather**. The **weather** is surprisingly good for autumn. Will the **weather** be affected by climate change?

Common errors	Actual meaning	Use in a sentence
thought	thought = past tense of the verb 'to think' OR a noun meaning 'idea'	I **thought** you were going to the movies tonight. He gave little **thought** to the matter.
taught	taught = past tense of the verb 'to teach'	He **taught** the lesson well today. What has she **taught** you?
except	except – with the exclusion of	They are all valid reasons, **except** the last one. All of you can come to the party, **except** for you, Peter.
accept	accept – to agree to	I **accept** your proposal. Why don't you **accept** the inevitable? He must **accept** the final decision.
affect	affect (verb) – to affect something (to influence, to change)	How does the weather **affect** people's moods? You cannot **affect** my decision!
effect	effect (noun) – the effect on something (the impact, the outcome)	The **effect** the weather has on mood is noticeable. We must determine the **effect** of the intervention. Note: '**effect**' is also occasionally used as a verb meaning 'to cause', e.g. The protesters tried to **effect** change.
advise	advise (verb) – to offer information on a particular topic	I **advise** you to take better care of your health. Please **advise** me about the correct course of action.
advice	advice (noun) – opinion or recommendation	My **advice** to you is to proofread carefully if you want to get good grades. His **advice** was gratefully received. She always gives me good **advice**.
than	than – used to compare	He is certainly much taller **than** I am. She wrote a much better assignment **than** her brother.
then	then – a different time from now, the next step, used in **if–then** sentence constructions	She was much richer **then**. Start with developing an outline and **then** move on to creating topic sentences. If we start slowly, **then** we will be better off.

Common errors	Actual meaning	Use in a sentence
number	number – use when the item under discussion is countable, such as people, reasons	The number of times he played football. The number of people who were in the team. There are a number of reasons why this topic is important.
amount	amount – use when the item under discussion is NOT countable – time, sand etc.	The amount of time I spent on this assignment was phenomenal. There is an unlimited amount of sand on the beach.
female/male	female/male – adjectives to describe gender – do not use these as nouns	Female and male footballers have different experiences in sport.
women/men	women/men – nouns	Women and men have different experiences in sport. 'Females and males have different experiences in sport' – poor expression.
where were	where – a location were – past tense of the verb 'to be'	Where do you come from? They were very happy to see their father. We were most surprised at the turn of events. You were saying something?
we're	we're – contraction of 'we are' (never use contractions in written work at university)	We're very pleased you came. We're off on holidays tomorrow.
lose loose	lose – to no longer have loose – not tight	Do not lose the money I gave you. I had some loose change in my pocket. After you lose weight, you might have some loose skin.
alot, alright –	These are not words! Should be a lot or all right	He has a lot of matches coming up. She felt all right about her exam.
huge/hugely massive/ massively big	Very poor word choices that drag down the quality of your writing. Better alternatives: for huge/big/massive try significant, important, notable	
looks at	Also a poor choice. Try examines, discusses, analyses, contends	
could of	This is an error that comes from people misunderstanding the spoken sound of could've, which is a contraction of could have. This mistake also applies to would of, might of, should of and so on.	

Common errors	Use in a formal sentence
Contractions **NEVER** use contractions – write out the words in full	**can't = cannot** **won't = will not** **it's = it is** **haven't = have not** **he'll = he will**
	Extra tip: There is NO occasion where 'it's' will appear in your written work. Look for it specifically as it is one of the most misused words in student assignments.
Numerals	The rules for numerals change across disciplines and institutions, but a good rule of thumb is that smaller numbers (up to one hundred) are written out in full, whereas larger ones are written as numerals (101)
	Sentences never begin with a numeral. Either write the number out in full or think of another way to begin the sentence.
	Incorrect: 520 athletes were surveyed in the study.
	Correct: Five hundred and twenty athletes were surveyed in the study.
	OR
	The survey was distributed to 520 athletes.
Percentages	In the social sciences, 'per cent' is always written out in the text, and the symbol is only used in parentheses:
	'Very few children (5%) . . .'
	'In Australia, twenty per cent of children . . . However, very few adults (5%) . . .'
	In the biophysical sciences, the percentage symbol is normally used in all cases.
Capitalization	Capital letters are used only for the beginning of sentences and to denote proper nouns (formal names, titles).
	Sports are typically not capitalized unless they contain a component that is a formal name – for example, American football or Australian rules. But note that basketball, soccer and track and field, to name a few, are not capitalized.
	Proper nouns include formal titles, but not job descriptions.
	The President opened the season, much to the dismay of the team manager.
Abbreviations/ symbols	Never use abbreviations or symbols in formal academic work. The words for which they stand should be written out in full.
	& – ampersands should never be used – write out 'and' in full
	e.g. – for example
	i.e. – that is
	Please note: **etc.** – should NEVER appear in formal written work. It is enough just to include a small selection of examples.

APOSTROPHES

Apostrophes are one of the most misused punctuation marks. Make sure you understand the basic principles of apostrophes in order to use them correctly. When proofreading, every time you see an apostrophe in your work look at it carefully. Is it supposed to be there? If you think you have forgotten an apostrophe, look at every word that ends in 's' – should there be an apostrophe?

Common errors	Actual meaning	Use in a sentence
Apostrophes ONLY do the following:		
– indicate possession – indicate missing letters, as in the case of contractions		
Possession	Apostrophes denote ownership. *Tip*: If you can substitute 'his', 'her', 'its', then you can be sure it is a possessive and that you need an apostrophe	**Mary's** book fell on the ground. **Sarah's** boyfriend was tall.
Missing letters	Apostrophes denote missing letters *Reminder*: NEVER use contractions in academic writing	**ten o'clock** = ten of the clock **don't** = do not **fish 'n' chips** = fish and chips **ne'er do well** = never do well
Plurals	Do not add apostrophes to create plurals, INCLUDING abbreviations	**books** NOT **book's** **sports** NOT **sport's** **CDs** NOT **CD's**
	If you are referring to decades, there is no apostrophe	1990s, 1960s, 1950s NOT 1990's, 1960's, 1950's
Dates	The way that dates are written in formal academic writing is regionally dependent	UK/IRL/AUS/NZ: **29 November 2012** USA: **November 29th, 2012**

ACTIVE VERSUS PASSIVE VOICE

When constructing sentences, you should predominantly use the 'active voice'. This style is strong and assertive and exudes confidence. Avoid the 'passive voice' as much as possible. It typically puts the emphasis on the wrong thing. There are some instances, particularly in scientific reporting, where the passive voice is used extensively. For most essays and reports, it is not appropriate.

Active voice	Emphasis is on the SUBJECT'S ACTION *Someone does something*	The car **hit** the boy. This essay **examines** three points. The article **influenced** me.
Passive voice	Emphasis is on the OBJECT *Something is done to someone*	The boy **was hit** by the car. Three points **are examined** by the essay. I **was influenced** by the article.

Formatting checklist

The following checklist can be used when proofreading your written work. Not all of the items will apply for every institution or lecturer, so you should customize the checklist to suit your requirements. Make sure you inform yourself about any formatting requirements your lecturer, department or institution might have.

❏ Cover sheet is attached.
❏ Assignment topic appears on first page of essay.
❏ Assignment is spaced appropriately (check with your professor).
❏ Page numbers are located in the top right-hand corner of each page.
❏ Margins conform to requirements.
❏ Appropriate font and point size are being used.
❏ Student number is on each page.
❏ Word count is listed at the end of the essay (if required).
❏ Assignment addresses the topic.
❏ Spell check has been completed (electronic AND manual).
❏ Assignment has been thoroughly proofread/edited (use list of common student errors in Appendix 3).
❏ Apostrophes are used correctly.
❏ Contractions are not used (it's, can't, won't, isn't).
❏ Abbreviations are not used (etc., e.g., i.e.).
❏ Dates are correctly formatted.
❏ Minimum number of references are cited in the text AND appear in the reference list.
❏ Quotes longer than three lines/forty words are indented.
❏ Reference list is in alphabetical order.
❏ Reference list is in the correct referencing format.
❏ Journal/book titles are *italicized* in the reference list AND in the essay.
❏ References throughout text are *correctly* formatted.
❏ References throughout text are *consistently* formatted.
❏ Quotation marks are consistent.

GLOSSARY

abstract a short synopsis of a research article that outlines the nature, methodology, results and key findings of the study.

active listening listening with purpose so that the listener is interpreting, analysing and evaluating what is being said.

anecdotal evidence unsubstantiated information that is based on hearsay or personal opinions or experiences rather than rigorous scientific enquiry. It is not an accepted source of information for research papers.

annotation a note, commentary or explanation that is added to another text, such as lecture notes, notes from readings or summaries of journal articles.

appendix supplementary material placed at the end of a paper that is useful for the reader to know but would disrupt the flow of the argument if included in the assignment.

applied research research that is intended to have a real-world application or solve an existing problem.

bibliography a list of all sources examined during the research for an assignment, regardless of whether the source is cited in the paper or not; presented in alphabetical order by surname of the first author.

biophysical sports sciences the disciplines of sports sciences that focus primarily on understanding the biological and physical aspects of the body as it moves, exercises and participates in sport. Includes exercise physiology, biomechanics, functional anatomy, motor learning, strength and conditioning.

biomechanics a field of study that applies the principles of physics and mechanics to the body.

blog a public, regularly updated online journal, on which readers can usually comment; short for 'weblog'.

brainstorm when a group of people generate a large number of creative ideas on a given topic to find a solution to a problem.

citation an in-text reference in a research paper or academic publication that acknowledges the original source of ideas, facts, quotes or other information.

content words the part of a research topic that specifies the subject matter of a written paper.

Cornell notes a note-taking system created by Walter Pauk in the 1950s that divides a page into three sections based on the five 'Rs' of record, reduce, recite, reflect and review.

critical thinking a process that relies on the application of logic to analyse and evaluate information. A critical thinker does not merely accept information without question but instead tries to determine its merit through reason and reflection.

curriculum vitae a record of an individual's education, work experience, skills and references. Also known as a CV, and is sometimes used interchangeably with résumé.

direct quote an exact replica of words, placed within inverted commas, that is copied from a source and added to a research paper.

discipline a coherent field of study that has accepted research conventions and subjects of interest. The study of sport (kinesiology, human movement studies, sport and exercise science) may be considered a discipline, though areas such as exercise physiology and sports history are sometimes regarded as sub-disciplines of the 'parent' disciplines of physiology or history respectively.

discussion board an online forum available to either closed or open groups where members can start threads and reply to messages to interact and discuss topics; also known as a discussion forum.

dissertation a lengthy submission based on primary research of a defined topic that contains an introduction, a review of literature, methods, results, discussion and a conclusion; also known as a thesis.

edited book a collection of chapters written by a series of authors that is collated into a single publication by editors who provide an introduction to contextualize the chapters.

essay a written paper that offers a coherent, reasoned argument based on research, usually in response to a set topic.

executive summary an overview of a report that provides the reader with all salient information contained within the report, including, most importantly, the key recommendations.

exercise physiology a field of study that examines the body's acute and chronic response to exercise.

experiential learning the process of learning through direct experience, such as through internships, placements, practicals and labs.

extra-curricular activities voluntary activities that fall out of the realm of the normal college curriculum, including sport, clubs and societies.

feedback constructive advice provided on submitted assessment or exams that aims to highlight areas of improvement and aid overall learning.

group roles the allocation of specific responsibilities to members of the group that benefit the overall functioning of the team.

group work working collaboratively in teams to create a single piece of assessment, often a written project and/or presentation.

independent learner someone who accepts the responsibility to take an active and autonomous role in their own learning regardless of the level of direct supervision. Independent learners place themselves at the centre of their learning experience by acquiring knowledge for themselves rather than waiting for information to be handed to them.

internship a paid or unpaid placement where students are offered real-world experience in a preferred industry.

in-text reference a citation in the text of a written paper that acknowledges the original source of ideas, quotes, facts or other information.

jargon specialist terminology that is understood by a group, but largely inaccessible to outsiders.

journal a scholarly periodical that publishes peer-reviewed academic research and related materials in a specific field or discipline.

journal article a paper written by one or more scholars or experts that is subjected to peer-review before being published in an academic journal.

kinesiology the scientific study of human movement, encompassing both biophysical and socio-cultural approaches to sport.

learning style theory a theory that argues that individuals have different ways of acquiring knowledge that are categorized into several main types, and offers suggestions for how to best learn according to each learning style.

lecture information delivered by a qualified lecturer to an audience of students at university or college.

limiting words words that establish the limits or boundaries of a research topic to provide a focus for the written paper.

literature review a critical analysis of the existing literature on a specific topic, focusing on the main themes or theoretical debates. A literature review is typically included in research studies and dissertations.

mind mapping a visual note-taking system that uses diagrams to map information on a single page, with sub-themes radiating out along branches that originate at a central key theme.

paraphrasing communicating ideas from a research source in your own words, but often misunderstood to mean simply changing one or two words to 'make it your own'.

peer-reviewed research research that is published in academic journals only after it has been scrutinized and evaluated by recognized experts in the field.

perusal time a short period of time before an examination starts to allow you to read through the paper carefully, but not start writing.

plagiarism the intentional or accidental act of copying words, ideas, diagrams or other material from another source without proper attribution, usually, though not always, with the intention to present the material as their own work.

primary data data that are raw and unprocessed – such as the results of experiments, field observations and archival materials – and that require analysis and interpretation by the researcher.

proofreading the careful review of a written paper with the specific purpose of identifying and correcting spelling, punctuation and grammatical errors.

podcast online audio content available on demand that can be downloaded to a portable media player.

pure research the exploration of research ideas that are driven by curiosity rather than any expectation of real-world application.

qualitative research research that seeks to interpret people's feelings, thoughts, behaviours and experiences

quantitative research the collection of numerical data that is analysed statistically to generalize results across a population.

reference list a full bibliographic record of all sources that are cited in the text of the paper, presented in alphabetical order by the surname of the first author; also known as a list of references.

referencing system specific, recognized systems of citing research sources, which differ according to the discipline and/or institutional preference.

reflective writing the process of capturing more than a simple description of an event, experience, observation or feeling. It includes a consideration of the context, motivation, outcomes and changes that might result from the experience, in order to develop an understanding of an individual's response to a specific situation, or to interrogate its meaning.

report a document that is produced in response to a specific question and is divided into identifiable sections. It typically ends with recommendations for future action.

research methods the established research protocols used by scientists to gather and interpret data.

résumé a brief description of a person's qualifications and work experience pertaining to the specific position being applied for; sometimes used interchangeably with curriculum vitae.

secondary data data that have already been analysed and interpreted by researchers; includes research studies, journal articles, academic books and other scholarly publications.

scientific research the systematic collection, organization and analysis of data based on accepted empirical or scientific research methods.

socio-cultural sports sciences the disciplines of sports sciences that focus primarily on understanding the social and cultural aspects of why people move, exercise and participate in sport; includes sports history, sociology of sport, philosophy of sport, sports psychology, sports pedagogy.

sociology of sport a field of study that examines how individuals, groups, institutions, organizations and cultures behave, interact and are expressed within the context of sport and tries to identify common patterns, values and other social relationships. This field focuses largely on analyzing contemporary issues, including gender, race and class.

sports history a field of study that traces the origin, development and transformation of sport over time and examines not only its significance within various historical contexts, but also its relationship with social, political, economic and other forces.

sports psychology a field that examines how cognitive function influences sports participation and performance.

sports studies an umbrella term used in this book to refer to the full range of disciplines associated with the study of sport, including both the bio-physical and socio-cultural sciences.

task words terms that typically appear at the beginning of a research topic to direct the structure of the response; also known as function words.

tertiary data data that are drawn from previously published materials, including textbooks and encyclopaedias.

thesaurus a reference book (or online resource) that lists words with their synonyms rather than their definition.

thesis statement a concise statement of the purpose of a published article or research assignment that appears in the introduction. It is often followed by more specific research objectives.

topic sentence usually the first sentence of a paragraph that asserts the main point of the paragraph and typically links it to the overall research topic.

tutorial a small group class where interaction is encouraged between students. These often accompany lectures and provide an opportunity for students to discuss the material delivered in class as well as relevant support materials and readings. Tutorials are more common in socio-cultural sciences, whereas labs are typically used for small group teaching in the biophysical sciences.

unscientific research the use of anecdotal evidence to support opinions.

virtual learning environment an online platform that supports virtual learning by housing support materials such as lecture notes and supplementary readings or by offering online interaction between students and/or academic staff.

wiki an interactive website where anyone with access can edit, modify or delete the content.

REFERENCES

Abernethy, P.J. and Wehr, M.S. (1997) Ammonia and lactate response to leg press work at 5 and 15 RM. *Journal of Strength and Conditioning Research*, 11(1): 40–44.

Allender, S., Cowburn, G. and Foster, C. (2006) Understanding participation in sport and physical activity among children and adults: a review of qualitative studies. *Health Education Research*, 21(6): 826–35.

American Psychological Association (2009) *Concise rules of APA style*, 6th edn. Washington DC: American Psychological Association.

Borowick, J. (2000) *How to write a lab report*. Upper Saddle River NJ: Prentice Hall.

Brown, D. (2004) Olympic legacies: sport, space and the practices of everyday life. In: J. Bale and M.K. Christensen (eds) *Post-Olympism: questioning sport in the twenty-first century* (pp. 99–118). Oxford: Berg.

Buzan, T. (2012) *The ultimate book of mind maps*. London: HarperCollins.

Chivers, B. and Schoolbred, M. (2007) *A student's guide to presentations: making your presentation count*. London: Sage.

Collins, T. and Vamplew, W. (2002) *Mud, sweat and beers: a cultural history of sport and alcohol*. Oxford: Berg.

Creme, P. and Lea, M.R. (2008) *Writing at university: a guide for students*. Maidenhead: McGraw-Hill.

Davids, K., Bennett, S.J. and Beak, S. (2002) Sensitivity of adults and children to haptic information in wielding tennis rackets. In: K. Davids, G.J.P. Savelsbergh, S.J. Bennett and J. Van der Camp (eds) *Interceptive actions in sport: information and movement* (pp. 195–211). Abingdon: Routledge.

Davison, K.G. (2000) Boys' bodies in school: physical education. *Journal of Men's Studies*, 8(2): 255–66.

Devine, A., Bolan, P. and Devine, F. (2010) Online destination marketing: maximising the tourism potential of a sports event. *International Journal of Sport Management and Marketing*, 7(1/2): 58–75.

Duarte, N. (2008) *Slide:ology: the art and science of creating great presentations*. Sebastopol CA: O'Reilly Media.

Emerson, L. and Hampton, J. (2005) *Writing guidelines for science and applied science students*. Melbourne: Thomson/Dunmore.

Fairbairn, G.J. and Fairbairn, S.A. (2001) *Reading at university: a guide for students*. Basingstoke: Open University Press.

Ferrett, S. (2012*) Peak performance: success in college and beyond*, 8th edn. New York: McGraw-Hill.

Fields, S.K. (2008) *Female gladiators: gender, law, and contact sport in America*. Champaign IL: University of Illinois Press.

Fullerton, S. (2007) *Sport marketing*. New York: McGraw Hill.

Gamble, P. (2012) *Strength and conditioning for team sports*, 2nd edn. Abingdon: Routledge.

Gibbs, G. (1988) *Learning by doing: a guide to teaching and learning methods*. Oxford: Further Education Unit.

Gratton, C. and Jones, I. (2010) *Research methods for sports studies*, 2nd edn. Abingdon: Routledge.

Guillet, E., Sarrazin, P. and Fontayne, P. (2000) 'If it contradicts my gender role, I'll stop': introducing survival analysis to study the effects of gender typing on the time of withdrawal from sport practice: a 3-year study. *European Review of Applied Psychology*, 50(4): 417–21.

Hackett, D.A., Johnson, N.A., Halaki, M. and Chow, C.M. (2012) A novel scale to assess resistance-exercise effort. *Journal of Sports Sciences*, 30(13): 1405–13.

Hamilton, D. (2003) *Passing exams: a guide for maximum success and minimum stress*. London: Cassell.

Holmlund, C. (1997) Visible difference and flex appeal: the body, sex, sexuality and race in the *Pumping Iron* films. In: A. Baker and T. Boyd (eds) *Out of bounds: sports, media, and the politics of identity* (pp. 145–60). Bloomington IN: Indiana University Press.

Jarvis, P., Holford, J. and Griffin, C. (eds) (2003) *The theory and practice of learning*, 2nd edn. Abingdon: Routledge.

Kesselman-Turkel, J. and Peterson, F. (2003) *Note-taking made easy*. Madison WI: University of Wisconsin Press.

Klein, S. (2012) *Learning: principles and applications*, 6th edn. London: Sage.

Learning Higher (2012) *Group work video resource*. Liverpool: Liverpool Hope University Centre for Excellence in Teaching and Learning. Available at: www.learn higher.ac.uk/groupwork//index.php (accessed 16 August 2012).

Levin, P. (2004) *Sail through exams! Preparing for traditional exams for undergraduates and taught postgraduates*. Basingstoke: Open University Press.

Levin, P. (2005) *Successful teamwork!* Maidenhead: Open University Press.

Light, R.J. (2001) *Making the most of college: students speak their minds*. Cambridge MA: Harvard University Press.

Locke, L.F., Silverman, S.J. and Spirduso, W.W. (2009) *Reading and understanding research*, 3rd edn. London: Sage.

McCarthy, P. and Hatcher, C. (2002) *Presentation skills: the essential guide for students*. London: Sage.

Magdalinski, T. (2008) *Sport, technology and the body: the nature of performance*. Abingdon: Routledge.

Mansfield, L. (2011) Fit, fat and feminine? The stigmatization of fat women in fitness gyms. In E. Kennedy and P. Markula (eds) *Women and exercise: the body, health and consumerism* (pp. 81–100). Abingdon: Routledge.

Miller, J. and Siedler, T.L. (2010) *A practical guide to sport management internships*. Durham NC: Carolina Academic Press.

Moon, A.J. (2005) *Reflection in learning and professional development*. Abingdon: Routledge Falmer.

Moore, K.M. and Cassel, S.L. (2011) *Techniques for college writing: the thesis statement and beyond*. Boston MA: Wadsworth.

Neville, C. (2007) *The complete guide to referencing and avoiding plagiarism*. Maidenhead: Open University Press.

Osmond, G. (2010) Photographs, materiality and sport history: Peter Norman and the 1968 Mexico City Black Power Salute. *Journal of Sport History*, 37(1): 119–37.

Patrias, K. and Wendling, D. (2007) *Citing medicine: the NLM style guide for authors, editors, and publishers*, 2nd edn. Bethesda MD: National Library of Medicine. Available at: www.ncbi.nlm.nih.gov/books/NBK7256/?redirect-on-error=__HOME__&depth=2 (accessed 3 July 2012).

Pauk, W. and Owens, R.J.Q. (2011) *How to study in college*, 10th edn. Boston MA: Wadsworth Cengage Learning.

Ricciardelli, L.A., McCabe, M.P. and Ridge, D. (2006) The construction of the adolescent male body through sport. *Journal of Health Psychology*, 11(4): 577–87.

Ryall, E. (2010) *Critical thinking for sports students*. Exeter: Learning Matters.

Schiller, K. and Young, C. (2010) *The 1972 Munich Olympics and the making of modern Germany*. Berkeley CA: University of California Press.

Smith, M.F. (2010) *Research methods in sport*. Exeter: Sage.

Sparrow, B. Liu, J. and Wegner, D.M. (2012) Google effects on memory: cognitive consequences of having information at our fingertips. *Science*, 333(6043): 776–8.

Thomlison, B. and Corcoran, K. (2008) *The evidence-based internship: a field manual*. Oxford: University of Oxford Press.

University of Chicago Press (2010) *The Chicago manual of style*. Chicago IL: University of Chicago Press.

University of Waterloo (2012) Curve of forgetting. Available at: http://uwaterloo.ca/counselling-services/curve-forgetting (accessed 17 September 2012).

Watkins, R. and Corry, M. (2011) *E-learning companion: a student's guide to online success*. Boston MA: Wadsworth.

Weinberg, R.S. and Gould, D. (2011) *Foundations of sport and exercise psychology*, 5th edn. Champaign IL: Human Kinetics.

Whitehead, S. and Biddle, S. (2008) Adolescent girls' perceptions of physical activity: a focus group study. *European Physical Education Review*, 14(2): 243–62.

Wong, G.M. (2013) *The comprehensive guide to careers in sports*. Burlington MA: Jones & Bartlett Learning.

INDEX